Romantic Narrative Art

ROMANTIC
Narrative
ART

****

Karl Kroeber

THE UNIVERSITY OF WISCONSIN PRESS

Madison, Milwaukee, and London: 1966

Published by The University of Wisconsin Press
Madison, Milwaukee, and London

U.S.A.: Box 1379, Madison, Wisconsin 53701
U.K.: 26-28 Hallam Street, London, W. 1

Paperback Edition 1966

Printed in the United States of America
Library of Congress Catalog Card Number 61-5190

To Krakie and Alfred

Prefatory Note

****

In this study I have deliberately concentrated upon the origins of *Romantic Narrative Art*. I had not planned to discuss story poems written after the first quarter of the nineteenth century; but I discovered that even adequate comment upon the narrative verse of Shelley and Keats would extend my book beyond the length appropriate to a single work of criticism. So I confine my attention to the beginnings of Romantic * narrative poetry—to those poems wherein principles and techniques that later developed and flourished and branched out diversely seem to have originated. The imposition of such limits has produced some problems of presentation.

While it is sometimes possible to isolate a specific poem in which a particular narrative tendency first appears, more often a single tendency is manifested in a number of different poems, and one's

* An explanation is required for my terminology. The words "Romantic," "Romanticism," "Romantic style," and the like are used frequently. I am aware that these terms are artificial and inexact and still subject to redefinition. Indeed, one of my purposes is to suggest ways in which these labels may be defined more precisely and used more meaningfully (see Chapter X). But terms like "Romantic," however vague and controversial they may be, are part of a convenient critical shorthand. To avoid them would be to indulge in an academic fastidiousness absurd in a work as exploratory as this.

choice for exemplification leads to apparently arbitrary emphases. Thus, as instances, I comment at length on *La Belle Dame sans Merci* but do not analyze any one of Scott's ballads in detail; though I am as specific as possible in talking about *The Prelude,* I keep my discussion of *The Excursion* focussed on general characteristics rather than on particularized details or interpretations; and I exclude several poems, such as Landor's *Gebir,* which, although interesting in themselves and relevant to my subject, do not help to clarify the major trends in Romantic narrative art.

Furthermore, it is not always possible to restrict commentary to a single poem, or, indeed, to a single stylistic phase. Byron's later work, for example, might properly be treated in relation to developments in narrative among the second generation of Romantic poets. I deliberately reduce to a minimum, however, my remarks on Shelley's and Keats's art in the belief that it merits comprehensive study in another work, particularly in regard to its influence upon later nineteenth-century poets like Tennyson. I believe also that Byron's different narrative techniques can be evaluated only in terms of their progressive evolution throughout his entire career. So I devote a chapter to the internal history of Byron's narrative verse and make no effort to study its relationship to the poems of his younger contemporaries.

I am forced, in fact, to pay scant heed to any problems of influence. Because I seek root causes of a poetic mode shared by many poets, I cannot, without tiresome repetition, discuss the ways in which one poet stimulated another. Nor can I arrange the works I comment upon in any simple chronological order. I organize topically, dividing my commentary into three parts. Part One, after the introductory chapter, traces the history of the literary ballad to its establishment as a recognized form within the lyricist's repertoire. Part Two deals with the relation of narrative form to the Romantic stress upon imagination. This section, though in some respects closest to the heart of the Romantic style, is least amenable to schematic organization, and I choose to divide the subject into three parts—the visionary lyric, the simple tale, and the personal epic—without attempting to impose upon these separate forms too strict a unity. Visionary lyrics, in fact, transcend mere story. The most valuable generalizations about this material, it seems to me, must await a detailed study of Keats's and Shelley's use of the narrative mode. In Part Three I describe the evolution of relatively realistic story poems, trying in particular to make clear the ways in which narrative verse during the Romantic era contributed to the development of new matter and new manners in prose fiction.

Such organization, though not so unified as I would like, at least makes it possible to suggest the critical and historical problems which have made this study so intriguing to me. I am exploring a subject which, so far as I know, has never been studied *in extenso*. My task, I believe, is to identify what appear to be the principal features in this new literary landscape—its boundaries, its major divisions, its conspicuous configurations. I trust that I neither mistake molehills for mountains nor propose delightful pathways which in fact lead only to gnat-infested swamps. I assume a tone of assurance and generalize and speculate freely, believing that the pioneer should, above all, arouse others to develop and improve whatever in his discoveries promises to be more than chimerical.

It is a pleasure to acknowledge my gratitude to Professors Jerome H. Buckley, James L. Clifford, and Mark Van Doren for guiding and encouraging me when I began my study of narrative poetry. I am grateful also to the Graduate School of the University of Wisconsin for a summer research grant in 1958. Most of all I wish to thank my wife for so cheerfully contributing nothing to the mechanical preparation of the manuscript; whatever in this book is more than technically correct reveals the influence of her civilized amiability.

Karl Kroeber

Madison, Wisconsin
April, 1960

Contents

PART I

Balladry

****

Chapter I

*

NARRATIVE POETRY AND THE ROMANTIC STYLE

Although few poets nowadays write any narrative verse, most poets of the nineteenth century delighted in every sort of poetic story. From Coleridge to Kipling the narrative mode stood pre-eminent, if not predominant, absorbing the lion's share of English poets' creative energies. In the eighteenth century, however, narrative verse occupied a position almost as modest as that it has retreated to today. The Augustans, to be sure, revived the ballad and proclaimed the glory of the epic, but they told few tales in poetry. To the great Augustans narrative was a vehicle for satire or wit. Not until we have pushed back into the seventeenth century and beyond the Restoration do we find poetic narrative re-assuming a significant role in its own right. We need pursue the history of the story in verse no further, for the rise and fall already outlined suggests the intimate association of narrative with the changing styles of English poetry. This association of mode and style deserves more intensive exploration than it has hitherto received.

Early nineteenth-century poetry promises the richest rewards to such investigation. We are concerned with a cyclic process; the significance of the mode wanes, waxes, then wanes again. We should consider one full cycle at least, but our primary attention must be directed to the phase in which narrative is ascendant. It is to the period of the earliest importance of a poetic form that one goes to find the reasons for its rise. In the Romantic era we find the origins of the nineteenth-century predilection for poetic narrative, and there we are most likely to discover some answers to the questions suggested by the history of verse narrative sketched in the preceding paragraph. Is the association of the narrative mode with shifting poetic styles accidental? If not, is the mode itself an efficient cause, or is it a by-product of extra-poetic circumstances? If the mode is not peripheral, is it narrative form or narrative subject which is most helpful in defining a shift in literary style?

Several collections of poems of the later eighteenth century, as well as many individual verse narratives of the Romantic era, throw light on these questions. Percy's *Reliques,* Coleridge's *The Rime of the Ancient Mariner,* Scott's *The Lay of the Last Minstrel,* and Keats's *Hyperion,* for example, will provide many of the answers we seek. Even more useful as an introduction to this problem is Robert Burns's *Tam o' Shanter.* Burns belongs to an early phase of Romanticism, if he belongs to Romanticism at all. His grounding in the traditions of Neo-classicism is strong. Yet no historian of literature would have the temerity to minimize the independence of his genius by classifying him as a transitional figure. And if our general estimate of Burns's work places it between two styles without reducing its individual integrity, specific attention to *Tam o' Shanter* will free us from involvement in problems raised by particular forms of narrative poetry, especially the ballad and the epic. Burns described *Tam o' Shanter* simply as "A Tale," and there appears to be no reason why we should not accept his description and regard the poem as an example of narrative verse in its purest, least formalized state.

With *Tam o' Shanter,* furthermore, we deal with a masterpiece, the poem in which Burns's genius attained its most complete fulfillment.[1] But *Tam o' Shanter* is his only sustained narrative poem. To what degree does this circumstance lessen its value for our purposes? In fact, its uniqueness in Burns's canon enhances its value for us. To the problem of why Burns wrote only one such narrative when that one is so successful only speculative solutions can be proposed.[2] Yet the very stating of this question suggests that if we could develop some reasonable explanation for the effectiveness of the poem, we might thereby establish more clearly Burns's relationship to both Neo-classicism and Romanticism. We may assume that the unique excellence of *Tam o' Shanter* cannot be detached from Burns's role as a precursor or initiator of Romanticism rather than as a complete participant in that style. Whatever we find to be a cause of the effectiveness of this poem will illuminate the position of narrative in the shift from the Neo-classic to the Romantic style.

Though much praised, *Tam o' Shanter* has been subjected to few critical analyses.[3] And no one has thought to study it as a narrative, as a poem, that is, whose basic structure is its story. Or, more accurately, critics have concerned themselves with the matter of its story and have disregarded its form.[4] The latter may be described as the system by which all the elements in the poem are organized to control and to direct our expectations about and our later reactions to the events which occur, these events being the matter of the story. The system of organization is created by the interrelation of three factors:

> . . . the general estimate we are induced to form . . . of the moral character and deserts of the hero . . . judgments we are led similarly to make about the nature of the events that actually befall the hero . . . as having either painful or pleasurable consequences . . . permanently or temporarily; . . . opinions we are made to entertain concerning the degree and kind of his responsibility for what happens to him. . . .[5]

Professor Crane, of course, applies these factors to *Tom Jones,* one of the longest of English novels, and we cannot expect his criteria to be completely appropriate to so brief a story as *Tam o' Shanter.* Yet Professor Crane's method does carry us beyond the mere rehearsal of incidents and goes far to explain why a poem about danger and death is universally regarded, like *Tom Jones,* as comic.

In the first place, no one rates Tam's moral character highly. We are curious about what will happen to him rather than fearful that a good man will suffer, and we sense that his responsibility for what occurs is limited.[6] So we laugh at Tam's harrowing adventures; whatever fear and pity we feel is mingled with disesteem. We learn rapidly, moreover, that the events in which Tam becomes involved are only temporarily painful and that they conclude happily.[7] When the chase to the bridge occurs our expectations have been trained to anticipate an amusing rather than a tragic result. Our assurance is reinforced by the tone and manner of the narrator, who dawdles and philosophizes as a man with a terrible tale could not.

Yet *Tam o' Shanter* is not merely comic; it is tinged by suggestions of authentic horror. Cowper's *John Gilpin,* which also tells of an exciting ride, is simply funny; Gilpin himself is ludicrous. Tam, though amusing in his drunkenness, never becomes an object of derision. We feel for Tam even as we laugh at him. If the narrator's irony detaches the reader from the events of the story by minimizing his fear and weakening his sympathetic identification, the wonder of *Tam o' Shanter* is that we do become involved in the fantastic escapade. "[Burns] makes us hear Nannie and her infernal crew come galloping from the kirk to the river in full cry after poor Tam. The reader is left wide-eyed and breathless...."[8]

It is a commentary upon the present low estate of narrative verse that most modern techniques of literary criticism are derived from investigations of lyric and dramatic poetry. These methods have only limited usefulness in the study of narrative poetry, the outstanding characteristic of which, when it is contrasted to lyric or dramatic verse, is its movement, its flow in time. Of necessity a play is concerned with a dramatic situation.[9] A lyric is—relatively—so brief that we may without danger of going far wrong consider it temporally self-contained, timeless in the way that a painting is timeless. But a narrative is a temporal process. As E. M. Forster observes, the question we ask of the storyteller is "What happens next?"[10] A verse story like *Tam o' Shanter* is, in fact, a dynamic system of probabilities created first of all by the order of the happenings which occur, and only secondarily by the nature of the protagonist whom they befall. If the brevity of a lyric makes it comparable in its timelessness to a painting, the dynamic continuity of narrative poetry makes it comparable to music.

Professor Crane derives his critical approach from a study of tragedy, in which the focus of expectations is the protagonist. But art may arouse expectations without focussing on a protagonist. There is no hero in a symphony. In *Tam o' Shanter,* as in much narrative verse, the protagonist is relatively unimportant. At the climax of the final chase our interest is directed more toward his horse than toward him. Let us call to mind the ballad *Edward,* which has been "accepted as pre-eminently characteristic"[11] of the best ballad narratives. Who is Edward? What kind of a person is he? Obviously such questions are not germane to a determination of the ballad's excellence. The same is approximately true of *Tam o' Shanter*. Tam's unimportance helps to explain why our emotions are so engaged by a poem whose general form is comic and much of whose appeal lies in the plain heartiness of its humor. In *Tam o' Shanter* the events in themselves (not, that is, regarded as happenings which befall a particular hero) are not so much funny as tense and exciting.

The funniest lines in the poem occur at moments crucial to our anticipations. Even humor increases tension by delaying an envisaged catastrophe or by rendering our expectations ambiguous, or by changing the reader's perspective. Movement of perspective or point of view appears to be the narrative equivalent of the dialectical tensions so important to lyric and dramatic poetry. The lyric is too brief, too concentrated, to allow much manipulation of the reader's point of view, and the drama, because of the nature of its physical presentation, must employ elaborate mechanisms if it is to modify the viewer's perspective on the action.[12] But the onward flow of narrative demands that some device which will not impede its progress be employed to keep the audience from sinking into the lethargy of mere passive suspense. That device, as all who have had the luck to hear a gifted *raconteur* well know, consists of the teller's manoeuvring of his audience—thrusting them into the center of the action, then withdrawing them, and then again plunging them into the rush of events. In *Tam o' Shanter* Burns interweaves shifts of perspective with his progressive narrowing and intensifying of our expectations to prevent these from hardening early into a rigid pattern, to prevent the reader from establishing a fixed basis for judging what has happened and thereby arriving at too objective and too detached an attitude toward what may happen.

The poem opens, as it closes, with the perspective of full generalization. At first we are kept well away from the events: the "sulky, sullen dame" is, alas, anybody's wife, the narrator apostrophizes the "gentle dames" and Tam, and keeps his description of his hero's behavior "removed" by portraying it through Kate's comments. Gradually we come closer to Tam's point of view, but we do not adopt it for our own. We feel, as Mr. Daiches suggests,[13] as if we were in the same pub with Tam. Our viewpoint during the trip to Kirk-Alloway is mostly that of the protagonist, but "inspiring bold John Barleycorn" lengthens our perspective so that we see Tam urge the reluctant Maggie toward the blazing kirk, whereas the more colloquial exclamation "And, wow! Tam saw an unco sight!" projects us back to Tam as he glowers in the window. We watch with him until the humorous apostrophe "Now, Tam! O Tam! had thae been queans" once more extends our perspective. Our movement back toward the action is then retarded by the poet's mock confession of enfeebled descriptive power, by the three formal (but now Scots) similes describing the outburst of "the hellish legion," and the ironic lament for that "woefu' woman" Kate. But as the chase nears its climax our distance from the action diminishes until, finally, we see only the "Carlin" catching poor Maggie's tail just as she makes her heroic leap. Then our involvement is disintegrated by the grotesquely absurd generalizations of the epilogue, and we think back over the poem in a good-humored, comic mood.

This is not the way poetry was written by the Neo-classicists, whose ideals of genre and decorum resisted such a method. Burns's method of organizing his narrative is ill-suited to a purely satiric purpose, whereas Neo-classic writers tended to use poetic narrative only as a vehicle for satire. Probably, and if so not unjustifiably, they felt themselves to be too civilized and too sophisticated to indulge in narrative for its own sake.[14] One premise of all classical literature, that art requires clarity,[15] is hostile to the movement of ambiguous expectations controlled by shifting aesthetic distances upon which *Tam o' Shanter* is based.

Yet to say this is not to classify *Tam o' Shanter* as a Romantic work. Complex, non-satiric narrative we do expect from the Romantics. But it is apparent that at least some of the techniques we have isolated, the use of humor, for example, distinguish Burns's story from the verse narratives of, say, Coleridge, Shelley, and Keats. The relation of narrator to protagonist in *Tam o' Shanter* is not typical of Romantic literature. The narrator is assured, omnipresent, and yet definitely a teller and not a participant. And the drunken anonymity of Burns's protagonist is different from the simplified but still individualized protagonists of *Alastor, The Ancient Mariner,* and *Michael.* The crude, almost bestial, lack of individuality of drunken Tam, whose experience partakes of the impersonality of authentic peasant life, is not paralleled in the poetry of Burns's successors. There is, furthermore, an immediacy to the supernatural elements in *Tam o' Shanter* which is lacking in most early Romantic *diablerie.* Burns laughs heartily, not playfully or superciliously, at Auld Nick and his witches, because, one guesses, genuine fear of demonic power is still embedded deep in his subconscious mind.[16] It is at least not psychologically paradoxical to suggest that the Romantics could give primitive superstition so large a role in their poetry because they were at root indifferent to its power.

Perhaps the key to the un-Romantic qualities of *Tam o' Shanter* is provided by the direction of Tam's journey. Tam, like a good Romantic, rides away from the city into the country. Like the Ancient Mariner, like Waverley, like Don Juan, he leaves the populous centers of civilization and penetrates into a domain where Nature's works are more important than those of Man. But what happens to Tam in the country is strikingly un-Romantic: he almost loses his soul. The

Romantic hero is imperilled by his experiences in Nature, he undergoes stress and privation physically, but he wins a spiritual triumph. There is no hint of such triumph for Tam, probably because he, like his Neo-classic predecessors, comes from the country. A modern critic has deplored the influence of *Tam o' Shanter* upon Scottish literature, arguing that Burns deflected the attention of northern writers toward rural matters and away from a proper concern with city life.[17] If this argument be true, the Scotch have misread *Tam o' Shanter,* for the poem is divided, representing a struggle between the urban and the rural which is inconclusive, because the protagonist is outside both worlds. It is true that the main emphasis falls upon Tam's ride back into his rural countryside, but we scarcely need the explicit praise of Ayr to realize that the goal of Tam's aspirations, the place where he seeks pleasure and comfort, is the town.

Tam belongs to the country (he rides to town only for the market day), but his taste for urban enjoyments accentuates the bleakness of his rural life. In Tam's world pleasure is, indeed, "secret" and "precious," for it is fleeting, it can be snatched only momentarily and surreptitiously from the harshness of an existence dominated by a savage Nature that is herself a "sullen, sulky dame." For an instant "Care" may be drowned in "nappy," but the illusion of being "O'er a' the ills of life victorious" is transient. Country life is untouched by the graces of art,[18] and it is a dark life. The cheery brightness of the tavern forms a single, short-lived refuge in the dusk, each of the four similes which send Tam into the night stresses the transience of color, and the only light in the countryside is the unearthly blaze piercing the chinks of Kirk-Alloway. This is not the way the Romantics picture rural life, and the cause of its bleakness is not one they preferred to stress as Burns does. He is explicit: country life is a life of poverty; the scantiness of Nannie's sark is symbolic.[19]

Poverty links the rural-urban contrast to an English-Scottish contrast, dramatized by the opposition of a formal, rhetorical, idyllic, English poetic style to a homely, realistic, colloquial Scots style. The opposition appears most plainly in the similes that end the tavern episode.

> But Pleasures are like poppies spread,
> You seize the flower, its bloom is shed;
> Or like the snow falls in the river,
> A moment white, then melts forever;

> Or like the Borealis' race,
> That flit ere you can point their place;
> Or like the rainbow's lovely form,
> Evanishing amid the storm.

These lines have been adduced as evidence that Scots poets felt in their own dialect and thought in formal English in the eighteenth century,[20] but the passage has a specific function in the structure of *Tam o' Shanter*. England (and English) reinforces and extends the urban half of the rural-urban conflict. English can afford the luxury of formal, traditional, semi-philosophical similes, can treat the brevity of pleasure as art. Tam can afford only the realistic platitude "Nae man can tether Time or Tide," for Tam "maun ride." In his catastrophic world the fine phrases of the *literati* become ironic underscorings of its sinister destitution of spiritual, as well as of material, benefits. In the comfort and security of Ayr minutes pass "As bees flee hame wi' lades [o'] treasure," but the witches swarm out of Kirk-Alloway "as bees bizz out wi' angry fyke," to pursue not a thief in a crowded market, but a lonely peasant struggling homeward through a stormy night. To fully describe what Tam sees upon the altar "wad be unlawfu'," presumably in cities civilized with English culture, where churches have not crumbled into haunted kirks as religion has disintegrated into superstitious dread of "bogles," and where the beauty and grandeur of Nature can be extolled in comfort without fear of "dub and mire," of "slaps and styles," of a neck-breaking fall, or of stumbling upon the corpse of a mutilated child.

One is tempted to wonder if Burns had in the back of his mind the idyllic poetry of Gray, Goldsmith, and Cowper, but such speculations are not germane, for the point of the savage realism of the Scots portion of *Tam o' Shanter* is that it is not introduced as social protest. Burns is not crying for rural reform. The horror of Tam's peasant world appears, as it were, unconsciously. The poem is humorous; it has darker aspects because Burns could not help writing about the life he knew as it appeared to him, and he was a clear-sighted and honest man. But, and this is the crux of our discussion, the life Burns knew and the way it appeared to him can be distinguished from the kind of life and the view of that life celebrated in most Romantic narrative poems. If Burns's artistic techniques in the narrative form separate him from Neo-classicism and link him to Romanticism, the subject-matter of his poem separates his work from that of the genuine Romantics.[21]

Presumably, then, the Romantic predisposition toward narrative verse arose not from extra-poetic concerns but from the very perceptions out of which Romantic poetry was created. It is in the connection between narrative form and narrative subject-matter that we may expect to find some of the major causes and meanings of the early nineteenth-century flowering of poetic narrative. In the following chapter we shall examine the form-subject relation in eighteenth-century ballad-imitations, for the ballad is in many respects the key to what Josephine Miles has defined as "The Romantic Mode."[22]

Chapter II

*

NEO-CLASSIC BALLAD-IMITATING

Our subject in this chapter is not anonymous, popular ballads but artificial ballad-imitations by sophisticated eighteenth-century poets. Interest in balladic subjects, themes, and techniques is characteristic of Romantic poets, witness Keats's *La Belle Dame sans Merci,* Scott's *Proud Maisie,* and the *Lyrical Ballads* of Coleridge and Wordsworth.[1] Most students of this Romantic predilection have concentrated upon the relationship of these Romantic poems to their primitive models. Our purpose is to trace the evolution of sophisticated ballad-imitating in itself, from its origin in the conservative aesthetic of the early eighteenth century to its emergence as a prominent feature in the revolutionary poetic movement of the early nineteenth century. We are interested, then, in the practice of ballad-imitating as a revelation of the way in which Neo-classic literary style was transformed into Romantic literary style.[2] In the succeeding chapter we shall try to evaluate the significance of this genre's contribution to that stylistic transformation.

"A ballad is a folk-song that tells a story with stress on the crucial situation, tells it by letting the action unfold itself in event and speech, and tells it objectively with little comment or intrusion of personal bias."[3] We may distinguish two principal classes of ballads: the historical and the adventurous.[4] Historical ballads are those most nearly allied to the epic; their subject, often an authentic historical event, concerns more than one or two private individuals, affecting larger social units, at least the clan, perhaps even the nation; an example is *Chevy Chase.* The adventurous ballad is more personal, less heroic, often trivial; it recounts merely "some event which is interesting; which is an adventure";[5] an example is *The Babes in the Wood.* These are not airtight categories, but it is surprising how little blending one finds among genuine ballads. In the ballad-imitations with which we are concerned, however, the separation or intermixing of these classes is often of paramount importance. For example, in the first significant ballad-imitation of the eighteenth century, Prior's recasting of *The Nutbrowne Maide* as *Henry and Emma,* we find the source of Prior's changes to be his endeavor to transform his adventurous original into an historical poem, almost a chivalric romance, in fact.

In *The Nutbrowne Maide,* one of the finest of English "dialogue" ballads, two singers dramatize the testing of the nutbrown maid's steadfast affection for her lover, who comes to her by night and tells her (falsely) that he has been banished and must leave her. She swears that she will accompany him, but he raises a series of objections. To his argument that she will be accused of lewdness, she replies,

> Theirs be the charge that speke so large
>   In hurting of my name.
> For I wyl prove that feythful love
>   It is devoyd of shame.

Next he asks if she is willing to become an outlaw like himself. To be with him, yes, she responds. In succeeding stanzas she declares that she will fight with him, endure privation, give up her comforts, even cut off her hair and take on man's dress. Then he argues that such willingness shows her to be merely lecherous, to which she replies that he had to labor long to gain her love, but once he had won it she proved her constancy by disregarding his "lowe degree" even though she is a baron's daughter. But he suggests that if she goes with him, later she will regret her loss of high estate and will revile him for betraying her. She answers that if he goes without her, he will be betraying her more certainly. He then says he possesses another paramour upon whom he dotes, but the nutbrown maid insists that she will still go with him and be the girl's servant to prove the trueness of her love. At this the man relents and confesses his trick, but she is still suspicious, thinking he has only found a new way to escape alone. He convinces her by admitting that he is no poor squire but has a rich heritage in "Westermerlande" to which "I wyl you bringe and wyth a rynge,/Be wey of maryage." Thus persuaded, she concludes the poem by observing that some women are faithful, not "variable," and by suggesting that men owe to God the kind of single-minded devotion she has shown her lover.[6]

Prior retains this plot as the core of *Henry and Emma,* devoting the central portion of his poem to a dialogue between the hero and heroine. But he precedes this colloquy with 261 lines of narrative scene-setting, and he appends another 54 lines of epilogue at its conclusion. If we examine these additions (which in large measure account for the striking difference in the length of the two poems, 360 lines in *The Nutbrowne Maide* and 784 in *Henry and Emma*), we find that their function is to locate the dialogue in a specific historical time and place and to reduce it to the central episode in a semi-epical, courtly romance. Thus in his prologue Prior identifies Emma's father as one of King Edward's supporters in his war against France (ll. 43–50), describes Emma's childhood and the origin of her title "The Nut-brown Maid," tells how "In tilts and tournaments the valiant strove,/By glorious deeds to purchase Emma's love" (ll. 80–81), explains how Henry won Emma's affection, and narrates the way in which the lovers arranged their nocturnal tryst.[7] And in his conclusion Prior insists that Emma's heroic steadfastness is symptomatic of that British sturdiness which not only enabled Edward to triumph but which sustained "unwearied Marlborough's toils," and deserves, therefore, an annual holiday with "everlasting marks of honour paid,/ To the true lover, and the Nut-Browne Maid" (ll. 783–84).

It is not alone Prior's expansion of the story of *The Nutbrowne Maide* which displays his hope of transforming an adventurous ballad into an heroic romance. His changes in form are as revealing. The ballad is composed of thirty twelve-line stanzas. The odd lines have four stresses, the even three. The four-stress lines rhyme internally; lines two, four, six, and eight all carry the same rhyme; and line ten in each stanza rhymes with the refrain of line twelve, either "Alone, a banysshid man" if the man is speaking, or, if it is the woman's part, "I love but you alone." This rigorously complex form becomes in *Henry and Emma,* of course, a procession of heroic couplets that permits variation in the length of speeches.[8] Not only has Prior framed the plot with beginning and concluding description and diffused the ballad's intense concentration upon the crucial episode—not allowed the action to unfold itself—but he has, by destroying the stiff stanzaic organization of his original, opened out a formalized debate into something like the slow-paced, line-by-line progress of an epic.

These changes in form are accompanied by a logical clarity not found in *The Nutbrowne Maide.* The variation in the length of the protagonists' speeches (from thirteen to fifty-three lines), for example, depends on the complexity of the ideas and feeling they express.

Prior, furthermore, modifies his version of the refrain, invariable in the ballad, to link succeeding portions of the colloquy. Thus Emma's fifth speech concludes: "That, leaving all mankind, I love but him alone."[9] Henry replies to this assertion: "O wildest thoughts of an abandon'd mind!" And he develops this suggestion that Emma has mistaken her own inclination, concluding not with his usual emphasis upon himself as "a banish'd man, condemn'd in woods to rove," but with an accusation:

> No longer loose desire for constant love
> Mistake; but say, 'tis man with whom thou long'st to rove.
> (ll. 533–34)

Prior sustains logical coherence with what we may call grammatical continuity. In the ballad, although the woman regularly replies to the specific objection that the man has raised in the preceding stanza, he seldom bases his next test upon her answer. The rigid stanzaic form requires that this should be so. Each pair of question and answer stanzas forms a unit which refers back not so much to what has immediately gone before as to the original situation. The unity of *Henry and Emma* derives from Prior's interlinking of the various stages of the debate into a continuous development. The unity of *The Nutbrowne Maide,* on the contrary, is that of a series of separate arguments about different aspects of the fundamental problem. *Henry and Emma* has the unity, so to speak, of a motion picture, the ballad of a series of slides of the same subject.

Increasing emotional intensity in *The Nutbrowne Maide* depends upon repetition. Prior, on the contrary, can increase intensity only by progressively exaggerating Henry's cruelty and Emma's affection. As a result, Henry comes to seem sadistic, and Emma, who is meant to be more refined and civilized than the ballad heroine,[10] becomes priggishly self-righteous,[11] then frantically emotional,

> Wanting the scissors, with these hands I'll tear
> (If that obstructs my flight) this load of hair.
> Black soot, or yellow walnut, shall disgrace
> This little red and white of Emma's face, (ll. 511–14)

and, finally, hyperbolically self-pitying and self-dramatizing:

> Yet, when increasing grief brings slow disease;
> And ebbing life, on terms severe as these,
> Will have its little lamp no longer fed;

> When Henry's mistress shews him Emma dead;
> Rescue my poor remains from vile neglect:
> With virgin honours let my hearse be deckt,
> With decent emblem; and at least persuade
> This happy nymph, that Emma may be laid
> Where thou, dear author of my death, where she,
> With frequent eye my sepulchre may see.[12] (ll. 624–33)

The meaning of these differences is symbolized by the titles of the poems. The hero and heroine of *The Nutbrowne Maide* are anonymous because they are unimportant except as participants in a story. They exist in a passive, fatalistic world, the world of the ballad. The man says he is banished, but gives no reason, and the woman asks for none, just as she accepts without protest the idea of her lover's new mistress, and, at the end, demands no explanation (none being offered) for the deception to which she has been subjected. Prior names his protagonists just as he locates them in a specific time and place. Henry provides a reason for his supposed banishing (he has killed a man), and he tries, with weakening feebleness, to justify the torture to which he has put Emma's feelings.[13] Emma, lacking her prototype's fatalistic acceptance, is forced to explain and to justify her feelings, and falls into the romanticizing sentimentality we have illustrated. Hence Emma finally appears less convincing, less realistic than her anonymous model. When, for example, she replies to Henry's urging of the hardship of forest life,

> When from the cave thou risest with the day,
> To beat the woods, and rouse the bounding prey;
> The cave with moss and branches I'll adorn,
> And cheerful sit, to wait my lord's return, (ll. 406–9)

we feel that Prior has robbed Emma of the ballad heroine's honest practicality, expressed in her response to the same difficulty: "And er we go, a bed or too/I can provide anoon" (ll. 213–14). In short, Prior shifts the emphasis from the unfolding of the story in itself to a stress upon how the characters feel about the event in which they are concerned.

Prior's stress upon the evolution of sentiment in his characters combined with the epic frame in which he centers the ballad episode excludes all supernatural enrichment of his story. *Henry and Emma* ends with an invocation of those tarnished literary divinities Venus and Mars, whereas *The Nutbrowne Maide* concludes with a simple but appropriate prayer to the Christian deity.[14] Lacking the ballad's passive fatalism and anonymity and its openness to supernatural reference, Prior's poem cannot be endowed with the kind of symbolic import which later renders *La Belle Dame sans Merci* and *The Ancient Mariner,* for example, so impressive. It is precisely this lack of symbolic import which defines most Neo-classic ballad-imitations, not merely *Henry and Emma,* as imitations.

Prior's concern for the way his characters feel about events rather than for the events in themselves cannot be dissociated from a stylistic "improvement" which he works upon his original. In *The Nutbrowne Maide* one finds few adjectives and almost no adverbs. The adjectives are of a stock, traditional kind: "wylde dere," "swete moder," "lowe degree." *Henry and Emma,* on the other hand, is filled with adverbs and adjectives, most of which attribute emotional qualities to the substantives they modify: "weary steps," "tedious day," "happy race," "dejected eyes," "wounded stone." Whereas objects and ideas in the ballad appear starkly, directly, and without modification, in *Henry and Emma* they are presented in terms of the emotions they arouse in the characters. Prior is able to introduce this subjective coloring into the baldness of the ballad story, first, because he conceives of that story as occurring to definite and particular individuals, and, second, because he possesses a rich vocabulary which he controls with exactitude. When he has Emma say that she will serve Henry "with humble duty and officious haste," or has Henry speak of "Th' ambrosial plenty of thy shining hair," Prior is not merely displaying elegance or padding out pentameter lines. He is also defining what these particular people think and feel under the pressure of specific circumstances. Such definition requires more than vocabulary; it demands complex grammar, skillful control of the relations of words. Prior can express complicated thoughts with grace and fluency, never losing track of his central idea while presenting it amidst all necessary qualifications and associations.

> When, chill'd by adverse snows and beating rain,
> We tread with weary steps the longsome plain;
> When with hard toil we seek our evening food,
> Berries and acorns, from the neighbouring wood;
> And find among the cliffs no other house,
> But the thin covert of some gathered boughs
> Wilt thou not then reluctant send thine eye
> Around the dreary waste; and weeping try

(Though then, alas! that trial be too late)
To find thy father's hospitable gate,
And seats, where ease and plenty brooding sate? (ll. 380–90)

Command of grammatical ordering enables Prior to freight single words with meaningful ambiguity, as in the phrase quoted above, "where ease and plenty *brooding* sate." He can, furthermore, manipulate long and complex metaphors, e.g., lines 397–402, and utilize devices such as metonymy and personification as well as compress complicated concepts into epigrammatic brevity. Prior is not in these abilities superior to other poets of his time, but he is better equipped than was the unknown author of *The Nutbrowne Maide*. The ballad writer has a small vocabulary, weak in latinate words and in terms for concepts, emotions, and states of mind. His syntax is simple, feeble in subordination, and without the flexibility to make single words function ambiguously. In brief, the ballad author is confined, as Prior is not, to a simplified and stylized language.

From that stylization of language arises, however, the effectiveness of the ballad's imagery.

For an outlawe this is the lawe,
That men hym take and binde,
Without pytee hanged to bee,
And waver with the wynde. (ll. 145–48)

Paucity of language enforces a directness, a definiteness in the figures of the ballad that is more striking than Prior's rationally extended and subtle similes. Compare, for example, the ballad's

O Lorde, what is this worldis blisse
That chaungeth as the mone!
My somers day in lusty May
Is derked before the none. (ll. 61–64)

with Prior's

What is our bliss, that changeth with the moon;
And day of life, that darkens ere 'tis noon. (ll. 289–90)

But, on the whole, figurative language is rare in *The Nutbrowne Maide,* for it lacks the richness of vocabulary and the complexity of syntax necessary to sustain comparisons and modifications. The typical ballad metaphor is formalized: "as cold as ony stone." The writer depends on definiteness of statement, on stark, objective presentation of an emotion-charged event. There is plenty of feeling in both *The*

Nutbrowne Maide and *Henry and Emma,* but in the latter poem, thanks to Prior's superior linguistic and grammatical gifts, we find a variety of emotions used to express personality. In the ballad there is the single, simple emotion arising from the intense situation.

Henry and Emma is nevertheless inferior to its original because the style and the content of the ballad are compatible and unified whereas they conflict in Prior's poem. With neither fanfare nor apology the ballad writer plunges into his story, absorbs himself in it, so to speak. Prior's chivalric embellishments show his sophisticated detachment from his subject. He can frame his story, manipulate its form, because he has not lost himself in it. Consequently, all his technical skill appears externally applied, ornamental, artificial. *Henry and Emma* illustrates a critical dilemma faced by the Neo-classic poet: his possession of a literary language of wonderful precision and flexibility derived from a civilized sophistication which prevented him from surrendering himself to his subject. Hence the artificiality of much Augustan verse, which frequently dramatizes trivialities with linguistic virtuosity. Hence, too, the unparalleled achievement of Alexander Pope, to whom (as to Racine) limitation of subject-matter happened to be congenial. A large part of Pope's satire consists in showing to be trivial that which most people regard as important. In *The Rape of the Lock* he systematically exploits the incongruity between his petty subject and his epic form.[15] A similar incongruity—unexploited—spoils *Henry and Emma.*

Henry and Emma, faulty as it may be, strives toward an organic organization. Prior is not mocking or satiric. He respects the authenticity of the emotion crystallized by his model. He does not, like his immediate successors, emphasize the contrast between crude ballad subject and sophisticated style. He does not turn ballads into songs. Nor does he, as mid-century poets were later to do, employ the ballad style to confine and diminish the richness of Neo-classic poetic language. Prior fails, paradoxically, because he endeavors to elevate the ballad *in toto,* matter and manner together, to the level of elegant literature.[16]

Although none of Prior's contemporaries tried his kind of ballad-imitating, the significance of his practice is defined by Joseph Addison's critical remarks upon the ballad in 1711. In that year Addison devoted two *Spectator* papers to praise and analysis of *Chevy Chase.*[17] In the first, Addison rejects Sir Philip Sidney's criticism of "the rude

Stile and evil Apparel of this Antiquated song," asserting, on the contrary, that

It is impossible that anything should be universally tasted and approved by a Multitude, tho' they are only the Rabble of a Nation, which hath not in it some particular Aptness to please and gratify the Mind of Man. . . . *Homer, Virgil,* or *Milton,* so far as the Language of their poems is understood, will please a Reader of plain common Sense, who would neither relish nor comprehend an Epigram of *Martial,* or a Poem of *Cowley.* So, on the contrary, an ordinary Song or Ballad that is the Delight of the Common People, cannot fail to please all such readers as are not unqualified for the Entertainment by their affectation or Ignorance; and the reason is plain, because the same Paintings of Nature which recommend it to the most ordinary Reader, will appear Beautiful to the most refined.[18]

In this passage Addison renders apparent the way in which the eighteenth century's faith in the soundness of the ordinary man's common-sense judgment validated both an interest in ballads and a taste for imitating them. But Addison does not rest his case solely on the approval of the multitude. *Chevy Chase,* he argues, is an epic, an epic comparable to *The Iliad* or *The Aeneid* in theme and "majestic simplicity" of sentiment. He points out numerous parallels between Virgil's poem and the ballad, insisting particularly that the final stanza of the ballad,

God save the King and bless the Land
In plenty, Joy, and Peace;
And grant henceforth that foul Debate
'Twixt Noblemen may cease,

satisfies Le Bossu's rule that "an heroick Poem should be founded upon some important Precept of Morality adapted to the constitution of the Country in which the Poet writes."[19] Addison did not know he was quoting from an "improved" version of *Chevy Chase.* Most of the epic parallels he cites are not in the original ballad we read today.[20] Addison, in fact, insists that the author of the ballad did not copy Virgil but was "directed by the same poetical genius, and by the same copyings after Nature." Addison, like Prior, sees the ballad as potential epic. This view is possible because neither critic nor poet is thinking historically about literature, but instead both are considering it in terms of genre.

But in 1711 faith in popular taste was not yet widespread. Just as Prior had no followers, Addison found few supporters. Indeed, his *Chevy Chase* articles were attacked, particularly by John Dennis,[21] and Addison never defended the position he had somewhat rashly assumed. Half a century later, however, his idea of the historical ballad as a kind of primitive epic was revived when historical and antiquarian knowledge increased; that revival led finally to *The Ancient Mariner.* That the historical ballad could be re-elevated in the mid-eighteenth century was due largely to the success of Addison's first proposition: that "an ordinary Song or Ballad that is the Delight of the Common People" is worthy of the sophisticated poet's attention. Two weeks after his *Chevy Chase* papers, Addison re-asserted this point.[22] Though on the defensive (he now admits the "despicable simplicity" of ballad language) and no longer pressing the claims of *Chevy Chase,* he continues to defend popular taste and the "genuine and unaffected" sentiments of ballads, arguing that they please because they are "a copy of Nature." In this paper, significantly, he produces as evidence an adventurous ballad, *The Babes in the Wood.*[23]

Addison's shift from the historical, epic-like ballad to the homely and adventurous kind is symptomatic of the early eighteenth-century attitude toward ballad-imitation. Until the time of Shenstone no poet attempted anything like the heroic narrative of *Henry and Emma* and no critic resumed Addison's defense of the heroic ballads. But the imitation of adventurous ballads flourished. Sophisticated poets turned ballads into songs, often exploiting that contrast between literary style and primitive subject we observed in *Henry and Emma.* This practice is well illustrated by Tickell's *Colin and Lucy* and Mallet's *Margaret's Ghost,* particularly the latter, because the story upon which it is based is the same one that Bürger later used for his *Lenore,* which was translated into seven English versions by five poets in one year, 1796.[24] All the Romantic versions emphasize the sensational narrative, whereas Mallet reduces the story to a single, sentimental, and rather elegantly described situation. But the master of this kind of imitation was John Gay.

The Beggar's Opera, of course, stands as the principal monument to Gay's genius for transforming ballad tunes, ballad characters, ballad situations, and ballad attitudes into polished, stingingly ironic verse.[25] *The Beggar's Opera* is too long and complex to be discussed here, but we can observe the essentials of Gay's technique in the following ballad from *The What D'Ye Call It.*[26]

'Twas when the seas were roaring
With hollow blasts of wind;

A damsel lay deploring,
  All on a rock reclined.
Wide o'er the rolling billows
  She cast a wistful look;
Her head was crowned with willows
  That tremble o'er the brook.

Twelve months are gone and over,
  And nine long tedious days.
Why didst thou, vent'rous lover,
  Why didst thou trust the seas?
Cease, cease, thou cruel ocean,
  And let my lover rest:
Ah! what's thy troubled motion
  To that within my breast?

The merchant, robbed of pleasure,
  Sees tempests in despair;
But what's the loss of treasure
  To losing of my dear?
Should you some coast be laid on
  Where gold and diamonds grow,
You'd find a richer maiden,
  But none that loves you so.

How can they say that nature
  Has nothing made in vain;
Why then beneath the water
  Should hideous rocks remain?
No eyes the rocks discover,
  That lurk beneath the deep,
To wreck the wand'ring lover,
  And leave the maid to weep.

All melancholy lying,
  Thus wailed she for her dear;
Repaid each blast with sighing,
  Each billow with a tear;
When, o'er the white wave stooping,
  His floating corpse she spied;
Then like a lily drooping,
  She bowed her head, and died.

Though very different from *Henry and Emma,* this delightful poem shows that Gay, like Prior, sought to elevate the ballad by improving its form. By aiming for the regularity and charm of a song rather than for the impressiveness of heroic verse Gay succeeds much better. In fact, he is so successful that we are likely to overlook the sensationalism of the incident which is the subject of the poem and to disregard the violence of the girl's emotion. Just as Emma in Prior's poem becomes almost hysterical in expressing her feelings (as contrasted to the restraint of the original nutbrown maid), so Gay's heroine indulges in a display of sentiment far more uninhibited and theatrical—"Repaid each blast with sighing,/Each billow with a tear"—than most ballad characters attempt.

We are not offended by this hyperemotionalism because it is presented in a formal manner that keeps us at once detached and charmed by the precise regularity of its movement. Like a five-act play, the five-stanza ballad has introduction, a central section of increasing emotional intensity, and a dramatic conclusion. Throughout the poem antithesis and parallelism, similitude and contrast provide a balanced and proportioned intellectual structure. In each stanza the first and third rhyme pairs are feminine, the second and fourth masculine. The imagery is skillfully linked. For example, the comparison of the girl in stanza five to "a lily drooping" carries the mind back to the picture of the willows "that tremble o'er the brook" in stanza one. The diction is carefully controlled: the "vent'rous lover" of stanza two becomes in stanza four "the wand'ring lover."

Gay achieves this control of form by reducing a potential narrative to a single situation, a single scene. By reducing narrative flow he attains formalized symmetry. His subject, as distinct from his form, is violently emotional; it is pure sentiment, a lovelorn girl's despairing lament. Contrast between formal manner and emotional matter is characteristic of Gay. In *The Beggar's Opera* the very title suggests an incongruity between the way of dramatizing and the subject dramatized. And that incongruity is sustained by the opera itself, in which the most savage passions, lust, avarice, fear, and treachery, appear in the glittering dress of the perfect verses.[27] But this technique is not Gay's possession alone; it is, in varying degrees, typical of most of his contemporaries. Its significance for the development of ballad-imitating which we are tracing can be illustrated by a comparison of Gay's poem with Wordsworth's *Alice Fell.*

Alice Fell, the story of the little girl who bemoaned her lost cloak, is surely one of Wordsworth's least attractive poems. It has none of the precision and formal structure which distinguish Gay's poem. It is as prosaically flat as an authentic second-rate ballad. Alice's lamentation for her miserable garment is as strenuous as that of Gay's heroine, but her grief is portrayed not with formal artistry but with bald repetitiveness:

> Insensible to all relief
> Sat the poor girl, and forth did send
> Sob after sob, as if her grief
> Could never, never, have an end.[28]

This insistence upon literal exactness arises, in part at least, from Wordsworth's treatment of the poem's central incident not as a self-contained dramatic situation but as one episode of a little story. And narrative, though producing objectionable awkwardness in form, enables him to develop the moral significance of the event. Wordsworth's point is that little Alice's grief for her cloak is as genuine and as harrowing to her as a more serious loss might be to an adult; it is our feelings for things that endow them with value. There is no such moral insight in Gay's poem; the incongruous relation of form to subject precludes the kind of particularized realism upon which Wordsworth's insight is founded. We feel that what happens in *Alice Fell* could happen in real life, although the event the poem narrates is unusual if not singular, because the poet relates simple, commonplace actions in the order and manner in which they do in fact occur. Probably a certain number of young men do drown every year leaving behind brokenhearted fiancées, but that literal reality, and the moral truth which resides within it, are of no interest to Gay. This difference between Gay's ballad and Wordsworth's dramatizes perhaps the most fundamental change that ballad-imitating underwent during the course of the later eighteenth century, and we must try now to describe some of the principal stages in that development.

The first timid step was taken by William Shenstone, whose contribution not only to the shaping of Percy's *Reliques* but to the whole mid-century climate of opinion concerning ballads has gained full recognition only in the last few years.[29] Shenstone, in fact, is the first literary man to state clearly the modern distinction between ballads and songs. "It has become habitual to me to call that a *Ballad* which describes or implies some *Action;* ... I term that a *Song,* which contains only an Expression of Sentiment."[30] Perhaps even more significant are some of Shenstone's general remarks about the poetry of his age. The following, for example, throws light upon the attitude of those "men of taste" whom Percy so ardently desired to please. "The public has seen all that art can do, and they want the more striking efforts of wild, original, enthusiastic genius."[31] When we turn to Shenstone's poetry, however, we find little that can be characterized as the work of a "wild, original, enthusiastic genius." But at least one of his poems, *Jemmy Dawson,* is of real importance to our study, and, though long, deserves full quotation.

1. Come listen to my mournful tale,
   Ye tender hearts and lovers dear!
   Nor will you scorn to heave a sigh,
   Nor need you blush to shed a tear.

2. And thou dear Kitty! peerless maid!
   Do thou a pensive ear incline;
   For thou canst weep at every woe,
   And pity every plaint—but mine.

3. Young Dawson was a gallant boy,
   A brighter never trod the plain;
   And well he loved one charming maid,
   And dearly was he loved again.

4. One tender maid, she loved him dear;
   Of gentle blood the damsel came;
   And faultless was her beauteous form,
   And spotless was her virgin fame.

5. But curse on party's hateful strife,
   That led the favour'd youth astray;
   The day the rebel clans appear'd—
   O had he never seen that day!

6. Their colours and their sash he wore,
   And in the fatal dress was found;
   And now he must that death endure
   Which gives the brave the keenest wound.

7. How pale was then his true love's cheek,
   When Jemmy's sentence reach'd her ear!
   For never yet did Alpine snows
   So pale, or yet so chill appear.

8. With faltering voice she, weeping, said,
   "O Dawson! monarch of my heart!

Think not thy death shall end our loves,
For thou and I will never part.

9. "Yet might sweet mercy find a place,
And bring relief to Jemmy's woes,
O George! without a prayer for thee,
My orisons should never close.

10. "The gracious prince that gave him life,
Would crown a never-dying flame;
And every tender babe I bore
Should learn to lisp the giver's name.

11. "But though he should be dragg'd in scorn
To yonder ignominious tree;
He shall not want one constant friend
To share the cruel Fates' decree."

12. Oh! then her mourning coach was call'd ;
The sledge moved slowly on before;
Though borne in a triumphal car,
She had not loved her favourite more.

13. She follow'd him, prepared to view
The terrible behests of law;
And the last scene of Jemmy's woes,
With calm and steadfast eye she saw.

14. Distorted was that blooming face,
Which she had fondly loved so long;
And stifled was that tuneful breath,
Which in her praise had sweetly sung:

15. And sever'd was that beauteous neck,
Round which her arms had fondly closed;
And mangled was that beauteous breast,
On which her lovesick head reposed:

16. And ravish'd was that constant heart,
She did to every heart prefer;
For though it could its king forget,
'Twas true and loyal still to her.

17. Amid those unrelenting flames
She bore this constant heart to see;
But when 'twas moulder'd into dust,
"Yet, yet," she cried, "I follow thee.

18. "My death, my death alone can show
    The pure, the lasting love I bore:
    Accept, O Heaven! of woes like ours,
    And let us, let us weep no more."

19. The dismal scene was o'er and past,
    The lover's mournful hearse retired;
    The maid drew back her languid head,
    And, sighing forth his name, expired.

20. Though justice ever must prevail,
    The tear my Kitty sheds is due;
    For seldom shall she hear a tale
    So sad, so tender, yet so true.[32]

Shenstone's principal interest, we observe, is Dawson's sweetheart. Many Augustan ballads deal with distressed heroines, whose clothing is likely to be "charmingly disarrayed." Only later in the century do ballad heroes come into their own. But Shenstone, although retaining in reduced form Prior's frame, and though, like Gay, containing violent emotion within prettiness of language, more nearly approached both the matter and the manner of genuine ballads than had his predecessors. As a result, his rhetoric and diction seem clumsy. It is difficult to decide what the first two lines of stanzas ten and seventeen mean, and throughout the poem there is an awkward mixing of artlessness and elegance. Stanza three is reasonably close to ballad rhetoric, whereas the simile of stanza seven and the epigram of stanza sixteen are learned. Shenstone loosens the tight versification of earlier ballad-imitators. He uses the ballad rhyme scheme but avoids the most familiar ballad meter, retaining four stresses in each line, although he sometimes has to pad his second and fourth lines with two-syllable adjectives or with repetitions (stanza eighteen). Equally inconsistent is his diction. He sometimes intrudes one formal, learned word into a stanza otherwise simple in language: "orisons" in stanza nine and "ignominious" in eleven.

Yet in two respects at least his imitation is more interesting than Prior's or Gay's. Shenstone's ballad is concerned with a real event and a real traitor; it was, as the subtitle says, "written about the time of his [Dawson's] execution, in the year 1745." This is important not so much because it shows Shenstone adhering to the habit of popular balladeers of turning current events into narrative songs, but because it tends to make him treat his subject as a story rather than as a situation. *Jemmy Dawson* unfolds an event. Significantly, there is no conversation between Dawson and his sweetheart, although Shenstone could have introduced it. That he did not is symptomatic of his concern with the unrolling of a series of incidents rather than with the presentation of statically sentimental characters. This concern produces something like the passivity or fatalism of genuine ballads. As we have observed before, Gay's heroine and Prior's Emma do little or nothing, but we do not have the sense that they are caught in an immutable chain of circumstances. That sense Shenstone arouses, if only mildly. And because he does so, he is able in his last stanza to pose, in gentle and tentative fashion, a moral problem: "Though justice ever must prevail,/The tear my Kitty sheds is due."

Jemmy Dawson, interesting though it is both as a step toward the realization of the valuable qualities in authentic ballads and as a step down from the formal excellence of earlier imitations, is perhaps most significant as an illustration of the limited value of the ballad to poets committed to the Neo-classic style. That style was founded on premises antithetical to ballad themes and techniques. As the fate of Addison's criticism demonstrates, in itself the Neo-classic manner resisted even innovation which was supported by the pressure of changing social and economic conditions.[33] We would scarcely predict on the basis of Shenstone's single, tentative experiment in 1745 that within a generation English literature would be teeming with literalistic imitations of every kind of popular ballad. For this to happen the impact of some alien force to which Neo-classicism was peculiarly vulnerable was required. That force was released by Thomas Gray, the retiring and fastidious scholar whose *Elegy Written in a Country Church-yard* has come in the popular mind to represent the essence of late Neoclassic art.

Chapter III

ROMANTIC BALLADRY

Thomas Gray, who opened the way for mid-eighteenth-century balladeers, wrote no ballads himself. This seeming paradox is only one manifestation of a profound psychological inconsistency or dividedness in Gray's personality. "...behind all those relics that testify to his fertile brain lies the drama of the mental conflict between the creative artist and the antiquarian." [1] This conflict is not peculiar to Gray; it is, in fact, characteristic of most mid-eighteenth-century English poets, the Wartons, Thomas Percy,[2] and Thomas Chatterton, for example. The struggle between antiquarianism and creativity in which so many literary men of this period engaged deserves more careful study than it has yet received. It is by no means an inevitable feature of literary endeavor. To Milton, for example, literary creation separated from scholarship would have been unthinkable. To Pope, however, scholarship, though a prerequisite to the writing of poetry, had no place in the finished verse. To him, as to most of the great Augustans, antiquarianism *per se* was the concern of dunces. To Wordsworth and his contemporaries the poet's creative act was an escape from a scholarly or antiquarian frame of mind, a regaining of the voice of "a Man speaking to men."

We may, then, regard the conjunction of Gray's influence upon ballad popularizers like Percy with his unwillingness to imitate ballads as symptomatic of a critical ambivalence in the mid-eighteenth-century sensibility. That ambivalence is further illustrated by Gray's response to the reception of his published poetry. He deplored the enthusiastic approval of his early poems, particularly the *Elegy*. Then, in 1757, he proudly and confidently published his Pindaric odes, *The Progress of Poesy* and *The Bard,* only to have them ignored or decried by the public.[3] The effect of this reception upon Gray was disastrous. He published no more original poetry, confining himself to a few small translations. Yet it was the Pindaric odes, particularly *The Bard,* which influenced those "men of letters" who were to determine the course of English poetry for the next quarter of a century. Evans, Mason, the Wartons, Percy, and Chatterton all were, in different ways, inspired by Gray's example.[4]

For our purposes the most striking feature of *The Bard* is the way in which it brings together without emphasis upon their incongruity a primitive subject and a classical form, a union implicitly encouraged by Addison's two papers praising the epic qualities of *Chevy Chase.* Ostensibly Gray employed his legendary Welsh subject-matter only as a vehicle for his experiment in the Pindaric form. But such a combination in itself implied a criticism of the purest Neo-classic standards. Gray would not have turned to the "sublime primitivism" of the Welsh heroic fable as a means of attaining something like the lofty grandeur of Pindar's verse had any of the more conventional Neo-classic subjects seemed as suitable. And of course sophisticated form and primitive subject became mingled in *The Bard;* Gray modified his Pindaric verses by introducing Welsh meters and enriched his ancient and provincial legend with references to Shakespeare and Milton, an image drawn from a painting by Raphael (I, 2), and even a reminiscence of Homer.[5] This interpenetration made it almost inevitable that those who were attracted to *The Bard* were at least as much impressed by its presentation of a sensational event as by its scholastic display of the technicalities of antique versification.

And if we compare the opening lines of *The Bard*—

> "Ruin seize thee, ruthless King!
> Confusion on thy banners wait,
> Though fanned by Conquest's crimson wing
> They mock the air with idle state,"—

with those of Prior's *Henry and Emma*—

> Thou, to whose eyes I bend, at whose command
> (Though low my voice, though artless be my hand)
> I take the sprightly reed, and sing, and play;
> Careless of what the censuring world may say;—

and with those of Coleridge's *The Ancient Mariner*—

> It is an ancient Mariner
> And he stoppeth one of three.
> "By thy long grey beard and glittering eye,
> Now wherefore stopp'st thou me?—

we see that it is not merely Gray's flexible use of the octosyllabic line and his manipulation of alliterative devices which link his verse more closely to that of his successor than to that of his predecessor. Gray and Coleridge begin in *medias res.* Prior begins with a formal and conventionalized address to Chloe. This difference illustrates a change in the attitudes of the poets toward their legendary subjects. Prior feels that only a skillful playfulness of presentation at first can justify a sophisticated poet's attention to a primitive story. Gray and Coleridge, much as they differ from one another, share the desire to re-enact the event that is their subject. Prior, re-casting a dramatic ballad, tempers it into formalized narration; Gray and Coleridge manoeuvre their narrative material to produce dramatic situations out of which the action of their stories may seem to unfold itself.

There is no detailed resemblance between *The Bard* and *The Ancient Mariner.* The contrast between these poems and Prior's illustrates how sharply Gray in his odes broke with his predecessors in his use of primitive and popular subjects while retaining some of their mannerisms of diction and of rhetoric. Gray was the first important English poet to re-enact stories derived from simple or uncultured periods or classes.[6] That is probably why his Pindaric odes inspired the literary antiquarians of his era. That these men wrote only poor, imitative, and undramatic verse should not blind us to the significance of Gray's pioneer attempt. In endeavoring to re-enact the situation of his legendary Welsh bard Gray was undertaking, certainly with awkwardness and probably with little awareness of the implications of his effort, to give literary expression to a new historical consciousness. Prior saw that his age was different from the age in which his ballad model had been composed. But he saw the difference as almost purely qualitative: *his* age was unquestionably superior. His task in *Henry and Emma,* therefore, was to improve his original, just as post-Restoration civilization as a whole had improved upon the "barbarism" of his ancestors. *The Bard,* on the contrary, shocked conventional Augustan taste because Gray's effort to re-enact the experience of his Welsh protagonist implied that a barbaric way of life might in some ways be equal or even superior to modern, civilized life. Gray was not fully liberated from the prevailing concepts of his age; he was free enough, however, to inaugurate not only what has been called sentimental medievalism and Gothic sensationalism but the idea that primitive civilizations may in some ways surpass sophisticated ones.

The primitive artist, in particular, may be superior to his learned and polished successors.

The Bard, like its companion ode, is above all a history of poetry. It is an assertion of the indestructible unity of poetic inspiration despite the turmoils of social and political life. In the final stanza primitive and anonymous Welsh bards are made to stand side by side not only with the "natural" genius Shakespeare but with the learned Milton. In one way this strikes a blow for true poetry. In another way it opens poetry to the inroads of antiquarianism. The verse of folk poets is far easier to imitate than that of Shakespeare. Furthermore, if Taliessen is comparable to Milton, the man who discovers or translates the Welsh bard's poetry will have performed a service to his society nearly equal to that of the great Puritan. And if no Taliessen is discoverable, one can, like James Macpherson, invent his equivalent. In *The Bard,* then, Gray's popularity as a writer who had proved his skill within the conventions of Neo-classic poetry joined with his reputation for learning to validate literary archaizing. Until Gray became interested in primitive literature, efforts to make antiquarianism justify poetry and poetry justify antiquarianism had met with little success. After his odes appeared, the archaizers swept the field, and for a generation English literature was plagued by fakes, forgeries, and slovenly scholarship.

In fairness to Gray it must be pointed out that he rejected the worst productions of the force he had unloosed. He did not, for example, fully believe in Macpherson. And in his single most significant contribution to ballad criticism he showed himself superior to his contemporaries in insight and taste. In a letter to William Mason in June, 1757, Gray observed:

> . . . I have got the old Scotch ballad [*Gil Morrice*] on which *Douglas* was founded; it is divine, . . . Have you never seen it? Aristotle's best rules are observed in it in a manner that shews the author never had heard of Aristotle. It begins in the fifth act of the play. You may read it two-thirds through without guessing what it is about; and yet, when you come to the end, it is impossible not to understand the whole story.[7]

Hustvedt, pointing out that these sentences came to be regarded as the classic statement of mid-century ballad criticism,[8] justly remarks that nearly half a century was to elapse before equally percipient judgments on the literary quality of ballads reappeared. And, as can be shown by a comparison with Addison's *Spectator* papers on ballads,

Gray's sentences reveal a decisive change in Neo-classic critical methods. Addison's primary example was the well-known and often-revised *Chevy Chase,* a ballad which bore the stamp of Sidney's approval. Addison made a direct comparison of an "improved" version of that ballad to classical epic, quoting as authority Le Bossu's treatise on the rules of heroic poetry. Gray's example is a less well known ballad: "Have you never seen it?" He is free of the most rigid kind of genre thinking: *Gil Morrice* accords with Aristotle's rules of drama. And Gray's reference to "Aristotle's best rules" illustrates how improved scholarship tended to weaken the authoritarianism of abstract critical dogma. Finally, whereas Addison had remarked that the anonymous author copies Nature in the same way that Virgil does, Gray insists more specifically on the ballad author's ignorance of classical precept as the cause of his successful practice of the "best rules." As we shall see later, Gray's position is different from that of the Romantics, but his critical attitude, like his practice in *The Bard,* marks a turning toward a sensibility sympathetic to popular verse.

There are so many premonitions of later literary developments in the writings of Gray that one is tempted to overestimate the range and solidity of his poetic accomplishments. Thomas Percy, the editor of *Reliques of Ancient English Poetry* (1763), provides no such temptation. One is more likely to underestimate the significance of the *Reliques,* a work of enormous literary importance, not in England alone but on the continent as well.[9] Percy's researches forced the traditional ballad into the English literary consciousness. Before the appearance of the *Reliques* few literary men knew much about unsophisticated ballads. After the publication of Percy's collection every educated Englishman had to take cognizance of the ancient popular literature of his country. Percy's limitations as an editor have been so assiduously cried up that it is only fair to point out that his collection includes a diversity of excellent story poems. And however much he mangled his originals in burnishing them for contemporary taste, he preserved intact more than he distorted. And even the modern reader, if he is not a ballad specialist, is likely to find the *Reliques* more entertaining than the compilations of scientific editors. Child's magnificent collection proves that scrupulousness and judiciousness do not necessarily make for the highest literary pleasure.

Indeed, though none would deny that the *Reliques* are the single most influential eighteenth-century ballad collection, few have given

Bishop Percy credit for his artful arranging of his materials. One reason, perhaps, that Percy so freely chopped up, rewrote, or deleted from the texts of his ballads [10] was that he sought aesthetic unity for his collection as a whole, not scientific accuracy in detail. One example may suffice for illustration. Percy places the "original" version of *Chevy Chase,* in his day the most famous and respected of British ballads, at the opening of his collection. Two books later he prints "the more modern Ballad of *Chevy-Chase,*" suggesting that "it will afford agreeable entertainment to the curious to compare them together." [11] By separating his variant texts Percy makes it possible for the general reader to enjoy both versions. Only the scholar can gain satisfaction from reading two renderings of the same poem in quick succession. Percy, moreover, follows the "modern" *Chevy Chase* with a song of James Shirley's, "inserted here," says Percy, "as a kind of Dirge to the foregoing piece." This third book of the first series, like the third books of the later two series, is made up in large part of modern songs by identifiable writers, with relatively modern versions of ballads sprinkled in. Thus by interlinking his different books, by tying his various pieces together with similarities of mood and sentiment, and by giving each section of his collection its own unity within the pattern of the work as a whole, Percy created the first, possibly the only, ballad compendium which makes even a modest claim to be a work of art in its own right.[12]

Only in the arrangement of his selections does Percy's artistic ability show to any advantage. His own ballads are wretched, and his editing shows deficiencies not merely in scholarship but also in literary sensitivity. As Leah Dennis has pointed out, Percy endeavored to compromise between literary elegance and antiquarianism, expecting "scholarship to subserve literature as a means to clerical advantage." [13] Percy contributed much to the archaizing spirit of his time which tended to debase poetry. Shenstone, Gay, and Prior were hampered in their ballad writing by their high regard for literature. In his notes and essays throughout the *Reliques* Percy treats poetry as a taste, an amusement, a relaxation. The ballad, in his hands, became a kind of weapon for attacking the worth of imaginative literature. There is a strong subversive element in the *Reliques.* Hustvedt has observed that Percy, like many of his contemporaries, while paying lip service to the idea of ballads as simple and artless and humble, in fact tended to reduce all poetry to the level of triviality.[14]

As regards later ballad imitations Percy is more important than any of his fellow men of taste in the middle years of the eighteenth century. Upon his collection the Romantic treatment of the ballad was founded. Wordsworth, though deploring Percy's failure "to follow his genius into the regions of true simplicity and genuine pathos," explicitly paid him tribute:

> ...for our own country, its poetry has been absolutely redeemed by it [the *Reliques*]. I do not think that there is an able writer in verse of the present day who would not be proud to acknowledge his obligations to the *Reliques;* I know that it is so with my friends; and, for myself, I am happy in this occasion to make public avowal of my own.[15]

Percy's influence upon Romantic ballad practice can be traced in less direct ways. In general the Romantics accepted his versions of old ballads. They followed his lead in excluding all the bawdy elements which play so large a part in popular balladry.[16] And like Percy they tended to use ballads as a means of sentimentalizing history, softening the definiteness and stiff brutality of their models with pathos and exotic descriptions. In short, Romantic employment of the ballad involves a heavy dependence upon the antiquarians—especially Percy—of the mid-eighteenth century and at the same time a complete reversal of those archaizers' implicit attitude toward imaginative literature. To the Romantics the attraction of ballads lay in the means they seemed to provide for once again making poetry a serious business of civilized life.

A change of attitude is apparent in the work of Thomas Chatterton, whose forged antiquities, the *Rowley Poems,* demonstrate his immersion in the archaizing spirit of his era. His fondness for grandiose historical subjects, e.g., *The Battle of Hastings,* likewise links him to the taste of his day, which was more delighted by the tumult of historical ballads than by the more domestic episodes of adventurous ballads. Yet even a quick comparison of the *Bristowe Tragedie* with Percy's *Hermit of Warkworth* or Gray's *Bard* validates Chatterton's claim to be a precursor of Romanticism. His subject is neither learned nor ostentatiously historical. His Rowleyan language, though philologically anachronistic, is animated by imaginative vitality. However unscholarly his conception of fourteenth-century life may have been, that conception was more real to him than the actuality of his ordinary existence. However blurred by false archaism, the *Bristowe Tragedie* is a poem, not antiquarianism in overdrive.

Because the *Bristowe Tragedie* tends toward Romantic treatment of balladic material, it provides illumination of the fully developed Romantic techniques when it is contrasted to one of the high Romantic ballads, Keats's *La Belle Dame sans Merci.* The first difference between the poems is their language, that of *La Belle Dame* being simple, abrupt, and arranged in a direct, uncomplicated syntax.

> Ah, what can ail thee, wretched wight,
> Alone and palely loitering;
> The sedge is wither'd from the lake,
> And no birds sing.

Chatterton's diction and syntax tend toward ornateness.

> Bolde as a lyon came Syr CHARLES,
> Drawne onne a clothe-layde sledde,
> Bye two blacke stedes ynne trappynges white,
> Wyth plumes uponne theyre hedde:
>
> Behynde hym fyve-and-twentye moe
> Of archers stronge and stoute,
> Wyth bended bowe echone ynne hande,
> Marched ynne goodlie route:
>
> Seincte JAMESES Freers marched next,
> Echone hys parte dydd chaunt;
> Behynde theyre backs syx mynstrelles came,
> Who tun'd the strunge bataunt:
>
> Thenne came the maior and eldermenne,
> Ynne clothe of scarlett deck't;
> And theyre attendyng menne echone,
> Lyke Easterne princes trickt:
>
> And after them, a multitude
> Of citizenns dydd thronge;
> The wyndowes were alle fulle of heddes,
> As hee dydd passe alonge.[17]

Here we have one sentence carried through twenty lines instead of two sentences in four lines, and a richness of sensuous description instead of austere selectivity. Yet Keats is fully engaged in his barren world. The pageant-like effect of the *Bristowe Tragedie* keeps poet and reader outside the world of the poem, as is the case with Gay's ballad, even though Chatterton has obliterated the Augustan incongruity between subject and language. We *watch* Sir Charles and listen to his words. We *share* the wretched wight's magical experience. The best part of Chatterton's poem is picturesque, a pageant of sound and color that we are invited to observe as a distant spectacle. Our enjoyment, like the poet's, must spring from the perception of the difference between past and present. The strange and exotic beauty of what once was and is no more enchants us. Keats's ballad plunges us into a severe world of limited and controlled sensations. Keats was not hostile to richly sensuous poetry, but like most Romantics he did not turn to the ballad form (as mid-eighteenth-century poets had) to escape from reality into a realm of magical lushness, pastoralism, and romance. The Romantics tended to value the ballad as a means of treating the harsh actualities of experience in dramatically symbolic fashion.

The ornate pageantry of the *Bristowe Tragedie* is accompanied by particularity of historical reference (real characters, period costumes, etc.), to which the Rowleyan language is meant to contribute. In Keats's poem there is no specific place or time. There is only the "cold hill side" and "the lake" to locate the place of the action and "the sedge is withered" and "the squirrel's granary is full" to identify the season. Keats's characters are unidentifiable, too. His often-lamented revision of "Knight at arms" to "wretched wight" at least has the virtue of emphasizing his protagonist's anonymity. This anonymity, an important feature of genuine ballads, is something upon which the Romantic ballads insist. Keats, in other words, has dropped the antiquarian quality so conspicuous in Chatterton. *La Belle Dame* is self-referent; its story is timeless. Because the language, situation, and manners of the *Bristowe Tragedie* refer to and are derived from a particular historical epoch, the poem must be a relatively literal account of a rationally coherent action. *La Belle Dame,* on the contrary, is a symbolic narrative of a supernatural experience essentially passive in character.

This passivity deserves special attention. However adventurous and daring the characters in authentic ballads may be, they almost always convey the sense of being trapped in circumstances against which their struggles are futile. Genuine ballads often are memorable because their sinewy narratives are pervaded by a profound and sombre fatalism. We have seen that the Nutbrown Maid, though alert and enterprising, accepts without inquiry or lamentation the situation into which her lover thrusts her. Similarly, Sir Patrick Spens guesses he has been betrayed and foresees his doom, yet sails unhesitatingly to his death. Such fatalistic passivity interlaces with, and tends to authenticate, the anonymity of ballad characters. Who is Edward? Lord Randal? The Wife of Usher's Well? The questions are irrelevant, not because what happens to these characters might happen to anyone (ballad stories, as we have noted previously, tend to concern unusual events) but because they inhabit a world full of unexpected hazards, a world not rationally and logically ordered, never under the control of an individual, a world not comprehended as historically coherent. In the world of the ballad one's actions may initiate a disastrous chain of events, but the particular nature of one's personality does not thereby become significant, for that destructive chain is as likely to begin somewhere else, and in any case the individual has no chance of guiding or adjusting to all the circumstances latent with danger which make up his environment.[18] Keats, no profound student of the ballad, like many Romantics captures the intertwined fatalistic philosophy and the stark anonymity of protagonist so characteristic of folk ballads. Yet the fatalistic passivity of *La Belle Dame,* although it may be derived from the ballad, is consciously exploited (as it never is in genuine ballads) for symbolic effect.

In Chatterton's poem, though Sir Charles passively undergoes his doom, he asserts his Christian resignation with the vigor of an inspired martyr. The movement of the action of the *Bristowe Tragedie* is like that of Shenstone's *Jemmy Dawson* and Prior's *Henry and Emma* in that there is a continuous development of emotional intensity which is based upon the individualized personalities of the characters. The strength of Sir Charles's spiritual heroism is progressively revealed through his speeches to Canterlone, Canynge, his wife, the king, and finally "the people" gathered around the scaffold. Hence the message of the *Bristowe Tragedie* is clear. It presents the moral beauty of political rectitude and Christian resignation in lucid and rational fashion. The structure of the poem is simple and rhetorical.

La Belle Dame is arranged differently. This poem is a symbolic narrative, that is, it will have a somewhat different meaning for each reader, whereas every reader will respond to the *Bristowe Tragedie* in approximately the same way, with admiration for the power of individual righteousness to assert its superiority to selfish passions.

No popular ballad tells a consciously symbolic story. The communal environment in which ballads thrive makes complex and subtle symbolism, the kind that stimulates individualized responses, undesirable. An editor or critic may discover symbolic content in a true ballad like *The Twa Corbies,* for example, but the unintentional or secondary nature of that symbolism becomes apparent as soon as one compares in detail the organization of an authentic ballad with a carefully wrought work such as *La Belle Dame.*

Most true ballads, which were, after all, recited publicly, exhibit the same kind of rhetorical organization [19] we find in the *Bristowe Tragedie.* Professor Gerould has shown that one of the most striking characteristics of many ballads, incremental repetition, is primarily an "effective rhetorical device," [20] and has argued further that "incremental repetition . . . though certainly the commonest is by no means the only rhetorical phenomenon that distinguishes the ballad." [21] The organization of *La Belle Dame,* on the contrary, is not merely subtle and complicated in a way that no popular ballad is, but produces an ambiguous response alien to the spirit of the ballad. It is the "structural drama" of *La Belle Dame,* as Professor Wasserman observes, which "compels a symbolic reading." [22] He points out that, while the twelve stanzas of the poem can be divided into prologue (1–3), central narrative (4–9), and epilogue (10–12),[23] the significant organization of the poem is more submerged and intricate. The introductory stanzas "serve to set the story of the knight's adventures in an additional narrative framework, a dialogue between the knight and the stranger, with whom the reader tends to identify himself." [24] Stanzas one and two, moreover, are identical in pattern, the first two lines posing a question about the condition of the knight, the last two commenting upon the condition of Nature. The third stanza takes its structure from the second part of the first two stanzas as it co-ordinates two images of Nature, the lily and the rose, but the subject of this third stanza is the condition of the knight.[25] Hence the prologue as a whole is organized about "the movement from a suggested but unstated relationship of man and nature in stanza one to an implied interrelationship in stanza two" to the third stanza where "the two terms are organically integrated." [26] In the "narrative core" of the poem there is another kind of movement, a progressive shrinkage of the "I" (the knight) as a power and a corresponding dominance of the "she" (the lady),[27] clearly marked by the stanza openings: "I met," "I made," "I sat," "She found," "She took," "And there she lulled."[28] And the epilogue reverses the movement of the prologue, concluding with a stanza almost identical to stanza one, with man and Nature again separated.

The functional intricacy of this organization is of course alien to the authentic folk ballad. And that intricacy assures us that Keats's subject will be unballadic in its tendency toward symbolism. Though *La Belle Dame* appears to draw closer to genuine ballads than the *Bristowe Tragedie* through its employment of a "magical" story, the way Keats employs supernaturalism demonstrates that he is less dependent upon the model of simple, popular poetry than was Chatterton. The *Bristowe Tragedie* is direct, definite, literal, and these are qualities of ballad narratives, the qualities, in fact, that make ballads seem refreshingly different from purely Neo-classic poetry. But ballads are definite, direct, and literal even when they deal with the supernatural. Ballad stories do not present supernaturalism as unusual or surprising in itself. Ballads treat the mysterious with matter-of-factness; they appear to arise from a milieu in which belief in the reality of supernatural events is both firm and traditional.[29] Almost all English and Scottish ballads of the supernatural involve exciting, entertaining, or interesting events—they do not depend for their effect upon an examination or exploration of supernaturalism in and for itself. If the dead return from the grave or a traveller is spirited into fairyland, so much the better chance for a thrilling story. In *La Belle Dame* no exciting action occurs except the supernatural journey to and from the "elfin grot." It is the strangeness, the mysteriousness of this event which Keats emphasizes and which we savor. Keats does not appeal to our credulity, as Chatterton does with his Rowleyan language. Keats provokes our response by presenting an "unnatural" story in which we become aware of an intricate and subtle coherence, and the co-existence of that coherence and that strangeness forces us to read *La Belle Dame* symbolically, to determine the significance of this systematic unreality. That is why Keats's pictorial images are so carefully selected and arranged with regard to their interrelations. Keats's images, like those of the popular ballad, are simple, but, unlike them, are the source of organizational coherence. We are not expected to believe literally in the wight's experience. We do not have to, because unmistakable contrasts in imagery, such as that between the cold, barren hillside and the warm, flowery atmosphere of the elfin grot, create an aesthetic reality, a purposeful coherence not dependent on literal credulity.

In short, Keats does not try to reproduce the effect of the popular ballad. He uses a variety of balladic elements, meter, simple diction, abrupt narrative action without stress on characterization, etc., as the basis for a symbolic narrative. To Chatterton imitation of older, popular poetry is the primary end; insofar as the *Bristowe Tragedie* is like authentic ballads it is successful. Insofar as Keats has transformed the manner of the authentic ballad into symbolic narrative *La Belle Dame* is successful. To Keats the folk ballad is a means, not an end.

The differences between Chatterton's ballad and Keats's are striking because Keats is not one of Chatterton's immediate successors. Keats belongs to the second generation of Romanticism in England. Not himself specially interested in the ballad, he was able to compose *La Belle Dame* as a similitude of the folk ballad because in the interval between Chatterton's death and the florescence of his own poetic gifts the literary ballad had been established as a valuable form of sophisticated lyricism by Wordsworth, Coleridge, and Scott.[30] The characteristics which we have observed in *La Belle Dame* are, in fact, the characteristics of almost all literary ballads since the beginning of the nineteenth century. Individual poets, of course, have wrought important variations, but if we look at the ballads of Rossetti and of Kipling, Pound's *Ballad of the Goodly Fere,* Cummings' *All in Green Went My Love Riding,* or Auden's "O what is that sound which so thrills the ear," to name some impressively different examples, we see that they share with Keats's poem the assumption that a literary ballad is a symbolic narrative whose value depends not on its historicity but on its success in embodying in plain diction, colloquial rhythm, and a simple metrical form the significance of an intense human experience.

La Belle Dame sans Merci in a sense marks the completion of the process which we have been studying, the process by which a new form of lyric poetry was introduced into polite literature. Although not, like the sonnet, definable in purely metrical terms, the literary ballad is now as definite and recognizable a form within the lyric mode. Since the early years of the nineteenth century it has held a position in the lyricist's repertoire equivalent to that of the more tradition-hallowed sonnet and canzone.

The single work which did most to establish the literary ballad as a respected form was the appropriately titled *Lyrical Ballads* of Coleridge and Wordsworth. We have called attention to Wordsworth's praise of Bishop Percy and to the difference between his handling of the ballad form and Gay's. In his preface to the second edition of the *Lyrical Ballads* Wordsworth attacks Dr. Johnson's denigration of *The Babes in the Wood*. Wordsworth quotes Johnson's mocking quatrain beginning "I put my hat upon my head," and then comments: "Dr. Johnson's stanza ... is neither interesting in itself, nor can *lead* to anything interesting; the images neither originate in that sane state of feeling which arises out of thought, nor can excite thought or feeling in the Reader." [31] Wordsworth does not defend the ballad on the ground that it has been "approved by the Multitude." His preface as a whole is an attack on the popular taste of the day. Nor does he try to justify the form of the ballad. "The words, and the order of the words, in no respect differ from the most unimpassioned conversation." To Wordsworth it is "the matter expressed," the subject, that makes *The Babes in the Wood* admirable and Johnson's stanza contemptible. In the context of the preface in its entirety it is plain why Wordsworth praised ballad subjects. He says early in his essay, "The principal object, then, proposed in these Poems, was to choose incidents and situations from common life, and to relate or describe them throughout, as far as was possible, in a selection of language really used by men, and, at the same time, to throw over them a certain colouring of the imagination ... and above all, to make these incidents and situations interesting by tracing in them, truly though not ostentatiously, the primary laws of our nature. ..." [32]

This passage could be read as a description of many authentic folk ballads, which do relate unusual events "from common life" in "a selection of language really used by men" and which are interesting as illustrations of "the primary laws of our nature." Wordsworth is not delighted by the "affecting sentiments" of the ballads, nor is he interested in their recollections of earlier historical situations. What he admires in the ballad—and aims for in his own poetry—is the simple, direct rendering of "the primary laws of our nature." Like Keats in *La Belle Dame sans Merci,* Wordsworth seizes on the simplicity of the ballad as a technique for dramatizing the essential conditions of human experience. Thus *We Are Seven* portrays that animal vitality, present in all human beings but most conspicuous in children, which is incapable of recognizing even the possibility of death; *Goody Blake and Harry Gill* dramatizes a psychic source of physical illness; *Simon Lee* examines a contrasting phenomenon, physical decay as a producer of spiritual anguish; and *The Idiot Boy* celebrates the restorative power of generous love. We mention some of Wordsworth's least popular contributions to the *Lyrical Ballads,* since these poems are stiff and awkward in part because they derive so immediately from his critical theories. These early pieces, furthermore, exhibit more clearly than do the complexities of such later poems as *Michael* and *Resolution and Independence* the fact that Wordsworth found in narrative lyricism a means of embodying significant moral and psychological insight without becoming meditative and abstractly philosophical. In poetry at the same time narrative and lyrical he could express "the primary laws of our nature" in a concrete, particularized, and (relatively) dramatic fashion. He aimed to support the pleasure of profound personal insight with the pleasure of an easily comprehended story.

Wordsworth wrote surprisingly few poems that qualify as thoroughgoing ballad imitations. But a major part of his lyric output is cast in the shape of simple narrative. Even when he attempted dramatic or heroic verse his manner was that of a lyricist, a singer whose songs originate in his private imaginings, his innermost feelings, his personal experience. As he says in the preface, "Another circumstance must be mentioned which distinguishes these Poems . . . that the feeling therein developed gives importance to the action and situation, and not the action and situation to the feeling."[33] What the poet feels, not the convenience of his audience and not the work of art as a separate entity, is to Wordsworth of paramount importance. But by fusing the simple narrative structure from the ballad into his lyricism he was able to free it from formalism and at the same time to give his individual emotional memories and private moral imaginings a relatively objective form derived from common experience rather than imposed upon it by a philosophic intelligence. Story enabled him to remain "a Man speaking to men" and to avoid becoming a specialist in psychological analysis.

Wordsworth's desire to provide lyric poetry with narrative organization relates to his theory that poetry should be written in a "selection of language really used by men." Through the bad offices of many critics, beginning with Coleridge, Wordsworth's principles of diction have been so obscured that we can scarcely hope to clarify them here. But we can observe one crucial point. Wordsworth never suggests that poetry should employ *only* the language of "humble and rustic life." That, indeed, is precisely what ballad-imitators of the latter part of the eighteenth century had done or tried to do. Wordsworth insists that simple and common language, properly arranged, can convey powerful feeling and valid moral insight. His argument is for a democratization of language. Alexander Pope's diction is, on the whole, as colloquial and naturalistic as Wordsworth's and is a good deal racier, but it is drawn from the conversational realities of only the educated upper classes of society. Wordsworth, in point of fact, uses many more learned and literary words than Pope as well as many more words drawn from the speech of the lower orders of society.[34] Wordsworth did not betray a theory he never held—that poetry should be written in the language of peasants—but demonstrated how a sophisticated poet could use both the resources of commonplace, everyday speech and the learned, complex language laboriously developed by educated writers since the Renaissance.[35] It was the inability to combine these linguistic resources which handicapped early ballad imitators like Prior. In fine, Wordsworth in his poetic diction exhibits the characteristic Romantic practice of employing the model of the ballad as a means of enriching sophisticated lyricism rather than as an object of historical curiosity or as a subject for literal imitation.[36]

Coleridge's principal contribution to the establishment of the literary ballad is, of course, *The Rime of the Ancient Mariner,* which both in meter and narrative mannerisms suggests the ballad. But to treat this masterpiece merely as a ballad would be absurd. For one thing, *The Ancient Mariner* marks the successful culmination of a long series of experiments, beginning with Prior, to transform an extended balladic narrative into something like an epic.[37] Coleridge succeeds where others failed because, though he takes advantage of eighteenth-century antiquarianism, he develops the poem in an anti-antiquarian fashion. For example, the past in which the mariner's adventures occur is not historically identifiable; it is a temporal perspective derived from a mythical conception, not from scientific research. Or, to focus on a more detailed point, most eighteenth-century poets, literally imitating ballad mannerisms, wrote as if the events described were recent occurrences. Though the mariner's story is told to the wedding guest as if it were a recent occurrence, the wedding itself is made to appear as an event of the distant past. Coleridge manipulates rather than imitates the manner of the ballad. Furthermore, although rich with pictorial and auditory images, his poem is animated by a tense onward pressure and is never halted by statically spectacular pageantry. Coleridge's narrative is rapid and nervous because it follows a symbolic rather than an antiquarian impulse. Yet, somewhat paradoxically, that symbolic impulse is conditioned and shaped by his historical imagination. Coleridge as a ballad-imitator differs from Prior and Gray and Percy in his comprehension of past and primitive civilizations as valid and respectable systems of thought, feeling, and belief, as ways of life unlike our own but not for that reason any less coherent or less true.

His familiarity with eighteenth-century historical studies combined with his eclectic reading in popular verse and older literatures apparently revealed to Coleridge the falsity of the Neo-classic assumption (which we observed in Prior) that primitive poetry was the expression of untutored minds groping toward civilization. *The Rime of the Ancient Mariner* accepts the primitive mentality as a systematic, coherent, fully developed state of mind that differs in kind—not degree—from the sophisticated, civilized mentality. The poem is an imaginative re-enactment of a way of thought, an emotional system, and a manner of expression foreign to Coleridge's own infinitely sophisticated and philosophic mind. It is scarcely reasonable to think Coleridge believed that albatrosses were birds of good omen whose destinies were watched over by supernatural spirits. Yet he presents us not with the quaint fact of such an albatross (which eighteenth-century poets were capable of doing) but with that state of mind which sincerely believes albatrosses to be so significant and so guarded. In reading *The Ancient Mariner* we do not suspend our disbelief in the supernatural attributes of the albatross (as eighteenth-century ballad-imitators demand, for example, that we suspend our disbelief in ghosts); we believe—because Coleridge has imagined himself into such an alien state of mind—that the mariner believes in the supernatural significance of the albatross.[38] *The Ancient Mariner,* like *La Belle Dame sans Merci,* is an imaginative re-enactment and in that sense an original creation, not, like Gray's *Bard* or Chatterton's *Bristowe Tragedie,* an imitation whose first appeal is to our credulity.

One can illustrate the nature of this imaginative re-enactment in another way. Some time after he had composed the poem Coleridge added the prose gloss which comments in an archaically learned way upon the verse, providing the illusion that an anonymous, antique poem has been explicated by a Renaissance scholar. "Illusion" is important. The prose of the gloss is poetic and unlike any genuine scholarly commentary. But in no earlier English ballad-imitation would such a gloss be appropriate or even possible, for not until *The Ancient Mariner* do we find a poem whose effect depends upon the poet's re-enacting of a culturally alien state of mind.

Such re-enactment produces artistic complexity. Although Coleridge confines himself to simple diction, a balladic meter, and an abrupt, magical narrative like those of many folk poems, he arranges these elements into a complicated structure which in aesthetic sophistication is perhaps further from the methods of authentic balladry than Prior's *Henry and Emma.* No folk ballad has the intricate symbolic patterning or the subtle metrical variation exhibited by *The Ancient Mariner.*[39] Although there are, for example, no words and few constructions in the poem which might not occur in an authentic ballad, there are few stanzas that do not interweave visual, tactile, and auditory sensations in such a way as to evoke a richness of psychological response totally different from that aroused by the stark simplicity of genuine ballads. Similarly, though the repetitions of *The Ancient Mariner* are like ballad repetitions, they are more delicately varied than those of popular verse, as when the crimson shadows in the quiet harbor "white with silent light" recall the scene where the mariner, surrounded by his dead comrades, watches the rising moon:

> Her beams bemocked the sultry main,
> Like April hoar-frost spread;
> But where the ship's huge shadow lay,
> The charmèd water burnt alway
> A still and awful red. (ll. 267–71)

The images, similes, and metaphors suggest the sensuous directness of ballad figures, but they are often expanded into almost epic proportions (e.g., ll. 45–50, 446–51). And the figures in *The Ancient Mariner* are supported by a range of connotation beyond the capacities of folk poetry, as when, for instance, the mariner's dead comrades leave him:

> This seraph-band, each waved his hand
> No voice did they impart—

No voice; but oh! the silence sank
Like music on my heart.[40] (ll. 496–99)

The achievement of Romantic balladry, then, was the establishing of a new form within the lyric mode: the literary ballad. This was part of a new interest in and a new value for a narrative lyricism symbolical rather than rhetorical in structure and purpose. In the following chapters we shall attempt to illustrate some significant ways in which this interest spread out from its balladic source into more extensive and elaborate poetic forms.[41]

PART II

Stories of Imagination

****

Chapter IV

*

VISIONARY LYRICS

The Romantics employed balladic forms, techniques, and themes as means of enriching their lyric poetry. It is misleading to speak of the Romantic revival of the ballad. The ballad was revived during the eighteenth century; the Romantics put the ballad to the service of lyricism. Consequently, Romantic interest in shorter narratives must often be understood as a preliminary, as it were, experimental, phase in the development of a new lyric method. Frequently the presence of narrative elements in a Romantic poem is less a sign of the poet's originality and progress beyond Neo-classicism than an indication of his artistic immaturity and of his failure to transmute older techniques into the sort of poetic vision which we would now define as fully Romantic. The evolution of Romantic lyricism is, in some measure at least, the gradual transformation of simple narrative structure as the basis of lyric organization into a discontinuous, non-narrative structure.[1] It is an evolution whose nature and direction are suggested by the Romantic poets' tendency to begin their careers writing literary ballads and to climax those careers with odes, to begin by writing literal fragments, obviously unfinished poems, and at the height of their powers to compose complete poems that embody a conception of vital experience as supra-rational.

The character of this development may be described through a consideration of what we shall call the visionary lyric, a poem which celebrates the experience, the insight, or simply the pattern of images occurring to the poet in a trance, when dreaming, or under the influence of a preternatural vision. Wordsworth's *A Night Piece* from the *Lyrical Ballads* will serve as a fair representative of the form.

> —The sky is overcast
> With a continuous cloud of texture close,
> Heavy and wan, all whitened by the Moon,

Which through that veil is indistinctly seen,
A dull, contracted circle, yielding light
So feebly spread, that not a shadow falls,
Chequering the ground—from rock, plant, tree, or tower.
At length a pleasant instantaneous gleam
Startles the pensive traveller while he treads
His lonesome path, with unobserving eye
Bent earthwards; he looks up—the clouds are split
Asunder,—and above his head he sees
The clear Moon, and the glory of the heavens.
There, in a black-blue vault she sails along,
Followed by multitudes of stars, that, small
And sharp, and bright, along the dark abyss
Drive as she drives: how fast they wheel away,
Yet vanish not!—the wind is in the trees,
But they are silent;—still they roll along
Immeasurably distant; and the vault,
Built round by those white clouds, enormous clouds,
Still deepens its unfathomable depth.
At length the Vision closes; and the mind,
Not undisturbed by the delight it feels,
Which slowly settles into peaceful calm,
Is left to muse upon the solemn scene.[2]

This poem, though thoroughly Wordsworthian in its exact, naturalistic detail and its prosaic, cumulative movement, is characteristic of the Romantic visionary lyric in several ways. We begin with the poet, or rather the pensive traveller, in an unusual state of mind, unobservant of the commonplace reality about him, unresponsive to the ordinary stimuli of perception: "with unobserving eye bent earthwards." From this state he is plunged by the "instantaneous gleam" into a marvellous and profound vision—the stars wheel but vanish not, *"immeasurably* distant" in a vault of *"unfathomable* depth" that is "built round" by white *"enormous* clouds." The effect of this vast vision is to leave "the mind/Not undisturbed by the delight it feels." The experience celebrated in this lyric, furthermore, is accidental, unexpected; its relevance to ordinary existence is neither stated nor readily discoverable. Though the vision is presented in its entirety, it impresses the reader with its transitoriness; it is but a fragment of experience, an almost random event, and hence its meaning is obscure, resisting purely rational interpretation. We may observe, finally, that the logical coherence of the lyric derives almost entirely from the narration of how the traveller's mind moves in harmony with the changes in the night sky. Wordsworth recognizes—indeed, almost emphasizes—the fragmentariness of the occurrence by narrating it as an unexpected incident. A Neo-classic poet would not, in all probability, have rendered such an event in poetry unless he could have buttressed the experience with philosophical expression, given rational as well as emotional coherence to his vision, changed the particular event into an exemplary situation. A modern poet, on the other hand, would probably suppress the more obvious narrative elements in *A Night Piece* and concentrate on dramatizing the traveller's emotions without locating that drama in the story of a particularized evening walk.

These characteristics of *A Night Piece* appear in many Romantic poems, but for illustration we will confine our attention to three lyrics, Shelley's *A Vision of the Sea,* Byron's *Darkness,* and Coleridge's *Kubla Khan,* which are based upon, respectively, a vision, a dream, and a trance. All three present vivid pictorial accounts of visionary marvels of doubtful import, are literally fragmentary or lack logical completeness, and contain half-transcended narrative elements. *A Vision of the Sea* is not one of Shelley's finest poems, but its very clumsiness exhibits his tendency to present his reader with what we might call dislocated allegory. An allegory is composed of fixed signs which refer to a system of ideas or beliefs. The signs derive their meaning, in fact, their very existence, from the ideas or beliefs to which they refer. One cannot understand an allegory unless one understands the system to which the signs refer and which exists independently of the poem. This referent is what Shelley leaves obscure, but that obscurity should not mislead us into calling a poem like *A Vision of the Sea* symbolic. A symbol is not merely a specific and definite reference to something else; it exists in its own right and can be understood without knowledge of a particular system of ideas or truths outside the work in which it appears. The multiple meanings of a symbol (as opposed to the single dominant meaning of an allegorical figure) are revealed by its context, by its interrelationship with other elements in the work of art. Hence, as Coleridge observed, the symbol "partakes of the reality which it renders intelligible" and "abides itself as a living part in that unity, of which it is the representative."[3] It follows, then, that a symbolic poem will tend to be dynamically interrelated and, as compared to allegory, realistic, though of course not necessarily naturalistic. *A Vision of the Sea,* like many of Shelley's poems such as *The Sensitive Plant,* is static and unrealistic. It describes a ship that is nine weeks becalmed, its crew wiped out by pestilence, and then struck by a terrible tempest. The only survivors are a beautiful woman, her infant child, and two tigers that have escaped from the hold. As the ship sinks one tiger engages in a fight with a sea snake. The other swims for shore but is shot by a boatload of rescuers heading for the wreck, where the woman, as she sinks, holds her child, "smiling and playing," above the waves. At this point the poem breaks off. Now those tigers, to leave aside mother, child, and snake, can only be described as allegorical. Yet what makes *A Vision of the Sea* unsatisfactory is that its allegorical signs are dislocated from any recognizable system of ideas and tend toward symbolic complexity. Thus when the tiger fights with the sea snake, "The foam and the smoke of the battle/Stain the clean air with sunbows." Similarly the child, supported by his mother's hand above the waves, "Is yet smiling, and playing, and murmuring; so smiled/The false deep ere the storm." Now one may dismiss Shelley as incompetent (some modern critics have already done so), or one may observe that the confusions of this poem are in several respects like contradictions or awkwardnesses found in other Romantic poems such as *A Night Piece*. Like Wordsworth's poem, Shelley's presents a strange and marvellous vision whose relevance to ordinary experience it is difficult to state concretely, because the coherence and order of the poem are only half revealed by a story which does not seem to be self-contained (and hence an obvious source of symbolic order), nor rationally fitted to the objective system of cause and effect which creates the design of ordinary, everyday living, nor immediately referable (except by lifelong students of Shelley's thought) to any extrinsic system of beliefs or truths.

A somewhat similar confusion occurs in *Kubla Khan,* surely the most famous fragment in English literature. Here we can at once identify the disturbing element as an evanescent narrative. The modern controversy [4] as to whether the poem is a fragment or a completed lyric masquerading as a fragment (which sounds improbable until one stops to consider Coleridge's almost unbelievably devious personality) would probably be decided in favor of the proponents of completeness were it not for lines fifteen and sixteen— "As e'er beneath a waning moon was haunted/ By woman wailing for her demon-lover" —whose echo of a specific ballad tale mingles with suggestions of a paradise story (the mingling strengthened by the "damsel . . . singing of Mount Abora"), and lines twenty-nine and thirty—"And 'mid this tumult Kubla heard from far/ Ancestral voices prophesying war!"—which suggest a particular character trapped in a relentless logic of events (Is Kubla perhaps playing the part of the doomed king of Greek tragedy and history, following the path from prosperity to overweening pride to fatal madness?). We are not proposing an interpretation of *Kubla Khan* but are simply pointing out that were it not for one or two faint suggestions of a story the lyric would be satisfactory and understandable merely as the description of a vividly pictorial dream.

Byron's *Darkness,* which portrays the sun and stars as suddenly extinguished and the earth being transformed into a dark, icy "lump of death," can so be read—merely as the account of a dream, despite Byron's warning: "I had a dream, which was not all a dream." Yet this lyric derives more nearly than the others we are considering from the tradition of the formal prophetic-dream poem, which can be traced back to the literature of antiquity. Unlike most poems in this tradition, however, *Darkness* does not give us the setting and situation in which the dream occurs, does not provide us with the present reality against which the direful prophecy is launched. The unsettling vividness of this poem does not come from its apocalyptic significance so much as from its concrete dramatization of pure fantasy. Byron seems more excited by the image of the terrific wasteland he has envisioned than concerned with its meaning.[5] *Darkness* appears to be baleful prophecy for the sake of baleful prophecy. The episodes of the one faithful dog and of the two enemies who die "even of their mutual hideousness," for example, contribute to the story of the world's final agony, to the drama of the progressive extinction of life, but they do not supply either allegoric order or symbolic coherence, though seeming to hint at both.

We believe that these incomplete and somewhat baffling visions are not evidence that the Romantics were philosophically muddle-headed and technically inept. They do show the dislocation and disintegration of much literary skill and knowledge that previously had been orderly, systematic, and hallowed by tradition. Our suggestion, however, is that the Romantic era was one of reconstruction and re-formation. Like all such eras it was based on the rejection of many ideas and techniques that had seemed to preceding generations to be the essence of civilized behavior and civilized thought. And these same ideas and skills seem to succeeding generations, who accept unconsciously the virtues of the era of reconstruction, to have been rejected needlessly by the reformers. We pursue the idea, in other words, that the awkwardnesses we have observed in the Romantic visionary lyric are not harbingers of fatal disease but signs of life, that the early nineteenth century was one of those periods of reorientation without which no art can escape stiffening into sterile rigidity and repetitiveness. If this be true, we must make clear in what ways the defects to which we have drawn attention foreshadow or lead into new and freer poetic techniques.

In each of the poems with which we are here concerned the vitality, the lyric intensity lies in vigorous personal feeling. Even the unsympathetic modern critic who dismisses these poems as phantasmagories or hallucinations in so denominating them pinpoints their origin in the private emotions and imaginings of their authors. Byron's absorption in the ghastliness of his dream weakens the prophetic purposefulness of his traditional form. In *A Vision of the Sea* and *Kubla Khan* Shelley and Coleridge seem more concerned with pursuing the private course of their intensified imaginings than with relating those emotion-charged streams of images to common experience. Even in Wordsworth's relatively naturalistic *A Night Piece* the mighty vision does not reveal eternal truth, either of Nature or of God, but is presented, as we have said, rather as a random personal experience, one memorable for the emotions aroused by the "grand vista"; but these emotions, though extraordinary, are memorable in and for themselves, not for their revelation of some higher truth. We may begin, then, to define the literary reorientation illustrated by these lyrics in terms of stress upon creative, spontaneous feelings with a corresponding de-emphasis on responsive emotions.[6]

Readers who turn back to re-read these poems are caught up in the verve and force of the creative, spontaneous emotions with which their images are charged; they are also left somewhat dissatisfied if not actually irritated by the poems because the emotional charge has not been fully grounded and harmonized. Emotion begets emotion, but successful art always releases or, as we say, satisfies the emotions it has aroused. The poems we are considering tend to evoke emotions without satisfying them. On the one hand, it is difficult to associate the feelings embodied in the poems with the sentiments and experiences of ordinary life—these are, after all, visionary lyrics. On the other hand, the feelings do not provide their own satisfaction, are not organized into a self-satisfying total harmony—they are, as we have seen, fragmentary poems.

This is not, however, to deny the value of writing poetry about a private trance, dream, or vision. These were serious-minded and important poets who attempted it; and their subjects appear not ill-suited to the welling up of powerful emotions. Yet such poetry should be self-organizing and self-satisfying. If the value of the visionary lyric is that it frees the poet from mere responsiveness, by the same token it imposes the duty upon him of supplying an inner coherence, an inner order. In the poems we are considering, lack of inner order would seem to derive from incompleteness in the stories that are the basis of the structure. A story, after all, must be rationally coherent to be a story; however improbable its events, it must follow some sort of sequential order. But the subject-matter of a poem such as *Kubla Khan* is not amenable to any sort of simple sequential ordering. The experience which is the core of a trance or dream or vision is not subject to the rational, logical, practical systems by which we arrange ordinary life and to which narrative, however indirectly, always refers. The source of whatever power is in these Romantic visionary lyrics, their creative emotion, is antagonistic to the relatively reasonable and objective form provided by their narrative structure. As a result the lyrics tend either to break off suddenly or, if they are completed, to appear bafflingly half-logical.

Despite their unsatisfactoriness these visionary lyrics are important, for they represent that point in modern literary history where the assumption that any poem should be more or less fully comprehensible at first reading begins to give way to the modern assumption that a good poem should at first reading be mysterious and provocative of deeper study. It is the point at which poetry changes from a predominantly rational method of discourse to a predominantly suprarational method.[7]

What the Romantic poets were striving toward and moving away from can be illustrated by an analogy with a development in nineteenth-century painting. From the Renaissance until well on in the nineteenth century painting was dominated by the idea that what a picture represents should be immediately comprehensible to the viewer. A Madonna should look like a woman. This idea did not, as critics like Mr. Berenson have shown, prevent the painters from being deeply concerned with "tactile values," the "organization of space," and the like. Still, any educated viewer can on demand at once supply a reasonable title for these pictures, since their apparent meaning, their surface, is clearly and unmistakably presented. Many modern paintings, on the contrary, are meant to be at first glance enigmatic, are meant to provoke contemplation of their mystery. A painting by Raphael takes as much skill and time to appreciate and to evaluate as does a Picasso, but the surface, the way into full understanding, so to speak, is different. Now a painter who is involved in the transition from one idea of painting to another, Cézanne let us say, is almost sure to do some awkward floundering which will bring down upon him the condemnation of his contemporaries and, later, of his successors who have not caught up with the times.

Our visionary lyrics, like Cézanne's early work, are not free from the manners and assumptions of earlier artistic traditions, although they strive toward a more intensely personal and private expression based upon a discontinuous organization. Narrative as it appears in these lyrics is an element of logical or rational organization; it implies a conception of experience as objectively apprehendable: "If I tell you what occurred you will know what happened to me." But the experiences which are the sources of the poems' energy are purely subjective and creative; they cannot be told about; we must be made to participate in the poet's vision. The fragmentary poem so characteristic of early Romanticism is, in other words, a lyric whose narrative elements have not been fully transmuted into the discontinuous structure demanded by the poets' efforts to express that which is not objective. That transmutation does occur, however, in the great odes of Wordsworth, Shelley, and Keats. Keats's *Ode to a Nightingale,* for example, is in many ways similar to the visionary lyrics we have been studying. It is a trance poem in which the poet frees himself (helped by the darkness of the evening) from the restrictions of ordinary perception and pursues imaginative sensations, which, finally, lead to "magic casements, opening on the foam/ Of perilous seas, in faery lands forlorn." But the *Ode to a Nightingale* is not a fragment and is not confused by conflicting orders of coherence. The emotions which well up in the poet are projected into as striking a stream of images as those of *Kubla Khan* and *Darkness,* but in Keats's poem the images create a self-satisfying inner order, a non-logical continuity. Although, like Wordsworth in *A Night Piece,* Keats locates the origin of his vision in a particular time and place, the coherence of his poem derives almost entirely from the unity of his liberated feelings, from the dramatic invasion and counter-invasion of his conflicting sentiments, which do not correlate directly with the objective, external circumstances surrounding his vision. Unlike *A Night Piece,* the *Ode to a Nightingale* subordinates the objective order of the situation in which the poet's trance originates to the necessities of that trance's interior order. As a result, Keats's poem does not, like *A Vision of the Sea,* hover on the allegorical edge of symbolism but is overtly and impressively symbolic, in the sense that it is self-consistent and the significance of that consistency is self-created. It challenges the reader with its systematized complexity in which the complications arise from the tense interrelations of the emotion-charged images and have no reference to abstractions not embodied in the poem.

The way in which the *Ode to a Nightingale* attains intensified subjective coherence by transmuting rational, continuous narrative into a discontinuous structure, a transmutation only partly attained in *Kubla Khan, Darkness,* and *A Vision of the Sea,* may be illustrated by contrasting Keats's poem to Mark Akenside's *Ode to the Evening Star,* which in some details of its last stanzas superficially resembles Keats's great ode and which is not untypical of the late eighteenth-century lyric manner.[8]

> But hark; I hear her liquid tone.
> Now, Hesper, guide my feet
> Down the red marl with moss o'ergrown,
> Through yon wild thicket next the plain,
> Whose hawthorns choke the winding lane
> Which leads to her retreat.
>
> See the green space: on either hand
> Inlarg'd it spreads around:
> See, in the midst she takes her stand,
> Where one old oak his awful shade
> Extends o'er half the level mead
> Inclos'd in woods profound.
>
> Hark, how through many a melting note
> She now prolongs her lays:
> How sweetly down the void they float!
> The breeze their magic path attends:
> The stars shine out; the forest bends;
> The wakeful heifers gaze.

Whoe'er thou art whom chance may bring
To this sequester'd spot,
If then the plaintive Siren sing,
O softly tread beneath her bower,
And think of heaven's disposing power,
Of man's uncertain lot.

O think, o'er all this mortal stage,
What mournful scenes arise:
What ruin waits on kingly rage;
How often virtue dwells with woe;
How many griefs from knowledge flow;
How swiftly pleasure flies.

O sacred bird, let me at eve,
Thus wandering all alone,
Thy tender counsel oft receive,
Bear witness to thy pensive airs,
And pity Nature's common cares
Till I forget my own.[9]

In these stanzas the poet does not escape from the situation which gives rise to the poem (which is perhaps why the evening Akenside describes is so much lighter than the evening of the *Ode to a Nightingale*). Akenside's emotions are responsive, are limited to what is directly stimulated by the twilight quietness of the scene. Hence his language is consistent, philosophically meditative rather than dramatic, never surprising or unexpected, and always plain, clear, and devoted to making apparent the logical compatibility of his inner mood with the external situation. The dim melancholy of the wood is equated with the poet's feeling of pensive tenderness. We are never in any doubt as to what the poet feels and what circumstances have given rise to those feelings. The feelings and circumstances are presented in the common language of ordinary rational discourse and are ordered according to the systematic coherence which a reasonable, logical understanding of the world affords. In the final two stanzas it is made clear that continued contemplation of the sadness of the solitary nightingale's song gradually transmutes the poet's "selfish" melancholy into a healthful, outgoing sympathy for the anguish of all other creatures in the world.

Keats, too, finds in the nightingale's song a means of transmuting his emotions. In the bird's song he finds relief from "The weariness, the fever, and the fret/ Here, where men sit and hear each other groan." But that relief comes in the form of a death-like trance, and, although "now more than ever seems it rich to die," that "drowsy numbness" of heartache springs, paradoxically, from the poet's "being too happy in thine happiness." In the *Ode to a Nightingale* we are drawn into a drama of conflicting emotions which begins in a particularized place and time but at once transports us "Away! away!" from "embalmed darkness" into bright, life-filled images "of the warm South" and "Provençal song, and sunburnt mirth!" Keats's ode is visionary and his emotions are creative, not controlled and shaped directly by the circumstances of his experience. The conflict, in fact, between the "drowsy numbness" of Keats's situation and the ecstatic intensity of the imaginings which emerge from that passivity supply the basic dialectic of the ode. Hence the discontinuity in the poem. Only to the degree that we participate in Keats's vision do we find consistency and continuity. Logically or objectively life and death, sorrow and mirth, bright Provençe and the dark English garden, and so forth, are irreconcilable contraries. Only at the expense of reasonable order do we experience the unified intensity of the poet's trance. Only by surrendering, or, perhaps better, transcending, the ordinary, reasonable processes of perception and conception can we apprehend those distinctions and similarities which form the private unity of the *Ode to a Nightingale*. As a result the poem is at first relatively difficult to respond to. We have, for example, no objective reference (as we would in Akenside's poem) by which to comprehend the last lines of stanza seven and the first lines of stanza eight.

> The same that oft-times hath
> Charm'd magic casements, opening on the foam
> Of perilous seas, in faery lands forlorn.
>
> Forlorn! the very word is like a bell
> To toll me back from thee to my sole self.[10]

To respond to these superb lines we must share the complex development of Keats's feeling as it appears in the whole poem, for the lines are not directed to the external, objective order of experience. We must share Keats's experience to appreciate it, for it is in essence a private trance, the projection of an individual creative imagination. But sharing is not to be accomplished instantaneously. We must read and re-read, contemplate and re-contemplate to enter this surprising and magical world. There is no easy way into the poem as there is into

Akenside's. And it is by abandoning any attempt to provide easy entrance, by abandoning even the magical narrative of *La Belle Dame sans Merci,* by making no direct connection between his unified visionary experience and the logical coherence of untranced living that Keats is able to build up a self-contained structure which creates its own enduring value.

In other words, the Romantic visionary lyric is a further step toward the conscious addressing of lyric poetry immediately to the imagination rather than to the imagination through the discursive intelligence. When the Romantics used balladic elements in their lyrics they were asserting, implicitly, that the function of poetry was to speak to more than the rationally sophisticated intellect. But they went further. They surrendered even the simple continuity provided by balladic narrative. The first phase of this advance [11] was the literal fragment, the unfinished story. In the next phase the literal fragment became, as it were, unnecessary,[12] for at this point the poets were willing to assert the logical discontinuity of intense experience, to begin with a recognition of the apparent unreasonableness, the incoherence from the point of view of ordinary discourse, of what they wished to express. They became willing to accept literal incomprehensibility or at least difficulty as the price for the inner, imaginative unity which they could thereby attain. As we have said, their fullest success is revealed by their odes. But even at their best the Romantics could only introduce such a profound change in the nature of poetic practice, a change which is, in all probability, founded upon a new philosophical conception of human nature and of the processes of individual experience. At any rate, the tendencies we have observed were developed and enriched throughout the nineteenth century and have been more thoroughly exploited in our own century.

Perhaps the real value of this Romantic transcendence of narrative can be appreciated if we glance ahead to modern practice. Yeats, for example, wrote many visionary lyrics which are superior to those we have analyzed, in the main because they carry out fully principles the Romantics at first treated experimentally. *The Second Coming,* for instance, is, like *Darkness,* a personal apocalyptic vision, but, despite the effort of helpful commentators to convince us that none of Yeats's poetry is enjoyable to a reader unsteeped in his private allegorical systems, it is a more complete, self-contained, and satisfying poem than Byron's. The basic assumption upon which the visionary lyric is based, as we have seen, is that the poem should be challenging and somewhat mysterious. That assumption Byron only partially accepted but Yeats adopted unashamedly. He concentrated upon attaining visionary coherence. As a result *The Second Coming* can be enjoyed in and for itself without reference to the poet's personal relation to his society (a reference we feel suggested in *Darkness* but never clarified) or to his private mystical system. We may not know what special meaning a gyre or *Spiritus Mundi* had for Yeats, but a memory of Lewis Carroll and of high-school Latin is sufficient to keep us within the poem's visionary system, which links the force of destruction latent in each human being to the instability of entire civilizations and makes us shudder at the meaningless triviality of those dark, blind forces which periodically break free from the inhibiting powers of training, tradition, and systematic religious and intellectual aspiration. Similarly, *Sailing to Byzantium* may be even harder to understand at first than *Kubla Khan,* but as the difficulty in Yeats's poem arises from properly relating images which are, if sufficiently contemplated, progressively interilluminating, even a sense that one partially comprehends its complexity is both satisfying and stimulating. The more we study Coleridge's poem, on the contrary, the stronger is likely to be our feeling that its unfinishedness is merely a symptom of an unresolved conflict between two orders of coherence, which conflict forces the reader's imagination out of the poem rather than drawing it into the intricacies of a unity profounder than that of ordinary experience.[13]

The Romantic visionary lyric, then, led toward a poetry of intense subjectivity organized solely by the inner logic of vision, a poetry whose discourse transcended rational consistency, a kind of poetry which has perhaps attained its fullest development in our own day, and which found its finest expression during the Romantic age in the great odes of Keats, Shelley, and Wordsworth. But this is only half the picture. The visionary lyric shows us the Romantics, having used narrative to free themselves from some limitations in the Neo-classic style, going on to transcend narrative. But story, particularly extended story, in and for itself had a positive attraction for the Romantics, and we must now turn our attention to the significance of that part of their practice.

Chapter V

*

THE POETIC TALE

In directing our attention now to the poetic tale, by which we mean a relatively brief story in verse not derived from a balladic model and not pretending to epic grandeur or formality, we return to some of the problems raised in Chapter One. In *Tam o' Shanter* we observed several elements that are not typical of Romantic practice in the poetic tale, that link Burns to the ways of Neo-classicism. We noted, in particular, that Burns's manner of presentation is earthy and realistic—even in his evocation of the supernatural; that both his humor and his understanding of authentic peasant life are important even to the form of his story; that a basic tension in *Tam o' Shanter* is created by the opposition between the bright, joyful town and the dark, hostile world of Nature. We identified, on the other hand, three characteristics in *Tam o' Shanter* which we recognized as linking the poem to Romanticism rather than to Neo-classicism. The narrative of Burns's poem is primary; it does not serve as the vehicle for something else, such as satiric comment. Then, too, Burns controls the movement of his story by creating a pattern of shifting perspectives, by manoeuvring the point of view. And the evolving expectations aroused by the poem are based more upon the events than upon the character of the protagonist.

These characteristics are discernible in Coleridge's *Christabel,* as typical a Romantic poetic tale as one could desire. In *Christabel* the story is so impressively an end in itself and without ulterior purpose that some critics regard it as meaningless.[1] Without subscribing to so harsh a judgment we may remark that the poem is more self-contained and intensely imaginative than *Tam o' Shanter*. The shifting of perspective in *Christabel* is more daring and complicated than in Burns's poem, though not so obvious, for Coleridge gives his narrator no definable personality or attitude. But a good part of the fascination of *Christabel* springs from the way in which Coleridge keeps moving us toward and away from the action. Observe how in the first five lines,

> 'Tis the middle of night by the castle clock,
> And the owls have awakened the crowing cock;
> Tu—whit!——Tu—whoo!
> And hark, again! the crowing cock,
> How drowsily it crew,

we begin with the objective distance of ordinary storytelling, are projected into the scene with the literalistic representation of the owls' call, are drawn back a little by the "hark, again!" which intrudes the narrator between us and the action and allows him to present us with the second crowing of the cock in terms of his response to the sound. Throughout the poem Coleridge manoeuvres the reader's relation to the action with rhetorical questions, appeals to local knowledge ("some say"), exclamations ("Jesu, Maria, shield her well!"), personal observations ("I guess, 'twas frightful there"), abrupt actions at first incomprehensible—

> She kneels beneath the huge oak tree,
> And in silence prayeth she.
>
> The lady sprang up suddenly,
> The lovely lady, Christabel!
> It moaned as near, as near can be,—

dramatic speeches, historical summaries, and even the re-creation of dreams. But we are less conscious of Coleridge's manoeuvrings than of Burns's, because the later poet in typical Romantic fashion embeds his changes of perspective more firmly in the texture of the story itself. Nor does Coleridge involve our expectations with his characters even as much as Burns does with Tam. Christabel is pure and innocent, Geraldine serpentinely evil, and Sir Leoline splenetic and foolish. It is not what these people are that intrigues us but the mysterious and doubtful situations in which they are entrapped.

There is one formal element in *Christabel,* however, which must be reckoned as more than an intensification of a characteristic already observable in *Tam o' Shanter:* experimental versification. The meter of *Christabel* is not, as Coleridge claimed in his preface, "founded on a new principle," but its accentualism does illustrate the Romantic tendency to use the poetic tale as a means for experimenting with verse forms. Besides the standard octosyllabic and pentameter couplets one finds employed in these poetic stories Spenserian stanzas, *ottava rima,* blank verse, *terza rima,* as well as several original stanza forms. Metrical experimentation expresses the imaginative freedom which informs the subject-matter of these stories. *Tam o' Shanter* follows exactly a traditional Ayrshire story. Most Romantic poetic tales are founded on their author's fantasy. Even when a Romantic poet bases his poem upon someone else's story he feels free to revise and to delete liberally, to invent and rearrange according to his own whim or special purpose.

Romantic invention and rearrangement of subject-matter tends to stress three factors: pictorial beauty, timelessness, and stylization of character. A further comparison of *Tam o' Shanter* with *Christabel* will illustrate this Romantic emphasis. There is little beauty in Burns's poem, in which Nature in particular is presented as harsh and cruel. There are, on the contrary, many lovely descriptions in *Christabel,* and even when Coleridge dramatizes the bleakness of Nature he does so by means of pictorially attractive images.

> There is not wind enough to twirl
> The one red leaf, the last of its clan,
> That dances as often as dance it can,
> Hanging so light, and hanging so high,
> On the topmost twig that looks up at the sky.

Then, too, Burns tells his story as if he were narrating a contemporary event, whereas *Christabel* is set in the past; but that past is unspecific, basically ahistorical. Such treatment is typical in the Romantic poetic tale, in which the occurrences, whether superficially located in modern times or in ancient days (usually the latter), are conditioned less by the circumstances of a particularized historical setting than by the inner logic of fantasy or of moral principle. We observe, finally, that while Coleridge and Burns both simplify their characters, they simplify them in different ways. Tam, as we remarked in the first chapter, bears the stamp of peasant anonymity. The blankness of his personality is imposed by the limitations of his stern and ungracious way of life. Christabel and Geraldine are not thus limited. Coleridge stylizes their characters, deliberately reduces their personalities to one or two central traits in order to fit them to the aesthetic (rather than naturalistic) structure of his narrative. The methods and purposes of this emphasis by reduction merit close attention.

Christabel and Geraldine are reduced to embodiments of two opposed moral forces. Christabel is good, innocent, passive, and motivated by spiritualized love. Geraldine is evil, experienced, active, and motivated by sensuality. But though these two characters are differentiated, their actions are not entirely separable; we sense, indeed, that one cannot exist without the other. They are like the positive and negative poles of an electrical system; without the activity created by their contrariety the system would be inert. Thus, for instance, it is right not merely according to folk traditions but according to the dynamics of the poem that Christabel should carry Geraldine across the threshold of the castle and that later Christabel should "passively... imitate" Geraldine's "look of dull and treacherous hate." Our feelings are not polarized by the absolute contrast of the two characters. Quite the contrary. We feel that Christabel must undergo the experience of evil, and we are not totally unsympathetic to Geraldine, who seems burdened by her evil:

> Yet Geraldine nor speaks nor stirs;
> Ah! what a stricken look was hers!
> Deep from within she seems half-way
> To lift some weight with sick assay,
> And eyes the maid and seeks delay....

What Coleridge has done is again typical of the Romantic poetic tale (compare, for example, Shelley's *The Sensitive Plant*): to present a moral problem reduced to its fundamental elements. So reduced, the problem tends to become representative of all moral situations. This moral reduction of the characters, considered as individuals, cannot be carried further. In herself Christabel is purely good, purely innocent, purely passive. Geraldine follows the dictates of pure evil, pure sensuality. From one pole flows only a positive charge, from the other only a negative. Out of the conflict of these moral absolutes arises, however, not a static situation but a dynamic process, an action. That action is the effect of one character upon the other, the changes wrought in one unalloyed moral element brought into the sphere of influence of its contrary.

Christabel narrates the birth and development of the process whereby goodness and innocence undergo the experience of evil. Because his subject is a process, a developing action, Coleridge's choice of the narrative mode of presentation is sound. The strength of narration, as opposed to drama and song, is its continuity, its power of moving with, so to speak, the evolution of an action. Or, because Coleridge portrays Christabel and Geraldine as the archetypes or essences of passive goodness and experienced evil, he must be more concerned with story, the relation of events in their time sequence, than with plot, wherein the idea of causality, as E. M. Forster says, overshadows the purely temporal order [2] and the complexity of character contorts the simple continuity of story. It should be clear, then, that the form and the subject of *Christabel* appear as they do because of two assumptions on Coleridge's part. He assumes that there are basic, indivisible elements in morality, that good and evil are integral and irreducible. And he assumes that morality is a process, that moral behavior must be judged as an action, not regarded as a thing, a condition, or a situation. The combination of these two assumptions is a valuable clue to the nature and purpose of the Romantic imaginative poetic tale.

All the Romantics, consciously or unconsciously, assumed a position that was opposed to the rational, abstract, scientific thinking which was so potent an intellectual force throughout the eighteenth century. Romantic narrative was founded on an artistic method almost explicitly opposed to that system of thought which stated the actions of the physical universe in mathematical formulae, as in Newton's law of gravity. The Romantics were by no means anti-intellectual, but they disliked analysis as an end in itself and disapproved of the overvaluation of rational discourse. Thus, to take the second point first, it is easy to see why scientifically unsophisticated poets should regard Newton's statement of the law of gravitation, for example, not simply as an abstraction but as a reduction of an individual action, the apple dropping in Sir Isaac's lap, let us say, to a generalized and static situation. Put in the form of an algebraic equation, the particular event of the falling fruit seems to the untrained to have been crystallized into an indefinite "thing." And improved scientific techniques, such as infinitesimal calculus (of which, it seems safe to say, no Romantic poet had any real understanding), was more threatening than traditional mathematics, for it enabled the mathematician to reduce more events to static formulae.

The Romantic rejection of abstract and analytic discourse was most clearly enunciated by Blake, perhaps because as an illustrator and engraver he was particularly concerned with lines. As Professor Bronowski observes,

It may seem odd that he should have coupled Newton's world of compulsion with the indefinite manner of engraving which he hated. He saw in both the same threat, that the actual would be lost in the manner or the system.... Newton's system was to him at once fixed and indefinite. Blake found a target for both dislikes in Newton's infinitesimals.[3]

And Mr. Bronowski goes on to quote Blake's observation that "a line is a line in its minutest subdivisions, straight or crooked. It is itself, not intermeasurable by anything else."[4] Now to the artist, especially one like Blake whose strength lies in the linear rhythm of his draughtsmanship, a line *is* a complete and indivisible unity, explicable only in terms of the totality of its entire movement. Newton's calculus appears to explain, that is, measure, a curve such as a parabola by dividing it into infinitesimals, immeasurably small segments. By thus analyzing the arc described by a cannon ball, for example, the method of calculus seems to reduce the complete, continuous action of the projectile's flight to a static situation, a formula, based upon the division of that action into an infinite number of separate parts, each of which is indefinite, not a finite, actual thing.

We suggest that the Romantic poetic tales express (unconsciously, of course) opposition to this method of thinking. Or, if that suggestion appears too extreme, we may say that the Romantics found in the poetic tale an effective means for asserting that the truths of intuitive art surpass anything that can be achieved by the methods of rationalistic science. At any rate, we see all the Romantic poets working against the methods of the eighteenth-century philosophers in treating of moral experience. They insist on the unified indivisibility of moral action and demand that it be judged in terms of its own entirety, as a total process. And they deny the ultimate utility of analysis, rejecting any suggestion of a moral calculus. To them good and evil, innocence and experience, sensual passion and spiritual passion are definite, irreducible components out of whose interactions the processes of human experience arise. Once these elements have been isolated, analysis cannot be carried further, and it becomes the poet's task to synthesize.

We proposed in the first chapter that the Romantic delight in the narrative mode sprang not from extrapoetic causes but from the very way in which the Romantics saw the world around them, from their basic assumptions about the function of art and the nature of human life. And we proposed, consequently, that it is in the connection between narrative form and narrative subject that causes and meanings of the shift from Neo-classic to Romantic style are to be located. We are here endeavoring to justify those proposals. In so doing, moreover, we are defining some traits of Romantic imaginative narrative verse, distinguishing those of its characteristics which make it different from the narrative verse of other periods rich in story poems—the Elizabethan era, for example. Thus we have seen that the continuity of the narrative form made it attractive to the Romantic poets, concerned as they were with the synthetic development of actions, with moral behavior as a temporal process, rather than with the analysis of static situations. We have seen, too, that the inherent unity of narrative (in which everything is controlled by the narrator, is the expression of his grasp of events[5]) was precious to these poets, who believed that the understanding of an action depended upon one's ability to judge its parts in terms of its totality. And, finally, we can say that the Romantics were pleased by the definiteness, the palpability of actions represented through narrative. The action of a play is something invisible, something which we deduce from the behavior, the movements, of the characters, the intricacies and complexities of whose composition we must observe carefully if we are to understand the nature and significance of the central action which they make visible, even as the moving leaves of a tree make visible the wind. In a narrative the story is the direct manifestation of the poem's action, and the characters necessarily tend to be simpler than in drama. A narrative in which we had to deduce the action, that is, the story, plainly would be a contradiction in terms. To the Romantics, interested in the moral absolutes of human experience, a form in which emphasis falls upon definiteness of action rather than upon mysterious complexity of the actors was a natural vehicle for artistic expression.

We have already drawn attention to one of William Blake's specifically anti-Newtonian ideas, and we must now see how he put his theory into literary practice. Blake wrote extensively in the narrative mode, and the changes that his treatment of story underwent in the course of his long life illustrate a characteristic Romantic development, one that can be traced through the successive poetic tales of Wordsworth, Shelley, and Keats, for example. The first poetic stories of these writers tend to be simple presentations of glamorized history. As the poets mature their stories become more original and more imaginative, less historical or pseudo-historical. Thus one of Blake's earliest narrative poems is *Gwin, King of Norway,* published in the *Poetical Sketches* of 1783 and probably written in 1778,[6] a ballad-imitation that tells how the tyrant Gwin was slain by the giant Gordred, who had raised an army to end "the son of Nore's" tyranny "over the nations of the North." The poem is relatively naturalistic—for Blake—and within the tradition of mid-century ballad-imitating. Yet there are one or two features of the poem worthy of attention in the light of Blake's later stories. The poem treats of revolt. Gwin and his nobles "did feed/ Upon the hungry Poor," who finally call out for succor, to which call

> Gordred the giant rous'd himself
> From sleeping in his cave.

Gordred raises an army in the south and marches against Gwin. The ensuing battle is one of terrific slaughter, not merely of the nobles but of the husbandman, merchant, shepherd, and workman. And the value of the revolt is made further uncertain in the final stanza, which tells us that the river Dorman rolled the blood of Gwin and his army

> Into the northern sea,
> Who mourn'd his sons, and overwhelm'd
> The pleasant south country.

Tyranny, revolt, and destruction of the revolutionists or the creation of a new tyranny is a cycle which we will see Blake later develop more fully, but still in terms that allow place (here "north" and "south") to represent psychic or spiritual qualities.

Tiriel is customarily treated as a part of the prophetic books, but Professor Robert Gleckner has demonstrated that this long and rather turgid narrative is better understood as forming a transition between the *Songs of Innocence* (which were published in 1789, the same year, apparently, in which *Tiriel* was composed) and the *Songs of Experience*.[7] The poem, which is written in the long, unrhymed, almost free-rhythmed line which Blake later handled expertly but which here is alternately over-tense and slack, opens with the aged, blind Tiriel, supporting his dying wife outside the gates of his palace, cursing his sons who have usurped his power. Though his sons offer him protection, Tiriel refuses their charity and "darkling o'er the mountains" seeks "his pathless way." His wanderings carry him to the vales of Har. Here dwell Har and Heva, actually the parents of Tiriel, who now live in a state of senile childishness, waited on by old Mnetha, the embodiment of maternalism. First frightened by Tiriel's appearance, Har and Heva seek the shelter of Mnetha's lap, but on being assured by Tiriel that he will not injure them, they accept him, invite him to stay in their pleasant valley, and almost recognize him as their son. But Tiriel denies his identity and the next day continues on his journey until he is captured by the savage Ijim "at entrance of the forest in a dark & lonely way." Ijim, who has worshipped Tiriel as a god, believes the blind beggar before him to be a "foul fiend" masquerading in the form of Tiriel, binds him, and carries him to the palace occupied by Tiriel's sons. There Ijim is finally convinced of his mistake, and, disillusioned, he

> ... gloomy turn'd his back, & silent sought
> The secret forests & all night wander'd in desolate ways.

Freed from Ijim's bonds, Tiriel curses his children, who die immediately or "wither in the palace," all but his daughter Hela, who is forced to lead him back to the vales of Har. Before they arrive there, however, they pass the caves of old Zazel, who mocks and scorns Tiriel and whose sons "threw dirt & stones as they pass'd by." Arrived at the peaceful valley of Har, Tiriel proclaims his identity: "I am Tiriel, king of the west." But when he actually comes before Har and Heva his curse on his children returns on himself and *his* father. Tiriel recounts his pride, sorrow, and evil, concluding:

> Such was Tiriel,
> Compell'd to pray repugnant & to humble the immortal spirit
> Till I am subtil as a serpent in a paradise,
> Consuming all, both flowers & fruits, insects & warbling birds.
> And now my paradise is fall'n, & a drear sandy plain
> Returns my thirsty hissings in a curse on thee, O Har.
> Mistaken father of a lawless race, my voice is past.
>
> He ceased, outstretch'd at Har and Heva's feet in awful death.

Clearly this strange story more closely resembles *Christabel* than *Gwin, King of Norway,* even though certain elements, the tyrant, the giant, and the cyclical pattern of disastrous revolution, are common to both of Blake's poems. The semi-realism and pseudo-historicity of *Gwin* have given way to a magical world where mythical coherence supersedes naturalistic logic. And the basic oppositions of *Tiriel* are similar to those of *Christabel:* action and passivity, innocence and experience, spiritual and sensual passion. Tiriel, a one-sided and irredeemable Lear, is a sensual tyrant, his blindness symbolizing his loss of spiritual vision. The rebellion of his children which ousts him from his "once delightful palace" has been created by his own tyranny, which has condemned his children to value only the worldly and the material. Children, the innocent, are blessed with a divine spiritual energy which shatters inhibiting laws and man-created morality and makes them natural revolutionaries. But unless they can become *aware* of their burgeoning selfhood, the sense of their own individuality which animates their rebellion, and consequently learn to cherish the condition of selfless innocence out of which they have grown, they will become, in their own turn, merely selfish, worldly tyrants, greedy for Tiriel's palace and power, and vulnerable finally to the blight of his curse, for they will have, in effect, accepted him as their creator, the creator not merely of their flesh but of their spirit.[8] The history of Tiriel and the history of his children are, in fact, the same. Tiriel is the creation of his parents, Har and Heva, who have implanted the curse in him, not as he did in his children through tyranny, but through the opposite and equally evil course of attempting to evade reality, of fleeing from, rather than facing up to, the terrible energy apparent in their offspring's original state of innocence. Har and Heva have been unable, as it were, to admit the awesome potency of their own creation. They avoid rebellion by abdicating. Inaction may be as corrupting as action. The "innocent life" to which Har and Heva have regressed is as false as the childishness of senility, and Har and Heva are shown to lack the characteristics of true innocence: their love, such as it is, lacks spontaneity; unwittingly they reveal that they are not freshly innocent but are withdrawn from experience, when they identify Tiriel as "the king of rotten wood and of the bones of death"; they recognize physicality as inferior to spirituality and they have learned of death; their hospitality is that of creature comforts; their greatest fear is of physical harm—they accept Tiriel when he lays down his staff: "He will not hurt us, Heva," whimpers Har. And so, finally, the curse descends upon them, too, and the cycle is complete, evil begetting evil upon innocence and breeding its own destruction.[9]

If such a reading of *Tiriel* be at all reasonable, it is plain that Blake, like Coleridge, has stylized his characters into the stark embodiments of the irreducible elements of moral behavior and has shown us those elements operating within the dynamics of a unified process. *Tiriel* is not a good poem, but it is a better story than *Gwin*. Every part of

Tiriel is narratively more efficient; its action is more nearly continuous, the effect of each event becoming the cause of the next. And the passage of time is not in *Tiriel,* as it is in *Gwin,* either distorted by indefiniteness or left blank, but functions as part of the unity of the story. We know, that is, why one event happens before or after another and why this occurrence took days and that only hours. Plainly this greater narrative efficiency is to be accounted for by Blake's deeper commitment to a purely imaginary story conceived of as a continuously unfolding action. As glamorized history is replaced by fantasy, static situation is transformed into mobile process. The complete evolution of this changing treatment of narrative can be illustrated by *The Mental Traveller,* probably written by Blake about 1803.[10]

This poem is too finely wrought and too densely symbolic to be explained fully by any brief interpretation, but the subject-matter of the poem as well as its structure is so revealing of the Romantic use of narrative that we must attempt at least the outline of an exegesis. The theme of the poem appears to be that the potency of creative power places in perpetual jeopardy that which it has created. There is no such thing as static living. That which is animate is capable of creation; hence so long as an individual or his civilization is alive it is in the process of transforming both itself and its environment. Blake's presentation of this theme, however, avoids all its mechanistic implications and asserts the freedom of mankind from the trammels of purely natural cycles. Man's development may reverse the rigid progress of biology, the old can become young again, and it is man's action that determines whether Nature flourishes or decays (stanzas 17, 21, 25). Three conditions of human life are described in *The Mental Traveller:* innocence represented by the babe, experience represented by youth, and wisdom represented by old age. There are, however, two active principles in human life: the principle of spiritual selfhood represented by the male and the principle of sensual selflessness represented by the female. These principles move in opposing directions,[11] and through these contrary movements a four-phase cycle of human life is formed, with two creative periods (stanzas 6–12 and 18–24) and two fallow periods (stanzas 1–5 and 13–17).

The poem begins with the "Woman Old," sensual selflessness in the condition of wisdom, apparently maltreating the boy babe, spiritual selfhood in the condition of innocence. Actually she is performing acts both useful and necessary. She teaches him to feel, to endure suffering, to grow stronger, while she, treasuring his shrieks and fingering his nerves, delighting in the violence of his emotions, is rejuvenated and becomes a "Virgin bright." The babe, matured by his suffering into youth, the condition of experience, then "binds her down for his delight." But his delight is not that of the crone reveling in the pure emotions of spiritual innocence: "she becomes his dwelling place/ And Garden fruitful seventy fold." From his delight spring fruitfulness of the earth and material possessions, but in thus acting creatively he exhausts the original strength of his emotion, his selfhood becomes dominant, and he wears out, as it were, the selfless sensuality of the maiden, who disappears. He is left with only the treasures of his experience (stanzas 8 and 9); he has reached the condition of wisdom, in which only his grief can bring happiness and relief to others, "Till from the fire on the hearth" around which "the Beggar & the Poor/ And the wayfaring Traveller" have found "eternal joy" the female babe, sensual selflessness in its innocent form, springs forth. Sensual innocence growing into experience drives away the wisdom of age (stanza 13), which is impotent until it can be rejuvenated by contact with the primal energies of innocence (stanza 14). This contact means that the male must surrender the dominion of selfhood, seeing the joys of cottage and garden, the treasures of experience, the grandeur of hospitality fade to nothing—"a dark desart all around." His nourishment is to be found only in his love. Feeding on innocent love, he gradually becomes a babe once more, while the maiden's innocence is transformed into the terrors of experience. Again the principle of spiritual selfhood has become impotent (this time through shrinking back to the essence of itself) but in so doing has impregnated the "desart" with its potency. Nature and civilization flourish (stanzas 22 and 23) until the babe is found, the creative principle again reveals itself, and again only through the severe ministrations of the old woman, sensual selflessness become wise through experience, can that creative energy once more be transformed from a force of destruction (withering the arms of those who rashly touch it) into fruitful experience.

If we compare *The Mental Traveller* with *Gwin* and *Tiriel* we see that Blake progressed from relatively naturalistic narrative to thoroughly imaginative narrative of a mythical kind. Granted Blake's purpose—which is the very opposite of naturalistic representation[12] —*The Mental Traveller* is a better story than *Gwin, Tiriel,* or even

Christabel. In *The Mental Traveller* the irreducible elements of moral action, sense and spirit, self and selflessness, innocence and experience, are completely stylized, but their simplification enables Blake to render the motions of their interaction with increased fluidity and to make clear that indivisible continuity which is to him the essence of moral activity. We may be puzzled as to how to interpret the poem, but we are never in any doubt that it possesses unified continuity. In it narrative becomes a fully effective means for portraying the unified process of human behavior which arises from the mutual influence of definitive contraries which (according to Blake) constitute the soul. *The Mental Traveller* is a kind of practical refutation of those aspects of Newtonian thinking which Blake loathed: it is definite but synthetic, dynamic but self-contained and self-explanatory.

Perhaps because of the fame of Byron and Scott, the influence of Victorians like Browning and Morris, and our memory of *The Canterbury Tales,* we have come to think of narrative poetry as inherently naturalistic. That idea is false. Blake does not in *The Mental Traveller* attempt to tell a story like that which Scott recounts in *The Lady of the Lake,* nor does Keats in *The Eve of St. Agnes* try to imitate Byron's *Lara,* any more than Spenser in *The Fairie Queene* tries to reproduce Chaucer's realistic narration. Many Romantic narrative poems seem tedious or inept to us because they are patently unrealistic and, consequently, lack the kind of excitement and tension we rightly expect from naturalistic stories. We have almost forgotten that narrative may be used for other purposes than realistic suspense. But in many Romantic poetic tales the naturalistic function of story is minimized or dropped altogether and narrative is employed as a means of expressing a philosophic position, a moral attitude, or a vision of what the poet believes to be genuine reality, a reality which transcends naturalistic appearance.

We can observe, moreover, that this visionary (rather than realistic) function of story tends to be stressed by different poets for the same reason. The dream-like quality of *Christabel,* the prophetic ecstasy of Blake's later narratives, and even, as we shall see in the next chapter, the accumulation of particularized, literal detail in Wordsworth's pastoral tales, are diverse expressions of a common belief: that the most essential and most rewarding human experience consists of active emotional projection rather than response. For all these poets the natural world in itself appears as something blank, something grimly mechanical in its operation according to cyclic laws. Only when the natural universe has been enlivened by the projection into it of human passions does it become a source of wonder, of solace, of joy. The external natural world is delightful to these poets because it provides a field for the exercise of their inner powers. The virtue of the flower, for example, is that human feeling can be bestowed upon it. Even when the poet is controlled and shaped by external scenes and objects and forces, it is the emotional charge, derived by the poet from an earlier experience or from a human tradition or from a supra-natural power, laid upon these scenes, objects, and forces that endows them with their molding power. For these poets story is the realization of value. Narrative tension springs not from naturalistic suspense but from the gradual emergence of a system of precious truth, profound insight.

This may be why so many Romantic imaginative tales—one is tempted to say all—involve travel. The traveller, the moving individual, is representative of the evolving unity of experience. At the same time that he passes through an exterior environment he undergoes an inner development, and "the eye altering alters all." Thus a reciprocal progress is created between the experiencer and that which he experiences, and the completion of the journey establishes a continuous significance and a dynamic coherence out of apparently random events and the inert determinism of natural law through which he has passed both as creator-organizer and observer-interpreter.

Chapter VI

*

WORDSWORTH: THE PERSONAL EPIC

The traveller motif links Wordsworth's tales to those of Blake and Coleridge. It is noteworthy, too, that, although Wordsworth's subjects are contemporary events, he presents them as occurrences which might happen at any time and emphasizes the eternality of the verities of psychology or morality which his tales illuminate. *The Idiot Boy* and *Peter Bell,* for example, are not circumscribed by the conditions of eighteenth-century life, and in his best narrative, *Michael,* Wordsworth creates out of a mass of particularized details an atmosphere of ahistorical timelessness. And like Coleridge and Blake he turns to the poetic story as a source of freedom, not alone in form but in subject-matter too. His desire for freedom carries him along a different path, however. In the prologue to *Peter Bell,* for instance, he explicitly rejects fantastic and ostentatiously romantic subjects because he feels that the simple, commonplace happenings of ordinary life have been too long neglected (lines 121–30 and 136–45). Yet for all the humbleness of his subjects and his determination to stay within the bounds of "life's daily prospect,"[1] Wordsworth celebrates the unusual beauties of Nature. Even in *Guilt and Sorrow,* which is concerned above all with suffering, he juxtaposes with scenes of poverty, degradation, and despair descriptions such as this:

> Ere long, from heaps of turf, before their sight,
> Together smoking in the sun's slant beam,
> Rise various wreaths that into one unite
> Which high and higher mounts with silver gleam.[2]

Dramatic contrasts between the lovely and the ugly are characteristic of Romantic imaginative narratives, though in the later work of the poets simple descriptive contrasts are made to interpenetrate more dynamically and to take on added symbolic significance and complexity, as in *The Mental Traveller.*[3] Finally, Wordsworth, like Coleridge and Blake, stylizes the characters in his stories. Perhaps Peter Bell is his nearest approach to genuine individuality, but even Peter is portrayed as a type, as the member of a class the characteristics of which are more important than his personal idiosyncrasies. Ordinarily the people of Wordsworth's stories appear as representatives of a condition—the idiot, the female vagrant—or a profession—the sailor, the shepherd, the potter.

Like Blake, Wordsworth begins with historical subjects treated more or less realistically and progresses to imaginative subjects rendered with symbolic significance. *Guilt and Sorrow,* which was written between 1791 and 1794,[4] is most interesting for the realism with which it dramatizes the condition of the lower classes in England in the 1790's and the harshness with which it attacks the complacent mores of bourgeois society and the inhuman rigor of antiquated laws. But as a narrative *Guilt and Sorrow* is confused. The interweaving of the separate histories of the Sailor and the Female Vagrant is strained and inept. There are disconcerting jumps in the time scheme because the life histories of the principal characters tend to crystallize into distinct scenes which do not convey the sense of continuity for which the poet so clearly aims. What might have been the dramatic representation of the struggle of individuals to resist the inhumanity of their society thus stiffens into melodramatic tableaux.

As a story *Peter Bell* (originally written in 1798 but much reworked and not finally published until 1819) is superior to *Guilt and Sorrow.* Wordsworth narrates with considerable skill the process by which the hardened nature of Peter Bell is softened into repentance by his discovery of a drowned man and his subsequent journey through the hills to the widow's house. Here Wordsworth subordinates the realistic aspects of his subject to the evolving interaction of Peter's mental struggles with the mysterious powers and influences exerted by natural phenomena, which, it must be noted, are always rendered effective as reforming agents by their association with human concerns. The wanderings of the Sailor and the Female Vagrant are nothing more than the random movements of the dispossessed. Peter's literal journey —he leaves the main road, becomes lost, finds the dead man, mounts the donkey and lets it choose his course, is carried past the wood-spirit-like hallooings of the dead man's son, past the tavern full of roisterers, past the vision of the Highland Girl he had deserted, past the Methodist meetinghouse from which issue the sounds of revivalistic prayers, and finally is carried back over the "stony lane" to the widow's house of grief and, paradoxically, of consolation—this journey is symbolic of Peter's spiritual travel. Symbolic orientation allows for something like the kind of moral simplification we have observed in Blake and Coleridge. The ass plainly represents[5] spiritual love, as Peter with his twelve wives represents sensuality. The dead man's son and daughter personify innocence, as his wife and the Highland Girl embody the grief of experience. Also interesting is Wordsworth's effort in *Peter Bell* to manoeuvre the reader's point of view, although he never approaches Coleridge's skill. Wordsworth's technique is to present the action in a kind of partial perspective. The story is not told objectively, for we hear it from the fictive narrator, who is not only supposed to be recounting the tale to little Bess, the Squire, Stephen Otter, and the others, but who has, in the prologue, told us of his magical flight in the "little Boat,/ Shaped like a crescent moon." But the fictive narrator's speech is sometimes interrupted by Wordsworth's own apostrophizings, e.g., lines 736–80. In part this method may originate in Wordsworth's uneasiness over what his contemporaries called the meanness of his subject-matter.[6] More important, in all probability, is his desire to put the reader in a position to appreciate the interaction between Peter's mental processes and the intensifying influences of the natural world. Nature and Peter's hardened mind are, like Geraldine and Christabel in Coleridge's poem, the two poles of this story, and it is necessary that neither appear merely as an aspect of the other, as they would tend to do if the action came to us either through Peter's eyes or in the full perspective of naturalistic narrative.

Michael, composed in 1800, is superior to *Peter Bell* and is, indeed, the high point of Wordsworth's narratives. The perspective here is simplified and more coherently organized. Wordsworth dispenses with the fictive narrator, beginning with a direct address to the reader: "If from the public way *you* turn your steps." Then, gradually, through the description of the solitary mountains and the unfinished sheepfold, he introduces the story as significant to *his* life:

> It was the first
> Of those domestic tales that spake to me
> Of Shepherds, dwellers in the valleys, men
> Whom I already loved;—not verily
> For their own sakes, but for the fields and hills
> Where was their occupation and abode.

And he concludes the prologue by placing his life within a larger, continuing tradition:

> Therefore, although it be a history
> Homely and rude, I will relate the same . . .
> . . . for the sake
> Of youthful Poets, who among these hills
> Will be my second self when I am gone.

Thereafter he tells the story as a neighbor of the shepherd might, though from time to time he unobtrusively reminds the reader that the story is, so to speak, second-hand and chiefly significant for its influence upon the poet (lines 93, 210, 451, etc.). This simplification and clarification is possible in *Michael* because Wordsworth, first, treats his story as pure story and, second, transcends naturalism by an intensified reiteration of selected naturalistic details instead of trying to impose upon a realistic narrative as a whole an arbitrary symbolic pattern.

When we say that *Michael* is pure story we mean that it has no plot. Causal relations between incidents are not dramatized. Events simply occur in temporal succession, and the question of why they occur as they do is virtually neglected.[7] A dramatist or novelist dealing with the subject of *Michael* would almost surely stress the conflict between the shepherd's love of his son and his love for his property. Wordsworth minimizes that conflict, and, finally, in Michael's last address to Luke blurs the two motives together (ll. 361–70). Likewise we are never told why Luke in the city becomes dissolute and finally goes abroad. Luke's defection is not made dramatic. His failure may be the most terrible happening in Michael's long life, but Wordsworth is emphasizing the frightfulness of the shepherd's life as a continuous unity, not focussing upon a single incident which might in a flash, as it were, illuminate the sombreness of his existence. Hence Michael lives on after Luke's failure and does not abandon once for all his work on the sheepfold "of which/His flock had need." Not every day "he thither went" and was unable to work but "many a day" he "never lifted up a single stone." It is the totality of Michael's life that concerns Wordsworth, not one dramatic part of it; his theme is the same as Tolstoy's in *The Death of Ivan Ilych:* "Ivan Ilych's life had been most simple and most ordinary and therefore most terrible."[8] Wordsworth needs not the complexity of dramatic plot but instead the simplicity of pure story.

It is, furthermore, the simplicity of the pure story form that enables Wordsworth to charge Michael's most ordinary life with mythical significance. "Myth" (which we have applied previously to the stories of Blake and Coleridge) is a kind of blank-check word—one fills in one's own meaning. But surely myth, as contrasted to symbol, is characterized by simplicity and largeness. Whereas the symbolic thing has multiple meanings that vary with the context in which it appears,[9] the mythical thing and its meaning are less separable; the mythical thing creates its own context. When we say that Prometheus is a mythical figure we mean that he is a figure invested with a particular significance by his participation in a particular action. He has no existence outside of that action; he is the embodiment of his own history. The symbolic object, the rose, for example, has an identity separable from its particular symbolic function and hence can operate with different significances in different contexts. The most usual form of the myth is the simple story, whereas symbolism flourishes in more complicated forms. Now whatever significance Michael possesses is the endowment of his participation in the continuity of his entire life. The poignancy of Michael sitting in the mute paralysis of grief beside the unfinished sheepfold, "his faithful Dog,/Then old, beside him, lying at his feet,"[10] resides in the fact that the gestureless pose embodies the shepherd's history. In saying this much of *Michael* we have, perhaps, justified our use of the word myth in regard to Blake's poems and to *Christabel,* wherein we observed a similar tendency to stress the unified continuity of story—rather than the dramatic complexities of plot—and an accompanying emphasis upon character as the crystallization of a moral absolute rather than upon the intricate dynamics of realistic personality.

We must still explain our remark that Wordsworth transcends naturalism by reiterated emphasis upon selected naturalistic details. *Michael* is filled with such details and the tone of the story is realistic: the diction and the imagery are ordinary, the structure of the narration follows commonplace chronology, and none of the occurrences is overtly impressive. There is, in fact, a disproportion between the wealth of unimpressive detail and the paucity of notable incidents in *Michael.* Because of that disproportion we come to comprehend the shepherd's life through the accretion of the many simple, physical particularities which surround it. These physical things—the spinning wheels, the lamp, the clipping tree, the sapling staff, the stones of the sheepfold, and so forth—become the enduring form or pattern of an ordinary life, a form which persists even when the life which took shape within it is no more. The very physical particularity of these objects, like a fossilized rock, preserves, and by preserving emphasizes, the form of Michael's life. Thus Wordsworth invests his protagonist's life with dignity, a mythical eternality, which transcends the apparent insignificance of his private, limited experience.

The success of *Michael* Wordsworth never repeated. Though a few later poems, *Resolution and Independence,* for example, employ effectively some of the narrative techniques of *Michael,* none attains the same degree of unified intensity. If we turn to *The White Doe of Rylstone* (first draft 1807, published 1815), we find, as we might expect, an increased emphasis upon the non-naturalistic function of narrative. Although treating a subject comparable to one of Scott's,[11] Wordsworth rejects the opportunity to develop a story of action. As he says in the preface: "Everything that is attempted by the principal personages in 'The White Doe' fails, so far as its object is external and substantial. So far as it is moral and spiritual it succeeds." But *The White Doe* fails as myth. Here the imaginative freedom of Wordsworth's earlier work seems to have stiffened into half-hearted allegory. The doe, the banner, and Emily herself are rigid and formalized signposts pointing to abstract and conventional beliefs. But Wordsworth does not fully accept the role of allegorist; the story of *The White Doe* is still partially an end in itself, still in part flowing and developing in its movement, not stylized in the fixed, formalistic designs of fully allegorical narrative. The weaknesses of *The White Doe* customarily are associated with the decline in Wordsworth's poetic powers after his thirty-fifth year.[12] But it is possible that the form of the poetic story which we have been considering was itself undergoing a transformation. The synthesis of a unified, continuous action out of the interinfluence of elemental contraries seems to have been congenial to the early Romantic poets because it enabled them to be at the same time personal and impersonal, subjective and objective. The simple imaginative story allows the teller to retain a central and controlling position while recounting that which has universal significance. Blake, Coleridge, and the young Wordsworth exploited this dual power to the full. That is why *Christabel, The Mental Traveller,* and *Michael* are, as we say, characteristic of their authors, without ever reverting to lyricism or degenerating into private monologues.

In *The White Doe* Wordsworth tries to write allegorically without giving up his central, controlling position as narrator of a simple, self-contained story. By definition allegorical narrative is something different from simple story, necessarily more formalized and less hospitable to subjectivity. The two kinds of narrative do not mix well, and we find in *The White Doe* a confusion of methods analogous to what we observed in poems like *Darkness* and *A Vision of the Sea.*[13]

The White Doe, in fact, not only belongs to a later phase in Wordsworth's career but stands on the threshold of a later phase of Romanticism in which the simple poetic tale ceased to exist.[14] We have noted that Wordsworth refused the opportunity to develop his story in the way in which Byron or Scott might have, and that deliberate refusal marks *The White Doe* as a significant dividing point in the history of Romantic narrative art. On one side, Byron and Scott, rejecting any pretense of epical significance and grandeur, developed what we shall call the adventurous narrative: a story poem concerned with physical action and adventure, usually based on historical fact, more or less realistic in manner, and most significant in its exploration of sociological reality—the relationship of the individual to the social group and the interaction of supra-individual forces. The adventurous narrative is most closely associated with (and contributed much to) the evolution of prose fiction during the early years of the nineteenth century. On the other side, the older Wordsworth, followed by Shelley and Keats, developed narrative poetically. Their stories became less and less like prose fiction and more and more the form or medium for the expression of personal, visionary experience. They became private myths. Whereas Byron's and Scott's language became progressively simpler and more colloquial as their subjects became more realistic, the language of Wordsworth, Shelley, and Keats became progressively richer and more literary as their subjects became less realistic. Byron and Scott moved in the direction of the novel. Wordsworth, Shelley, and Keats (who were, we may note, the Romantics most influenced by Milton) moved in the direction of the epic.

Romantic epics,[15] however, are not like the traditional epics of the Renaissance and antiquity. They express personal rather than social experience; their truth is not that of reason but of supra-rational vision; their manner is mythical and dynamic, not formal and conventional. No single form is more characteristic of Romantic poetry than these personal epics, but like all types of Romantic verse they originate in reactions against specific Neo-classic theories and in modifications of specific Neo-classic practices, and to understand them we must understand something of their literary antecedents.

Of all narrative forms genuine epic is the most impressive and enduring. That tenet of Renaissance genre theory was not profoundly challenged by either Neo-classic or Romantic poets,[16] who, nevertheless, if they were competent artists, almost ostentatiously eschewed the traditions of the form. A good writer knows his limitations as an inferior one may not. But we recognize in the history of eighteenth-century literature an increasing pressure upon poets to write epically. Partly the pressure was economic; Pope's *Iliad* was a money-making venture, and some atrocious original epics of the period sold reasonably well. Partly it was critical; one could scarcely accept the doctrine of epic supremacy and not urge practicing poets to prove their worth by attempting that "highest" genre. And partly it was philosophical; the growing appreciation of sublimity in art pointed toward epic grandeur. By the end of the eighteenth century these combined pressures could not be ignored, and Romantic poets had either consciously to deny any epic intention, as Scott and Byron did, or to try their hand at something like epic, as Wordsworth, Shelley, and Keats did.

If we are to discuss intelligently the fortunes of the epic during this period we must have some definite idea of what constitutes genuine epic. As touchstones of authentic epic we propose three characteristics.[17] First, an epic is a narrative poem. About this point all critics since Aristotle have agreed. Second, the story of an epic must be real, that is, in Professor Abercrombie's words, "must be founded deep in the general experience of men.... No [mere] fiction will ever have the air... not merely of representing, but of unmistakably *being,* human experience" (pp. 44–45). About this point there has been some critical quibbling, but most of it a matter of word-chopping. But our third touchstone, although probably acceptable to most modern students of epic literature, is one that many early critics might have had trouble understanding: The epic story must embody some profoundly significant idea. By "idea" we do not mean merely a rational abstraction, nor do we mean exactly what Milton, for instance, called his "argument." Rather we mean that sort of implicit lesson which Goethe said he learned from *The Iliad:* "From Homer I learn every day more clearly, that in our life here above ground we have, properly speaking, to enact Hell."

If we apply these touchstones to the epics or pseudo-epics of the eighteenth century we see why an age that talked so much about epics is so barren of genuine heroic poetry.[18] It has become a platitude to say that in the Augustan era poets and critics alike tended to distinguish between imaginative truth and rational truth, assigning reality to the sphere of the latter alone. Even if modern scholarship has exaggerated that tendency, its existence is indisputable and even in latent form is bound to be fatal to the creation of epic stories that are "real" in the sense of our definition. For related reasons the Augustans thought of the animating force of epic as its argument or fable rather than as its idea. Hence eighteenth-century criticism and practice seldom penetrated beyond the ornaments of epic—its obvious subject-matter, its supernatural machinery, its special diction. The Augustan discussions of the rules and techniques of epic (largely derived from Le Bossu) make tedious reading today not because they are silly (they are not) but because they never come near the experience we feel when we read epic poetry.[19] One is struck, for instance, by the Augustan reluctance to condemn poetry which even superficially meets the formal requirements of its particular genre. The eighteenth-century epics of Blackmore, Glover, and Willkie are bad by any standards because they are destitute of genuine poetic feeling. But that charge, as Macneile Dixon pointed out long ago, was only seldom and feebly raised against them by eighteenth-century critics, who wasted most of their energies on discussions of the appropriateness of their "machinery."[20]

One may examine the problem from a different angle. In a very real sense the true epics of the late seventeenth and early eighteenth centuries are Dryden's translation of the *Aeneid* and Pope's translation of the *Iliad*. Douglas Knight has argued persuasively that to the degree that Pope's *Iliad* is not Homer it is a positive and original contribution to the European heroic tradition.[21] One can only agree with Dr. Knight, but one may feel, as he does not, that Pope's translation is too like its original to contribute much to the European tradition of heroic poetry. In what large sense, after all, is Pope's *Iliad* not like Homer's? Richard Bentley, the classical scholar, is reputed to have remarked, "A very pretty poem, Mr. Pope, but you mustn't call it Homer." Seldom has pedantic hostility to poetry been better disguised in aphoristic grace. If the story, characters, and setting of Pope's *Iliad* are not Homer's, whose are they? If Bentley meant that

Pope's diction differs from Homer's he could have saved breath by confining himself to the observation that Greek and English are different languages. If he meant that Pope's translation is animated by a different spirit from that which animates Homer's poem he is in one obvious way correct, in another way ambiguous, but mostly obtuse. To the degree that Pope's version is faithful it necessarily must be animated by the same spirit as Homer's original. But the fact that Pope translates means that nothing in his version can embody Homer's spirit, which does not exist separately from the Greek language which expresses it. Bentley's comment deserves belaboring because, if we are interested in poetry rather than in scholarship, we must recognize that the fault of Pope's *Iliad* is that it is too faithful to Homer. Pope was a poetic genius of the first order, yet his one contribution to the European heroic tradition is a careful translation, which is as much as to say no contribution. Had Pope treated Homer with the happy freedom that some medieval translators used toward their originals, his contribution to epic would surely have been more significant and viable. That he did not do so may be ascribed to his being infected by the same kind of anti-poetic pedantry which Bentley exhibits in his criticism. Insofar as he was a poet Pope wasted his talents trying to copy, literally copy, another man's verse. His *Iliad* is actually a manifestation of, rather than as Dr. Knight contends, a protest against, his age's "growing opposition [to] the idea that one can look to poetry for an expression of human significance and value."[22]

Faith in the power of poetry to express the profoundest kind of truth is the necessary condition of all Romantic attempts at epic. Something of the nature of that faith is suggested by the distinctively antihistorical character of the Romantic personal epic. From the time of Pope until the writing of *The Prelude*[23] all epic poetry was to some degree historical or pseudo-historical.[24] A growing historical consciousness, one of the most significant eighteenth-century developments, perhaps most climactically exemplified by Gibbon's monumental *Decline and Fall* (published between 1776 and 1788), worked against the creation of authentic epic. Not only is the idea of a rational history hostile to faith in poetic truth, but also the historical method is antagonistic to the epical method. The essence of the historical method is research, research to discover factual truth. The essence of the epical method lies in its imposition of an imaginative ideal upon the facts of history. Epic asserts or celebrates rather than discovering; it is anti-historical. It can work only with that kind of history which has been transformed by tradition or imaginative enthusiasm into legend.[25] The historian's "grand design" is always, in theory at least, a tentative one.[26] It is always subject to modification, however slight, through the introduction of new evidence. The epic writer's grand design, being a function of his art, not an organization of external facts, cannot be dependent on extrinsic materials. Recent discoveries of Mycenean civilization do not affect the value of the *Iliad*. Or, to put the matter differently, the opinion of some modern historians that what Homer describes as the siege of Troy was in fact merely a freebooters' raid has no bearing on our opinion of Homer's poem but does affect our judgment of Thucydides' discussion of the Trojan War at the opening of his history. This is so well understood as to be scarcely worth repeating, except that the effort to treat history epically defines the basic fault in many eighteenth-century and early nineteenth-century long narrative poems, most of which are burdened by too great a respect for the grandeur of history. More important, the effort to escape the limiting conditions of history goes far to explain the form and the subject of Wordsworth's most ambitious poem, *The Prelude,* which attempts a new kind of epic system.

We are not the first by any means to call attention to the epic nature and structure of *The Prelude,*[27] although our definition of the poem as epic is perhaps derived from a more particularized consideration of its place amidst the many historical verse narratives of Wordsworth's era. *The Prelude* is, in part, a history of the French Revolution, but Wordsworth subordinates that history to his autobiography. The mighty events of contemporary history are presented only as they appear to, and exert influence upon, the life of a private individual. But without the French Revolution there would be no *Prelude*. *The Prelude* is not in any sense literal, consistent autobiography, as Wordsworth's later biographers have all had to emphasize. Wordsworth distorts his autobiography, in the first place, by suppressing certain important occurrences in his personal life. Many of his omissions, most strikingly, of course, that of his affair with Annette, reveal his determination not to treat of exclusively private matters. What critics of *The Prelude* have stressed insufficiently is that the organization of the poem is founded upon a continuous and systematic dialectic between public and private affairs, between social developments and personal growth, between the objective drama of political events and the subjective drama of psychological change. At no point is either term in the dialectic dismissed. The public and the private may interpenetrate or may stand in opposition, or may be more complexly related, but neither exists without reference to the other. Hence Wordsworth, besides suppressing some matters important to him personally, freely rearranges the actual chronology of his experience to make it accord with the social evolution he dramatizes. To take a famous example, the climactic vision from the top of Snowdon in Book XIV records an experience that in fact took place before—not after—the poet had undergone the psychic travail of abandoning his faith in revolutionary reform.[28] If in *The Prelude* public events are subordinated to the individual's vision of them, both public and private history are adjusted to the demands of Wordsworth's narrative embodiment of a profound and enduring conception of "the general experience of men."

The subject of *The Prelude* is power. Wordsworth is first of all interested in the power of the imagination, an individual power and one peculiarly the attribute of the poet. But in *The Prelude* the power of imagination is defined, dramatized, and evaluated according to its relationship to other kinds of power, most notably, on the one hand, the power of Nature, which is the "express resemblance" of the individual's imagination—

> The power, which all
> Acknowledge when thus moved, which Nature thus
> To bodily sense exhibits, is the express
> Resemblance of that glorious faculty
> That higher minds bear with them as their own. (XIV, 86–90)—

and, on the other hand, the contrasting power of social action, heroic service to one's fellow men, a power which Wordsworth tasted in the fervid days of revolutionary ardor:

> I began
> To meditate with ardour on the rule
> And management of nations; what it is
> And ought to be; and strove to learn how far
> Their power or weakness, wealth or poverty,
> Their happiness or misery, depends
> Upon their laws, and fashion of the State.
> . . . .
> Now was it that *both* found, the meek and lofty
> Did both find helpers to their hearts' desire,
> And stuff at hand, plastic as they could wish,—

> Were called upon to exercise their skill,
> Not in Utopia,—subterranean fields,—
> Or some secreted island, Heaven knows where!
> But in the very world, which is the world
> Of all of us,—the place where, in the end,
> We find our happiness, or not at all! (XI, 98–104, 136–44)

Imagination, as Wordsworth conceives it, is not restricted to aesthetic matters. The poet, we must remember, is to Wordsworth's way of thinking the least specialized of human beings. He is simply "a man speaking to men." He addresses himself not to one particular faculty nor to a limited range of experience but to those capacities and experiences which are common to all human beings.

> The Poet writes under one restriction only, namely, the necessity of giving immediate pleasure to a human Being possessed of that information which may be expected from him, not as a lawyer, a physician, a mariner, an astronomer, or a natural philosopher, but as a Man. Except this one restriction, there is no object standing between the Poet and the image of things; between this, and the Biographer and Historian, there are a thousand.[29]

In choosing as his subject the power of imagination, Wordsworth was not, as it may at first appear, confining himself to the egotistical and aesthetic, but was, rather, selecting what seemed to him the best available means of conveying the whole truth about the place and function of the individual in both the macrocosm of Nature and the microcosm of his society.

The story *The Prelude* tells, then, is of the birth and early growth of the imaginative power (Books I–VI), its impairment (Books VII–XI), and its eventual restoration (Books XII–XIV). The "idea" which the story embodies is that modern civilization, the human creation which is meant to foster and to protect man's dignity as man, is itself the most dangerous enemy of those "civil" virtues which distinguish man from beast. Thus in *The Prelude* we find the first expression of the typically modern conviction that only by resisting his civilization can a man preserve his individuality and all the common decencies that appertain thereto. Wordsworth as he appears in *The Prelude* is the prototype of the contemporary hero: the man who fights against his culture.

Because we have become accustomed to identifying heroism with the capacity to resist, instead of to represent, the culture of which one is a part,[30] we underestimate the vigor of self-consciousness required by such heroism 150 years ago. It demands, above all, that we become conscious of our culture as a culture. What makes that difficult is that any culture is pervasive and all-encompassing. If a salmon were to become aware that it is swimming in water and then further that the river it swims up in order to spawn is fresh rather than salt water, its awareness, however impressive an achievement for a fish, would be less astonishing than a man's consciousness of the culture in which he operates. For human culture is not only an external environment, it is also a way of thinking and feeling, and it determines to a large extent what we perceive and how we respond to those perceptions. To become aware of one's culture and then to reject it, even partially, is, in consequence, an enormous experience and a shattering one. For on what grounds can we reject that which is essential to us? If we deny the civilization that makes us what we are, to what standard or ideal can we turn?

Nature, says Wordsworth. But what does he mean by Nature? Better heads than ours have analyzed Wordsworth's conception in more detail than we can here afford, and we shall do no more than indicate the general outline of Wordsworth's ideal. To him Nature is certainly not merely the biological order, bestiality. He never recommends the law of the jungle. Nature, which fosters and nourishes imaginative power, is inferior to imagination, is, in fact, its servant, as the older, stronger nurse is servant to the child. The dramatic conclusion of *The Prelude* is Wordsworth's vision from the top of Snowdon, and of that view of Nature he says: "There I beheld the emblem of a mind" (XIV, 70). He goes on to insist that what "Nature thus/To bodily sense exhibits" is but the "Resemblance" of the "glorious faculty/That higher minds bear with them as their own." Whether Wordsworth is here being Platonic or Christianly mystical need not now concern us. His point is that "higher minds" are superior to Nature, are "By sensible impressions not enthralled" (XIV, 106). The power of imagination, though nurtured by association with "the beauteous forms" of Nature, derives from a higher, more enduring source, and is, in fact, the specifically human endowment which enables us to transcend the limits of our animal nature.

> Such minds are truly from the Deity,
> For they are Powers; and hence the highest bliss
> That flesh can know is theirs—the consciousness
> Of Whom they are, habitually infused

> Through every image and through every thought,
> And all affections by communion raised
> From earth to heaven, from human to divine.... (XIV, 112–18)

The temptation, then, is to say that the ideal upon which Wordsworth bases his rejection of his civilization is not, after all, Nature in itself but Nature as a revelation of God, that *The Prelude* turns from faith in civilization to reliance in a mystical union with a transcendent deity whose influence is visible in the natural world. This is true, and critics like Professor Trilling who urge us to attend to the quietistic elements in Wordsworth's thought are surely right. But it is easy to oversimplify the complexity of Wordsworth's ideal. For example, it appears to us that orthodox Christians have every justification for regarding *The Prelude* with suspicion. Wordsworth seems to have expended very little effort in making his poem represent systematically the basic tenets of Christianity. And Wordsworth's mysticism, as scholars like Professor Havens have shown, is of a peculiar kind. It is certainly not the mysticism of self-obliteration. Imagination in *The Prelude* is the power of intensified consciousness of one's own individuality, and that power is not aided or drawn forth by God's grace.

> Here must thou be, O Man!
> Power to thyself; no Helper hast thou here;
> Here keepest thou in singleness thy state:
> No other can divide with thee this work:
> No secondary hand can intervene
> To fashion this ability; 'tis thine,
> The prime and vital principle is thine
> In the recesses of thy nature, far
> From any reach of outward fellowship,
> Else is not thine at all. (XIV, 209–18)

In reviewing in Book XIV what the "long labour" of *The Prelude* has accomplished, Wordsworth describes the course of the developing imagination thus:

> we have traced the stream
> From the blind cavern whence is faintly heard
> Its natal murmur; followed it to light
> And open day; accompanied its course
> Among the ways of Nature, for a time
> Lost sight of it bewildered and engulphed:
> Then given it greeting as it rose once more

> In strength, reflecting from its placid breast
> The works of man and face of human life;
> And lastly, from its progress have we drawn
> Faith in life endless, the sustaining thought
> Of human Being, Eternity, and God. (XIV, 194–205)

From contemplation of the journey we have drawn "the sustaining thought" of God, but the journey itself, the poet quite rightly observes, has been "among the ways of Nature" and "the works of man and face of human life." We do Wordsworth an injustice when we isolate what we believe to be statements of his mystical faith from their narrative context in *The Prelude*. The ideal upon which the individual bases his resistance to his culture is created for us not so much by scattered passages in which Wordsworth states his mystical doctrine as by our experience of reading his poem as a continuous whole. If one were to study in isolation those passages from *The Iliad* in which Homer speaks explicitly of the gods, one would scarcely arrive at Goethe's conclusion as to the central "idea" of the poem.

Books I–VI of *The Prelude* tell of the genesis and early flowering of the poet's imagination. Dominant here are his experiences in the world of Nature, a world older and more primary than that of his particular society. Most of the incidents narrated in these first books are trivial. By trivial we mean relatively unimportant to the formation of Wordsworth's character—the outward or social aspect of his personality. As illustrations of the principles of imaginative power, or of stages in its growth, however, the incidents are the very opposite of trivial. In all of them, nevertheless, we are made conscious, sometimes directly, sometimes by implication, of the poet as a human being whose experience is inescapably conditioned by his relation to his fellow creatures. His first experiences of the natural world in infancy, for example, are shaped and controlled by the maternal emotions through which alone the child perceives.

> Blest the infant Babe,
> (For with my best conjecture I would trace
> Our Being's earthly progress,) blest the Babe,
> Nursed in his Mother's arms, who sinks to sleep
> Rocked on his Mother's breast; who with his soul
> Drinks in the feelings of his Mother's eye!
> For him, in one dear Presence, there exists
> A virtue which irradiates and exalts
> Objects through widest intercourse of sense.

> No outcast he, bewildered and depressed:
> Along his infant veins are interfused
> The gravitation and the filial bond
> Of nature that connect him with the world.
> Is there a flower, to which he points with hand
> Too weak to gather it, already love
> Drawn from love's purest earthly fount for him
> Hath beautified that flower.... (II, 233–49)

Even when celebrating the "Presences of Nature," Wordsworth links them to a human environment.

> Was it for this
> That one, the fairest of all rivers, loved
> To blend his murmurs with my nurse's song.... (I, 269–71)

Nor should Wordsworth's emphasis upon solitariness and loneliness mislead us. Wordsworth felt, and makes us feel, the "power of Solitude" by contrast. Most of the poet's childhood as it is described in the first books of *The Prelude* was spent in the company of many other children. The great scenes of solitariness, the ice-skating and boat-stealing episodes, for instance (I, 425–60 and 357–400), stand out in Wordsworth's mind, and in his poem, because they are unusual. Moreover, the operative element in these episodes is Wordsworth's consciousness of being alone, of freeing himself for a moment from the pressures created by his fellow creatures. The value of solitude is determined by its relation to the pleasures and responsibilities of gregariousness.

This same pattern persists throughout Wordsworth's story of his later youth, his time at Cambridge, his vacations, his reading, and finally his trip abroad. Alone amidst Nature or lost in the solitary perusal of a book, the poet responds to the power of emotions and perceptions more intense and more revealing of truth than the feelings and observations of ordinary social intercourse. But in each case the experience in solitude leads toward a deepening sense of commitment to the lives of his fellow creatures. The often-praised flood and waste-land nightmare motivated by his reading of *Don Quixote* (V, 50–140), for example, leads to this conclusion:

> Full often, taking from the world of sleep
> This Arab phantom, which I thus beheld,
> This semi-Quixote, I to him have given
> A substance, fancied him a living man,
> . . . .

Nor have I pitied him; but rather felt
Reverence was due to a being thus employed;
And thought that, in the blind and awful lair
Of such a madness, reason did lie couched.

. . . .

yea, will I say,
Contemplating in soberness the approach
Of an event so dire, by signs in earth
Or heaven made manifest, that I could share
That maniac's fond anxiety, and go
Upon like errand. (V, 141–61)

It is, indeed, the misdirection or misleading of his developing power of imagination through too superficial sympathy with other men which creates Wordsworth's later crisis. At the time of his famous dedication, for instance, he misunderstands the nature of his commitment. He associates the moving experience of the glorious sunrise with the gay sociability of the party he has left and with the "labourers going forth to till the fields."

'Mid a throng
Of maids and youths, old men, and matrons staid,
A medley of all tempers, I had passed
The night in dancing, gaiety, and mirth,
With din of instruments and shuffling feet,
And glancing forms, and tapers glittering,
And unaimed prattle flying up and down;
Spirits upon the stretch, and here and there
Slight shocks of young love-liking interspersed,
Whose transient pleasure mounted to the head,
And tingled through the veins. Ere we retired,
The cock had crowed, and now the eastern sky
Was kindling, not unseen, from humble copse
And open field, through which the pathway wound,
And homeward led my steps. Magnificent
The morning rose, in memorable pomp,
Glorious as e'er I had beheld—in front,
The sea lay laughing at a distance; near,
The solid mountains shone, bright as the clouds,
Grain-tinctured, drenched in empyrean light;
And in the meadows and the lower grounds
Was all the sweetness of a common dawn—
Dews, vapours, and the melody of birds,
And labourers going forth to till the fields.

> . . . to the brim
> My heart was full; I made no vows, but vows
> Were then made for me; bond unknown to me
> Was given, that I should be, else sinning greatly,
> A dedicated Spirit. (IV, 309–37)

Only later, when the "glorious birth" of the French Revolution has deteriorated into Napoleon's tyranny, does Wordsworth understand that "bond unknown." He mistakenly had thought his dedication was to revolutionary social action; now he understands the earlier vows were to private, not to public service. The betrayal of France's (and his own) revolutionary idealism is painted for us in an image meant to recall his original dedication:

> when the sun
> That rose in splendour, was alive, and moved
> In exultation with a living pomp
> Of clouds—his glory's natural retinue—
> Hath dropped all functions by the gods bestowed,
> And, turned into a gewgaw, a machine,
> Sets like an Opera phantom. (XI, 364–70)

But Wordsworth's revolutionary experiences have not been wasted. Through them he has gained increased consciousness of his own role in life, of the dangers of what we may call too easy social heroism. The principal fact about all of the poet's early experiences described in Books I–VI is that he did not, at the time of their occurrence, understand their meaning and significance. In retrospect he sees how they contributed to the development of his imaginative power. But until that power had developed he had no means of fully understanding what had happened to him. He was the victim of experience, not its master. Hence the impairment of his imaginative power is, ultimately, useful and productive. Through wrongly pursuing the temptation of heroic action for social betterment, Wordsworth learns that the individual's highest duty is to himself. The great lesson of *The Prelude* is self-reliance. But self-reliance requires self-understanding, and self-understanding is precisely what revolutionary ardor makes impossible. Yet, ironically, without the experience of blind revolutionary fervor the poet might never have awakened to complete self-understanding.

Until the last books of *The Prelude,*[31] then, the reader is given a double vision of the action of the poem: what Wordsworth experienced at the time and what he now realizes the significance of that experience to have been. This is most vividly illustrated, perhaps, by the poet's description of the event which concludes the first part of *The Prelude*—his crossing of the Alps. Here, as Mr. Foakes has observed, "as the poet *wrote* of crossing the Alps, he was seized by an imaginative vision . . . the vision does not belong to the moment of crossing the mountains, but to the moment of writing."[32] At the time the poet, as he says, "was lost." Crossing the Alps accidentally, as it were, symbolizes his lack of self-awareness. Only now, as he writes after the event, is he capable of recognizing the meaning of his experience.

> Imagination—here the Power so called
> Through sad incompetence of human speech,
> That awful Power rose from the mind's abyss
> Like an unfathered vapour that enwraps,
> At once, some lonely traveller. I was lost;
> Halted without an effort to break through;
> But to my conscious soul I now can say—
> 'I recognise thy glory.' (VI, 592–99)

Though valuable as a foundation for imaginative power, the "natural" experiences described in the first six books of *The Prelude* cannot of themselves produce the highest development of that power. Only the grim crucible of social action can temper the poet's individual consciousness to full and enduring strength.

Books VII–XI define the epic heroism *The Prelude* as a whole celebrates. Here is tested that imaginative consciousness so soundly based upon the poet's early communion with Nature. The preliminary test comes with his residence in the crowded loneliness of London (Book VII). Here Wordsworth's ardent youthfulness is injured and insulted by the nature of urban industrial society—indifferent, fragmented, dehumanized.

> Thousands upon thousands of her sons,
> Living amid the same perpetual whirl
> Of trivial objects, melted and reduced
> To one identity, by differences
> That have no law, no meaning, and no end—
> Oppression, under which even highest minds
> Must labour, whence the strongest are not free. (VII, 724–30)

For this systematized perversion of individuality the blind beggar and St. Bartholomew's Fair—"A Parliament of Monsters"—are Wordsworth's symbols. Yet to the imagination properly nourished and developed the horror of modern society is not in itself defeating. Rather, as the poet explains in Book VIII, "Love of Nature Leading to Love of Man," it calls forth the idealism of the youthful spirit, for

> among the multitudes
> Of that huge city, oftentimes was seen
> Affectingly set forth, more than elsewhere
> Is possible, the unity of man,
> One spirit over ignorance and vice
> Predominant, in good and evil hearts. . . . (VIII, 665–70)

But in conquering the dehumanizing force of contemporary urban society the idealistic youth is led into a worse danger—the temptation to revolt.

The attraction in revolution, Wordsworth argues, is that it promises a release for idealism and heroic energy, it seems to assure, along with the reformation of the most stultifying and dehumanizing characteristics of modern society, fulfillment of individual aspiration—not in the future but here and now.

> Bliss was it in that dawn to be alive,
> But to be young was very Heaven! O times,
> In which the meagre, stale, forbidding ways
> Of custom, law, and statute, took at once
> The attraction of a country in romance! (XI, 108–12)

The first blow which Wordsworth's revolutionary ardor sustains is the Terror, when "blasts/From hell came sanctified like airs from heaven" (X, 337–38). Here the weak give up the revolutionary cause, unable to face the reality of the basic doctrine of all revolt, that the end justifies the means. The weak lack

> the faith of those
> Who doubted not that Providence had times
> Of vengeful retribution. . . . (X, 339–41)

Much more painful is the experience of those who, like Wordsworth, are made of sterner stuff, who refuse to be discouraged. When the charge is levelled:

> 'Behold the harvest that we reap
> From popular government and equality,' (X, 471–72)

Wordsworth's response is:

I clearly saw that neither these nor aught
Of wild belief engrafted on their names
By false philosophy had caused the woe,
But a terrific reservoir of guilt
And ignorance filled up from age to age,
That could no longer hold its loathsome charge,
But burst and spread in deluge through the land. (X, 473–79)

He will not easily be driven from the ground of heroic action. It is after the Terror and during the wearisome, day-to-day establishing of the revolution as an accomplished fact that those who have held firm suffer the anguish of realizing that their heroic determination to overthrow oppression, ignorance, and inhumanity has led them to destroy the idealistic sense of humanity which originally animated their revolutionary fervor. In lines 223–305 of Book XI Wordsworth begins the tradition of revolutionary literature which extends down to our own day.

This was the time, when, all things tending fast
To depravation, speculative schemes—
That promised to abstract the hopes of Man
Out of his feelings, to be fixed thenceforth
For ever in a purer element—
Found ready welcome. Tempting region *that*
For Zeal to enter and refresh herself,
Where passions had the privilege to work,
And never hear the sound of their own names. (XI, 223–31)

This passage, particularly the last two lines, states explicitly and exactly the dilemma given extensive dramatization, for example, in Koestler's *Darkness at Noon*.[33] And it is noteworthy that Wordsworth in describing the moral agonies he suffered when he tried to "abstract the hopes of Man/Out of his feelings" insists as unflinchingly as Koestler's Rubashov that the origin of his faith was justified.

Enough, 'tis true . . .
had the clamorous friends
Of ancient Institutions said and done
To bring disgrace upon their very names;
Disgrace, of which, custom and written law,
And sundry moral sentiments as props
Or emanations of those institutes,
Too justly bore a part. A veil had been
Uplifted; why deceive ourselves? (XI, 259–67)

But the fact remains that the poet's revolutionary ardor is based upon a lack of self-mastery, a failure of individual consciousness. "I was lost,/Halted without an effort to break through," he had said of himself among the Alps. He has now made the effort to break through, but not on the basis of self-understanding. Without self-understanding one cannot comprehend the true nature of social responsibility. The poet has plunged blindly ahead, giving his passions "the privilege to work" without ever hearing "the sound of their own names." Like all rational revolutionaries Wordsworth is the victim of blind emotion, not its master. Hence his agony persists, the agony of having lost in the easy expression of heroic energy the moral basis and nourishment of that energy.

So I fared,
Dragging all precepts, judgments, maxims, creeds,
Like culprits to the bar; calling the mind,
Suspiciously, to establish in plain day
Her titles and her honours, now believing,
Now disbelieving; endlessly perplexed

. . . .

till, demanding formal *proof,*
And seeking it in every thing, I lost
All feeling of conviction, and, in fine,
Sick, wearied out with contrarieties,
Yielded up moral questions in despair. (XI, 293–305)

This is "the crisis of that strong disease" (XI, 306) which is not merely Godwinian rationalism but something much more fundamental, persistent, and virulent. The disease is, in fact, the ravaged spiritual condition of a man driven to take arms against his culture who discovers that the very fact of his revolt has destroyed the moral justification for his rebellion. It is the disease which destroys Nejdanov in Turgenev's *Virgin Soil* and Hyacinth Robinson in *The Princess Casamassima* and forces Pietro Spina, the hero of Silone's *Bread and Wine* and *The Seed Beneath the Snow,* to the verge of yielding "up moral questions in despair." [34]

Alas for all professions that have for their ultimate aim the salvation of the world! For the sake of saving others, you ended by losing yourself.... Don Paolo saw clearly now that his return to Italy had been at heart an attempt to escape from that profession ... to return to the rank-and-file and recapture in action the enthusiasm that had originally led him into the movement. This discovery left him perplexed.

. . . .

"Has not truth, for me, become party truth? [He wrote] Has not justice, for me, become party justice? Have not party interests ended by deadening all my discriminations between moral values? . . .

"What has become of my enthusiasm? . . . have I not impoverished, sterilized my life?"

. . . .

When he came to the end of the page Don Paolo read through what he had written. He noticed that all he had done was to draw up a list of questions to which his divided mind could give no certain answer.[35]

Wordsworth finally recovers, and the means and meaning of his recovery he describes in the last books of *The Prelude*. He recovers because his mind, born and nourished amidst the simple values, elemental rhythms, and enduring presences of rural life,[36] now shocked and sickened, turns instinctively for solace to

> the unassuming things that hold
> A silent station in this beauteous world. (XIII, 46–47)

Yet Wordsworth makes it clear that without the revolutionary experiences his imaginative power could never have attained full maturity:

> my trust
> Became more firm in feelings that had stood
> The test of such a trial. . . . (XIII, 55–57)

Through participation in heroic social action he has learned

> that I could no more
> Trust the elevation which had made me one
> With the great family that still survives
> To illuminate the abyss of ages past,
> Sage, warrior, patriot, hero; for it seemed
> That their best virtues were not free from taint
> Of something false and weak, that could not stand
> The open eye of Reason. (XII, 60–67)

That lesson, at the time a source of anguish, becomes finally the foundation of his happiness. The heroes of his culture are not his heroes. He has learned through experience that heroic action aimed at social betterment produces

> the mind intoxicate
> With present objects, and the busy dance
> Of things that pass away, (XIII, 29–31)

whereas the self-mastery resulting from imaginative consciousness presents "a temperate show/Of objects that endure" (XIII, 31–32).

Through his participation in actual history in the making Wordsworth has come to distrust the heroic record of cultural achievement embodied in the historian's celebration of his civilization's progress.

> Above all
> Were re-established now those watchful thoughts
> Which, seeing little worthy or sublime
> In what the Historian's pen so much delights
> To blazon—power and energy detached
> From moral purpose—early tutored me
> To look with feelings of fraternal love
> Upon the unassuming things that hold
> A silent station in this beauteous world. (XIII, 39–47)

Without denying the value of his original revolutionary motivations or defending the social abuses which the revolution had aimed to correct, the poet finds in himself, in his own fully developed power of imaginative insight, the one sure source for righteous action.

> The promise of the present time retired
> Into its true proportion; sanguine schemes,
> Ambitious projects, pleased me less; I sought
> For present good in life's familiar face,
> And built thereon my hopes of good to come. (XIII, 59–63)

His epic journey, like that of Silone's Spina a century and a half later, thus ends where it began, in his own heart, where, unbeknown to himself, his salvation had always lain waiting to be recognized.

> . . . as soon as my eyes became accustomed to the semi-darkness and I began to distinguish its contents—the wooden trough against the far wall, the old donkey lying between the straw and his manure on the ground, the pack-saddle, the halter . . . the broken lantern in one corner, and, just above my head, the faded picture of Saint Anthony Abbot, protector of animals—an indescribable feeling of serenity and repose came over me, a deep sense of peace such as I had never known in all my life before. . . . 'Here I have come to rest, *Inveni portum,*' I thought; this was the end of my long pilgrimage, the supreme reality. . . .
>
> . . . As I thought back to my lazy schooldays, the escape from my family, the turbulent years lost,—yes, lost is the word for them—with women and in sterile and desolate exile abroad, my whole life seemed a gradual stripping of all the gross pretences that most people adopt to make it worth living. . . . The place seemed to be familiar, as if I had carried it inside me for many years. . . .[37]

The Prelude, then, is epic in its rejection of the traditional principles of epic narrative. Quietism is celebrated over heroic activity; imagination is rated above physical prowess; autobiography supersedes political history; individual adherence to basic, perhaps even primitive, loyalties is praised beyond individual sacrifice to social causes. Yet it is precisely these reversals of conventional epic standards, not Wordsworth's half-century of labor on his poem or references to and echoes of previous epic poems, that command for *The Prelude* the title of epic. *The Aeneid* is an authentic epic in part, perhaps largely, because it embodies a conception of virtue and an ideal of life unalterably hostile to the virtues and ideals of life embodied in previous epics, most notably the *Iliad*. And in *Paradise Lost* Milton rejects the Virgilian ideal. Genuine literary epic, that is, epic written by a poet conscious of earlier examples of the form, must be inspired by the pressing sense that the great literary monuments of the past convey only a partial, a limited, and hence a misleading consciousness of the human predicament. That sense pervades every line of Wordsworth's *Prelude.*

Even if one finds it difficult to accept *The Prelude* as part of the old European epic tradition, one must recognize that it has given its form to much of the heroic literature of revolution that has succeeded it. *The Prelude,* in fact, is one of the first representatives of a form created in the early years of the nineteenth century which, whether or not itself a kind of epic, has usurped the function of traditional epic. That form we may call the mythical journey. It is a form characterized by its tendency to find the profoundest order, significance, and satisfaction in individual experience, in the fulfillments or defeats of the individual soul operating amidst the chaotic impersonalities of modern civilization. Its hero rejects, or is rejected by, his civilization; hence his journey is above all a spiritual journey through "The Heart of Darkness" to a personal salvation that may—but need not—be Christian salvation.

But if we grant the epic-like character of *The Prelude,* what are we to say of *The Excursion* (1814)? Why is it so unepical? Why was Wordsworth unable to continue or to develop the methods and purposes he established in the earlier poem? These questions have troubled most critics of Wordsworth's verse, but no one seems to have found satisfactory answers.[38] Perhaps we can contribute to a solution by confining ourselves to two simpler and more concrete questions: what is the primary difference between *The Prelude* and *The Excursion,* and what is the significance of that difference?

Wordsworthian scholars are almost unanimous in asserting that the fundamental weakness of *The Excursion* is its lack of definite and satisfying form. "*The Excursion* ... has no unity at all," objects Sir Herbert Read.[39] Judson Lyon in his excellent full-length study locates the formal weakness of the poem more precisely: "There is even something creaky and archaic about the towering and intricate structure of the poem."[40] And he goes on to point out that when Wordsworth "came to organize and complete *The Excursion,* he inadvertently dropped into the structural habits of the eighteenth century."[41] This seems to be the primary difference between *The Prelude* and *The Excursion*. The latter poem is structurally similar to the many descriptive, didactic poems in blank verse written during the eighteenth century, of which Thomson's *The Seasons* and Cowper's *The Task* are the most important representatives. In essence *The Prelude* is a narrative poem; it tells the story of Wordsworth's spiritual development. *The Excursion* is a philosophical or reflective poem; included within it are many subordinate stories, but its total organization is not narrative.

Stylistically, too, *The Excursion* seems to bear closer affinities to the Neo-classic descriptive poem than to most earlier Romantic works, even *The Prelude*.

> Perhaps the most surprising fact that emerges from a study of the style of *The Excursion* is the astonishing resemblance the poem bears to much that has always been called classical. It may seem a gross solecism to suggest that in *The Excursion* a classical Wordsworth emerges ... but when the evidence is reviewed this conclusion seems almost inevitable. The points of resemblance between *The Excursion* ... and eighteenth-century poetry are numerous, and the evidence that Wordsworth was seeking to elevate and dignify his style in *The Excursion* by the use of traditional artifices is overwhelming. Certainly the simplicity, concreteness, and homeliness of the early Wordsworth are not altogether superseded by this impulse, but it does represent a new and important departure ....[42]

But even if we admit that the difference between *The Prelude* and *The Excursion* is the latter's apparent reversion to the structure and style of the eighteenth-century descriptive-reflective blank verse poem, we may still feel that our distinction has not been finely enough drawn. Taken all in all, *The Excursion* is much more like *The Prelude* than like *The Seasons* or *The Task*. And even Professor Lyon, whose research has done more than that of any other scholar to establish the "reactionary" form of *The Excursion,* insists that the poem shows Wordsworth to be still lively and original as a thinker and still passionately dedicated to a vital and experiential art.

> ...*The Excursion* cannot be dismissed as the dull and pompous preaching of an aged poet in his decline.... *The Excursion* should be almost exempt from the common accusation of excessive orthodoxy and Toryism.... Wordsworth himself was intellectually and emotionally involved in almost every line of it, much as he was in *The Prelude*.[43]

In point of fact, the Neo-classic quality of *The Excursion* is more apparent than real; Wordsworth's reversion is to some degree illusory; the structural and stylistic similarities between *The Excursion* and eighteenth-century reflective-descriptive poetry are partly fortuitous. Perhaps we can justify these assertions and make some sense of *The Excursion* as a successor to *The Prelude* by considering in brief and generalized fashion the relationship of both poems to the tradition of the descriptive-reflective poem of the eighteenth century.

The two most significant and popular works in this tradition are Thomson's *Seasons,* the first part of which was published in 1726 and the complete, fully revised edition of which was published in 1744, and William Cowper's *The Task,* printed in 1785. Thomson's poem belongs to the era in which Neo-classicism was at its height, and Cowper's to an era that was both post-Augustan and pre-Romantic.

Although *The Seasons* is customarily called a descriptive poem, the epithet is misleading, because Thomson seldom describes an actual landscape. He is not interested in representing the sensory impression of particular scenes he has observed. His descriptions are ideal. In "Summer," for example, structure is provided by the progress not of a particular summer day in England but of a typical summer day which includes all the phenomena characteristic of the summer season anywhere. Consequently, Thomson is not limited to descriptions of specific places. On the contrary, it is appropriate to the economy of his poem to range the globe for climates and geographical features which will represent the idea of the season which is his true subject. So in "Summer" he devotes many lines to scenes in the tropics and in "Winter" includes a long passage on the arctic.

The Seasons is more reflective than descriptive, because even when Thomson describes he appeals to the mind rather than to the senses. He wishes to create, as we have said, the idea of each season, and such an idea is an abstraction, not a sensory fact. Hence the organization of *The Seasons* is non-organic, is formal, intellectual, abstract. The ideal day of "Summer" is obviously an arbitrary structure in that, while it commits Thomson to a temporal progression, it leaves him free to move spatially from England to the equator and from cheerful scenes of sheepherding to the picture of a lonely exile gazing mournfully across the empty sea. The Argument to "Spring" illustrates as well the purely rational order which Thomson establishes for each part of the poem, and which is, in fact, suggested by the "mechanical" system of the whole.

> The Season is described as it affects the various parts of nature, ascending from the lower to the higher; and mixed with digressions arising from the subject. Its influence on inanimate matter, on vegetables, on brute animals, and last on Man; concluding with a dissuasive from the wild and irregular passion of Love, opposed to that of a pure and happy kind.

An aspect of the idealistic character of *The Seasons* is its impersonality. Only rarely does Thomson use the first person, since to speak of himself and his own experience would be to reduce his presentation of the typical and the ideal to the particularized and idiosyncratic. Even more revealing of the impersonality of the work is Thomson's diction, which is usually (and correctly) described as literary and Miltonic.

> All nature feels the renovating force
> Of Winter—only to the thoughtless eye
> Is ruin seen. The frost-concocted glebe
> Draws in abundant vegetable soul,
> And gathers vigour for the coming year;
> A stronger glow sits on the lively cheek
> Of ruddy fire; and luculent along
> The purer rivers flow: their sullen deeps,
> Transparent, open to the shepherd's gaze,
> And murmur hoarser at the fixing frost.[44]

This latinate and heavily adjectival diction is appropriate not only to Thomson's abstract structure and impersonal tone but also to the philosophic import of his poem. For Thomson contemplation of the seasons leads to complacency, in the older sense of that term —tranquil, self-satisfied pleasure. The seasons, regarded in their ideal form, reveal the vanity of human wishes, the complex harmony of the natural universe, and God's mysteriously abundant and diverse beneficence. There are in *The Seasons* passages of political commentary, moral exhortation, and social satire, but the bulk of the poem is devoted to matters which transcend the personal, trivial concerns of ordinary life. This is why the poem is hospitable to the kind of scientific speculation which is least practical and most nearly philosophical, the origin of fountains, for example.[45] Both the charm and the worth of *The Seasons* lie in the poem's capacity to carry us away from our private, selfish interests into a complacent vision of Nature in its ideal form.

Real Nature rather than ideal Nature is Cowper's subject in *The Task*. Not only is the basic opposition between God's glorious creations and dreary man-made towns (a contrast that can play but a subordinate role in Thomson's abstract idealization) but that opposition, and, indeed, everything in *The Task,* is presented in concrete, specific, and personal terms. Cowper speaks directly to us in his own voice. Nature in *The Task* is neither abstract nor ideal, but the particular sights and sounds the poet has experienced. There is, consequently, less formal order to *The Task* than to *The Seasons,* less in the way of broad, generalized divisions, but a closer-knit continuity in the texture of the poem. Cowper's reflections are the thoughts of a particular man who thinks and muses in a particular way; the coherence of his mind provides the coherence of his poem. Hence the complacency of *The Seasons,* which is less Thomson's private possession than a generic attribute of the philosophic mind, is transformed in *The Task*. Nature is a solace for Cowper, a solace for the pains and evils of his existence. In *The Task* the problems of life are not transcended, as they are in *The Seasons,* by a grand philosophical vision. They are put into a more distant and perhaps truer perspective through the meditations of a man living a retired and tranquil life. So, too, the religion of *The Task* is personal and experiential rather than philosophical. Cowper's God is not, like Thomson's, the wondrous architect of the macrocosm, but the comforter of his soul whose private agonies, though usually kept latent in *The Task,* we always feel behind the quiet, unextraordinary circumstances of his withdrawn life.

Cowper's language is homely, direct, and precise. He observes carefully and describes with concise accuracy what he has seen. And such description constitutes a major portion of *The Task*. Because Cowper does not transcend the vanity of human wishes, he is often satiric, but even here he is homely and colloquial and eschews sensational rhetorical effects. His diction, compared to that of Thomson, is completely non-literary[46]—with a single exception, his Miltonisms. The difference between Thomson's Miltonisms and Cowper's is that the latter's are almost purely ironic. *The Task,* among other things, is a superb because loving parody of *Paradise Lost* and *Paradise Regained.*

The first hundred lines of *The Task,* an "historical deduction of seats, from the stool to the sofa," is in both its total massiveness of movement and its particularized verbal echoings as clever a piece of irony as the eighteenth century produced.

> Time was, when clothing sumptuous or for use,
> Save their own painted skins, our sires had none.
> As yet black breeches were not; satin smooth,
> Or velvet soft, or plush with shaggy pile:
> The hardy chief upon the rugged rock
> Wash'd by the sea, or on the grav'ly bank
> Thrown up by wintry torrents roaring loud,
> Fearless of wrong, repos'd his weary strength.
> Those barb'rous ages past, succeeded next
> The birth-day of invention; weak at first,
> Dull in design, and clumsy to perform.
> Joint-stools were then created; on three legs
> Upborne they stood. Three legs upholding firm
> A massy slab, in fashion square or round.[47]

But all six books of *The Task,* not only the opening panegyric to the sofa, depend upon Cowper's gentle but skillful use of Milton's epic mode and organ-toned language as dramatic counterpoint to his own most unepical existence and simple diction. When, for example, in Book IV Cowper describes how the women of his household, "though eloquent themselves," must keep silent when he is absorbed in the evening newspaper, he appeals ironically to our memory of Adam and Eve's ceremoniously hierarchical relationship with his implication of how postlapsarian his household is at other times.

In *The Prelude* Wordsworth uses narrative to combine the reflectiveness of Thomson with the descriptiveness of Cowper. *The Prelude* is an epic, but an epic which subsumes much of the matter treated by the eighteenth-century reflective-descriptive poets, and much of their manner, too. Wordsworth is anti-Miltonic in the sense that his poem consciously transcends the idea of *Paradise Lost;* he is not merely an ironic parodist of the Miltonic style. What Miltonisms there are in *The Prelude* are serious, in the same way that the Miltonisms of *The Seasons* are serious, but they are no longer merely literary, because they are used only when they help to express Wordsworth's private experience and personal faith.[48] On the other hand, that experience and that faith are not, as in Cowper, only private and personal. The narrative structure of *The Prelude* enables Wordsworth to endow specific experiences with more general significance. But this philosophic import is arrived at through meditation upon particularities. It is not, as in *The Seasons,* the origin of the poetic impulse. In *The Prelude* sensory fact (description) is charged with philosophic meaning (reflection). Hence for Wordsworth Nature is neither something beyond (or outside of) ordinary, private experiences—as for Thomson—nor—as for Cowper—a solace for personal suffering; properly understood, Nature enables the tortured poet to solve his anguishing problems. In *The Prelude,* to take an obvious illustration, Nature and politics (for Cowper, "the town") are not kept separate but intermingle and interact. They do so, of course, in the mind of the poet, and it is the growth of Wordsworth's mind, the story of his imaginative development, which unifies them. In *The Prelude* narrative organizes description and reflection into a complex harmony.

The Excursion, as we have already observed, is not truly narrative; one never thinks of it as a story but rather as a meditative or descriptive poem which includes a good many subordinate stories. There is a great deal of narration in *The Excursion,* twenty-two distinguishable stories, in fact,[49] but as a whole the poem is not animated by a narrative impulse. This is interesting, because much of the best poetry occurs in narrative passages, and the original poem was, in Helen Darbishire's words, "a stark, sad tale of humble life."[50] Most important, however, is the fact that because the single, unified and unifying story of *The Prelude* has given way to the several separate stories, description and reflection, interspersed among those stories, once again appear in their pure form untransmuted by subordination to an encompassing principle of organization. As a result the language of *The Excursion* often seems to revert to the Miltonic literariness of eighteenth-century descriptive-reflective poems. Reflection or description unassimilated to narrative movement perhaps demands the formality of complex sentence structure and a relatively massive diction. Certainly *The Excursion* is less colloquial and more deliberately poetic than *The Prelude;* but what is deliberately poetic to Wordsworth is very different from what is deliberately poetic to Neo-classicists like Thomson. Professor Lyon has observed that there is more concrete and sensuous detail in *The Excursion* than in *The Prelude*[51] and that the increase in the number of latinate and polysyllabic words in *The Excursion* is an addition to, rather than a replacement of, the simple and homely words of Wordsworth's earlier vocabulary.[52] *The Ex-*

cursion is consciously unprosaic, but the purposes and characteristics of Wordsworth's unprosaicness are very different from those of Neoclassic poets like Thomson, who also thought it important to distinguish clearly between poetic and prosaic styles.

Another sign of the fragmentariness of *The Excursion* is its division of *The Prelude's* single protagonist into four characters—the Wanderer, the Solitary, the Poet, and the Pastor—each of whom is an aspect of Wordsworth's personality.[53] Accompanying this dissolution of *The Prelude's* unity is a corresponding shift in philosophic emphasis. In *The Prelude* it is the poet's love of Nature which engages him with the problems of humanity; Nature is a means of commitment. In *The Excursion* it is a refuge, a means of withdrawal—but it does not function as a source of complacency or solace. The mere presence of the Solitary is enough to assure us that retirement in *The Excursion* carries a different philosophic import from that which it bears in *The Seasons* or in *The Task*. In *The Excursion* retirement is achieved, or perhaps better, deliberately chosen in full consciousness of the worth and pleasure of engagement in public life. Hence the ideal of detachment expressed in Wordsworth's poem is a positive, one might say creative, ideal, as it is not in Cowper's and Thomson's poems. If the poet of *The Excursion* is classical, his classicism is of a very different sort from that of his eighteenth-century predecessors. His serenity, his control, even his orthodoxy spring from private vision and personal faith based upon his experience of truth as vital, particular, and supra-rational, in short, as poetic truth. The poetry of Thomson and Cowper always appeals for confirmation to something higher than itself, to the philosophic view or to God. *The Excursion* asserts the validity of the poetic vision as the profoundest of revelations, as the truth to which all else must appeal for confirmation. If in *The Excursion* Wordsworth has detached himself from the busy world of political revolution and social reform that plays so large a part in *The Prelude,* he does so because he begins with the conviction that the genuinely creative man, the most human of men, finds spiritual truth expressed in the language of private experience—and only there. The difference between *The Prelude* and the *Excursion,* then, lies in Wordsworth's intensified belief in the latter poem that true reality is the private reality of poetic vision.

This difference carries us back to our discussion of the visionary lyric, where we observed the Romantic tendency to replace narrative with vision. And the central weakness of *The Excursion* is analogous to the weakness of some of the lyrics we considered there. If the poem is not fully narrative, neither is it, in its entirety, fully visionary. In it two styles of presentation co-exist awkwardly and uneasily. Neither narrative nor vision controls its structure. Professor Lyon calls attention to the chief cause for unsatisfactoriness of the various stories.

> ... Wordsworth gave a great deal more attention to explaining the moral purposes of the stories in *The Excursion* than has been generally recognized. Most of the tales ... have some remarks either in the course of the narration, in the subsequent conversation, or in the Argument at the beginning of the particular book, which indicate clearly the purpose they are intended to serve (p. 83).

Wordsworth will not let the narratives speak for themselves as they do, for example, in the *Lyrical Ballads*. On the other hand, visionary significance never succeeds in transcending story; we are constantly asked to regard *The Excursion* as literal, realistic narrative. Jeffrey's rather snobbish stricture on the Wanderer is not entirely off the mark.[54] He is, in fact, complaining about the kind of half-allegorizing or half-mythicizing which we noted to be so enfeebling in *The White Doe* and which is so conspicuously absent from Wordsworth's earlier tales and from *The Prelude*. Relatively simple narrative, which operated to unify diverse impulses in *The Prelude,* fragments in *The Excursion* and can no longer operate as a unifying force. But it has not been thoroughly transmuted or transcended—as it is in the later *River Duddon* sonnet series, where story is replaced by the geographical movement of the river.[55] *The Excursion* pretends, as it were, to be literal epic, a realistic account of how man may fortify his mind.

Without engaging ourselves in the futile question of whether *Hyperion,* for example, is a better work of art than *The Excursion,* we may remark that Keats's poem (like his *Lamia* and Shelley's *The Revolt of Islam* and *The Sensitive Plant*) makes no appeal to superficial credulity and to this extent at least is more coherent. We are not expected to believe in the war of the Gods and the Titans. The epicness of that conflict is not literal; it is the majestic form appropriate to the profundity of Keats's vision. In Keats's longest and most ambitious poems (and Shelley's, too) story is subordinated to the requirements of envisioned truth and functions as a mythic form that enables the poet to express a dynamically complex reality transcending that of natural perception and of natural appearances.

Stated so baldly, the point may seem obvious, even trivial. That it is not and that it deserves fuller development we may suggest by observing that Tennyson's *Idylls of the King,* to take an outstanding instance in later nineteenth-century poetry, like *Hyperion,* makes no appeal to literal credulity. Because Tennyson is not concerned with the superficial reality of King Arthur and his associates, he can make their stories expressive of complex philosophic truths—such as the meaning of social responsibility—which are not so amenable to rational statement or to succinct lyric presentation but require, rather, the flexible and evolving form of mythical narrative.[56]

We may suggest, then, that the significance of the differences between *The Prelude* and *The Excursion* is not their illustration of Wordsworth's hardening into conservatism and reverting to Neo-classic mannerisms, but, instead, their illustration of his effort to achieve a more intense expression of a more thoroughly Romantic conception of poetic truth, to give mythical shape to imaginative intuitions of a transcendent reality. In *The Excursion* Wordsworth tries to pass beyond the relatively rational and objective unity of *The Prelude's* story. That he is not entirely successful should not lead us to call *The Excursion* reactionary. It is anything but prosaic; where it fails it fails through too conscious, too artificial poetry; at its worst it is too ostentatiously literary; but it strives toward a supra-realistic art.[57]

So, to anticipate our conclusions in the following chapters, we can say that Wordsworth's development is precisely contrary to that of Byron and Scott. Their development was in the direction of narratives that contributed to the shaping of the nineteenth-century novel. Wordsworth's narrative verse led toward the mythical expression of subjective vision. His bias was antithetical to novelistic subjects and novelistic forms. It tended, rather, toward pure poetry, supra-rational art. Indeed, the later Wordsworth, the Wordsworth of *The Excursion* and *Laodamia,* in his relatively opulent imagery, his willingness to be literary, his insistence upon the value of private poetic vision as essential truth, and his preference for imaginative rather than naturalistic order, is perhaps closer to the practice of Shelley and Keats than to his own manner at the beginning of his career. In fine, *The Excursion* shows that Romantic narrative did not follow a single, unitary development. It divided. One branch, our subject in the following chapters, led toward the enriching of the novel. The other led toward a more consciously anti-prosaic style of visionary poetry, whose most impressive form, derived from the simple poetic stories of early Romanticism, became the mythical journey, the personal epic of the poet's individual experience of a transcendent reality.

PART III

Realistic Adventures

****

Chapter VII

*

REALISM AND ESCAPE IN SOME MINOR POETS

The poetic stories discussed in Chapters Five and Six represent only one part of the narrative verse written during the early years of the nineteenth century. Related to these poetic stories, but clearly distinguishable from them, are the adventurous narratives of Byron and Scott. And in the verse tales of three minor poets, George Crabbe, Leigh Hunt, and Thomas Hood, characteristics of both the poetic story and the adventurous narrative coexist in uneasy balance. The first-rank poet almost by definition transcends his time. The second-rank poet is less able to escape the pressures exerted by his period. His work is likely to exhibit the variety of impulses and motives operating on artists of his era, impulses and motives which are transmuted (and hence disguised) by his greater contemporaries. Crabbe, Hunt, and Hood were concerned with the social problems and attitudes of their age, which are not of interest to us today. But if we are to understand the verse stories of any of the early nineteenth-century poets we must comprehend the social context in which they wrote and which conditioned their more-than-personal fears and aspirations.[1]

Although George Crabbe lived until 1832, his allegiance as an artist was always to the standards and principles of Neo-classicism. He is, in fact, the last English poet whose career was determined by the old-fashioned system of patronage.[2] But if we examine the chronological development of his work we discover that Crabbe's Neo-classicism underwent some revealing changes. His first important poem is called *The Library* (1781), quite appropriately, for its subject is the shelves of books in an imaginary library. At its best it is epigrammatically satiric; mostly it is tediously didactic, for it is a simplification and exaggeration of Augustan literary commonplaces both of philosophic thought and of poetic technique.

Crabbe's next major poem, *The Village* (1783), while descriptive and satirical and aimed at the intellect rather than the emotions, substitutes for reworkings of a tired literary convention truthful and original observations. It is an anti-pastoral poem which contrasts the idyllic rustic life portrayed by the traditional pastoral with the sordid realities of existence in a Suffolk village. This realism is Neo-classical in its one-sidedness and intellectuality. Attacking satirically the unreality, the artificiality, of pastoral poetry, as so many Augustan writers did, most notably, perhaps, Dr. Johnson, is like cursing the locked door of a safe the combination of which one has forgotten. It is the function of the door to remain closed to those who do not know its secret. The purpose of pastoral poetry is to be artificial; it does not pretend to represent the actualities of life—that is its charm. Anti-pastoral realism is always limited by the speciousness of its originating impulse. Then, too, Crabbe's portrait of rural existence is an external and rational one. He describes poor laborers and outcasts as an outsider might see them; he cannot, like Burns in *Tam o' Shanter,* project his reader into the mind of a peasant.[3]

The Village is structurally feeble. It is a series of descriptions of the same general subject: a village. And this inorganic presentation is symptomatic of a split in Crabbe's conception of his subject. He attempts, on the one hand, to arouse our pity for the humble and the degraded, for example, in his powerful description of the poorhouse.[4] In other scenes, such as that of quarrels on the village green, he urges us to contempt for the lower classes. And in the latter portion of the poem he goes so far as to tell the poor that they are wrong to "lament their fate" and "to envy the great," for all mankind are doomed to be "the victims of distress." These inconsistencies arise because Crabbe, the very reverse of a reformer, does not consider the lower classes as victims of injustices created by social dislocations; he regards them simply as the lowest level of the traditionally stratified and hierarchical society of Augustan England. But Crabbe's subject is rural England in 1780, which was very different from the rural England of half a century earlier. The poverty, drunkenness, and degradation he observes are in large measure a product of the burgeoning complexities of the Industrial Revolution. The lower classes he portrays are in fact victims of social dislocations which Crabbe's Augustan concept of a fixed, relatively simple society did not permit him to recognize. Crabbe, indeed, has no conception of society as an organic whole. He portrays village life in guidebook fashion because he does not recognize it to be a social organism capable of disease or maladjustment. To him the village is a collection of separate individuals who inhabit the same geographical location.

After *The Village* Crabbe did not publish another major work of poetry for twenty-four years.[5] And *The Parish Register* (1807) appears to have little more unity than *The Village,* being a description by a parson of the parishioners whose names he finds in his register. But whereas the personages in *The Village* are only described, in *The Parish Register* the various characters are presented narratively, as the protagonists of little stories. Significantly, the dominant tense of the earlier poem is the present; in the latter it is the past, which, as Suzanne Langer has argued,[6] is the distinguishing mark of English narrative verse. There is a diminution of satiric comment. Crabbe is now more interested in the processes by which people come to be what they are—both in themselves and in society—than in abstract, anti-historical judgments which they can be made to illustrate. He still has no sense for the life of a community, but his treatment of individual lives is no longer purely schematic.

The Borough (1810)[7] lacks the unity and the biting vigor of *The Village,* and, like *The Parish Register,* concentrates on stories of separate individuals. This is one reason why *The Borough* is so lengthy, the history of Peter Grimes, for example, although it takes up only one of the poem's twenty-four sections, being nearly as long as *The Village* in its entirety. But while "Peter Grimes" is, like most of the stories in *The Parish Register,* merely a life history, what happened to a single man, it is more involved with the attitudes and activities of the community in which it occurs than any of the *Register's* biographies. Peter's society is one in which sadistic brutality to helpless boys is tolerated to a point but which, once that point is passed, can exert the force of unified repulsion toward the brutal master. In a different society, one more fastidious or one less closely interlinked, the particular private history of Peter Grimes could not occur.

All of Crabbe's poetry after *The Borough* is narrative. *Tales in Verse* (1812) is a series of stories in which, for the first time, he ventures beyond the life history, each of the twenty-one tales involving the interactions of three or four characters. In *Tales of the Hall* (1819) Crabbe provides unity for his several stories by having them told by two brothers who are reunited after a separation of many years and who tell one another their own experiences and those of former friends and dependents. This device enables Crabbe to give narrative depth to his work.[8] Here, as in the *Posthumous Tales,* we find the portrayal of a complex relation between the individual and his society. What happens to Peter Grimes is determined by his society, but Peter, like all of Crabbe's earlier protagonists, is responsible for his ruin. In the earlier stories there is no unjustified suffering; the cause of every event is ascribed to the character of the agent.[9] In some of the *Tales of the Hall,* notably "Ruth," "Smugglers and Poachers," and "The Sisters," characters fall into disaster not because of their own faults but because of pressures exerted by their society. Ruth, for example, is driven to commit suicide not by her own sin (she bears an illegitimate child) but by the avarice of her father, who threatens to turn her from his house if she does not marry a lustful Methodist preacher of pious tongue but sadistic instincts. As Huchon observes,[10] Ruth as a victim of others rather than as the architect of her own degradation is a sympathetic individual instead of a personified moral lesson.

The chronological development of Crabbe's art illustrates the way in which the eighteenth-century liking for satirically descriptive verse oriented toward moral didacticism evolved into the early nineteenth-century preference for narrative presentation, not so much of traditional moral doctrines, but rather of newly perceived moral dilemmas. Early nineteenth-century poets raise questions rather than provide answers, and this tendency is connected with their fondness for narrative forms. A story can be both coherent and unified without doing more than making apparent a moral problem.[11] Satiric, didactic, and even descriptive poetry (or a combination of all three) requires a definite and determined moral stance, indeed, is almost always inspired by a decisive moral commitment. Crabbe's poetry reveals these early nineteenth-century transformations of form and purpose without ever becoming fully engaged in the new style. Why and how it does not become engaged is worth some attention.

The basic pattern of all Crabbe's narratives, from his earliest to his latest, is that of the Progress, which enumerates in defined stages the course of punishments attendant upon a particular vice. The Progress is a mechanical form. It illustrates movement in only one direction—downward. The Progress is abstract, is not derived from the development of a specific life history but is imposed upon the individual's biography. Biography is made to fit a moral pattern. The Progress is a didactic form, the moral lesson is inherent in the pattern, which, furthermore, presupposes an hierarchically static society. The evil results of vice can scarcely be illustrated by a character's descent from wealth, position, and "good" company to poverty and unrespectable companionship unless the strata of society are differentiated and roughly equated with moral health. A socialistic writer will make the descent of a gentleman into the "lower depths" a means of moral regeneration.

The Progress, as Hogarth's paintings demonstrate, is best suited to a technique of descriptive realism, which, in turn, encourages the presentation of simplified characterizations. Seen only as he appears to external view, the protagonist of a Progress may become a more and more vivid personality as he emerges from the shifting background of his environment, but he is an arresting figure because he remains unchanged. This is true of Crabbe's characters, all of whom are, as Huchon says, "incorrigible" and who "never can escape the fatality which pursues them and which they themselves have let loose." [12] There is no hope for the protagonist of a Progress; his doom is inevitable, for it is the consequent of unchangeable flaws in his character. Crabbe is a superb descriptive psychologist, but the realism of his portraits seems to us superficial because he treats crucial traits as inherent and inexplicable. In "Jachin, the Parish Clerk" we see how pride in rectitude corrupts itself and produces destructive indulgence in trivial vices, but we are never shown the causes of the protagonist's fatal pride. The individual in Crabbe's stories cannot grow or develop or change; he can only follow to their inevitable conclusion impulses and motives which are given, which are determining factors in his personality from the beginning of his career. Crabbe's stories describe reality but never explain it, and his scientific accuracy becomes ultimately wearisome. His emphasis upon sordidness and ugliness (an emphasis tinged, as in Swift and Smollett, with morbidity and melancholia) is part of his method of descriptive realism. Focussing on consequences not causes, portraying not exploring, Crabbe for increasing intensity must insist with increasing vehemence upon physical and moral ugliness.

Temperamentally pessimistic and with some experience of the seamy side of life, Crabbe might have found both the Progress form and the technique of descriptive realism satisfying. Had he done so he might now be esteemed more than he is. But from the time of *The Parish Register* he seems to be struggling to work free of the restrictions of his literary heritage. While none of the later stories is gay or cheerful, repulsive conditions and moral perversities receive less stress. Some of the tales are told with sympathy rather than with austere intellectual objectivity.[13]

Technical developments in Crabbe's style illustrate the same effort to transform his literary tradition. The heroic couplet becomes more flexible in the later tales, Alexandrines and triplets occur frequently, and the caesura, instead of appearing monotonously in the middle of the line, moves freely. More important, as Huchon has shown,[14] Crabbe disengages himself from the brief, antithetical sentence structure favored by Pope. But Crabbe's development is only partial. His language remains that of denotation. His images are clear, precise, and intellectually conceived, never chromatically blurred, as it were, by what Wordsworth called "coloring of the imagination."

Crabbe's poetry shows, from one point of view, the limits beyond which Augustan conceptions and techniques could not be fitted to the narrative mode. From the opposite point of view, Crabbe's art shows that Romantic narrative techniques arose from changed conceptions of the individual's relation to his society and changed conceptions of the way in which poetry can best represent that relation. Crabbe's subject-matter is realistic only in the sense that it is accurately described. His verse is poetic only in the sense that it is rhymed and metrically regular. Yet Crabbe was insensibly drawn toward new conceptions of both realism and poetry. His descriptive didacticism yields to sympathetic narration. His later tales begin, however tentatively, to raise moral questions and to arouse, however slightly, our wonder at the mysteriousness of human behavior. His later poems arouse ambivalent emotions, instead of appealing purely to our power to anticipate logical consequences and to our intellectual ability to comprehend the remorseless progress of sinful souls from prosperity to degradation.

The evolution of Crabbe's art marks a transformation not only of eighteenth-century descriptive-satiric verse but also of Augustan prose fiction. The Progress is a characteristic element in the structure of Richardson's novels and influenced the form of both Fielding's and Smollett's. Moreover, the descriptive realism, psychological portraiture, and moral didacticism which accompany Crabbe's Progress form are not unlike those of the great Augustan novelists. So Crabbe's art should not be considered solely within the context of poetry but should also be related to prose fiction. The more complex his narrative poetry became, the less like eighteenth-century prose narrative it became, without ever attaining truly poetic intensity. His advance, therefore, is at least as significant for the development of narrative as narrative, story in either prose or verse, as for the progress of poetry.

Leigh Hunt's work, on the contrary, would seem to belong completely to the history of poetic art. But if we understand the central motives in his narrative verse we are likely to recognize the significance of the influence of his—and his contemporaries'—poetic stories upon prose fiction.[15] More particularly, with some sense for Hunt's role in the evolution of Romantic narrative art we can appreciate the importance of Thomas Hood's contribution to nineteenth-century transformations of the novel. But Hunt's place in literary history is difficult to define, partly because he lived a long active life in association (or conflict) with most of the leading literary men of the first half of the nineteenth century.[16] And, though not himself a poet of the first rank, he had an uncanny flair for discovering and encouraging first-rate poets when, early in their careers, they were neglected or despised. Finally, Hunt's relation to British society as a whole was a paradoxical one.

In 1812 Hunt was tried, convicted, and imprisoned for libel of the Prince Regent. In 1850, after Wordsworth's death, he was supported for the position of poet laureate. Anyone who knows Hunt only through his poetry must find both events inexplicable. Neither the anthology pieces like *Abou Ben Adhem* and *Jenny Kissed Me* nor substantial works like *The Story of Rimini* suggest a seditious libeller of royalty or an artist to be singled out for royal favor. Other of Hunt's poems, such as his re-rendering of *The Choice,* reveal only an amiably competent writer unabashedly suburban in his tastes. The explanation, we suggest, for Hunt's early persecutions [17] and later acceptance is to be found in his being a spokesman for those elements in British society which, moving with the crest of the Industrial Revolution, rose to power in the early part of the nineteenth century and by 1850 had become entrenched. When one compares Hunt with his friend Shelley one sees at once the difference between the liberal and the radical, between the reformer and the revolutionary. In the period of the Napoleonic wars it was the liberal reformer who was dangerous, because he spoke for a social group of increasing economic and political significance. The government could safely assume that no one would listen to or comprehend Shelley's exhortations for a philosophical utopia. But Hunt, a true-blue Englishman of straightforward, middle-class aspirations, was troublesome when he demanded the reform of particular abuses, even of such an apparently trivial matter as military floggings, for Hunt gave voice to the moral attitudes of a newly powerful class determined to obtain its share of British wealth and to establish the respectability of its mores and tastes.

Much about the nature of those mores and tastes is revealed by Hunt's poetry, particularly by his story poems. Although Hunt wrote a good deal of narrative verse, and translated more,[18] we need concern ourselves only with his most substantial and best-known non-lyric work, *The Story of Rimini* (1816). The story is derived, as we all say, from the Paolo and Francesca episode in the *Divine Comedy,* although M. Landré has quite rightly pointed out that Hunt's story follows Boccaccio's commentary more closely than Dante's verse.[19] The observation is worth making if only to spare Hunt's lax, lush treatment from invidious contrasts with Dante's supremely compressed poetry.[20] But Hunt's inspiration is literary and his subject taken from the remote past. Nothing could differ more from the tales of Crabbe. Hunt's narrative is a piece of belletristic escapism.

What is Hunt escaping from? In part from the sordid reality described by Crabbe. Certainly the gorgeous pageantry of medieval Italy carries the mind far from the damp and sooty England of the Industrial Revolution.

> A suitable attire the horses shew;
> Their golden bits keep wrangling as they go;
> The bridles glance about with gold and gems;
> And the rich housing-cloths, above the hems
> Which comb along the ground with golden pegs,
> Are half of net, to shew the hinder legs.
> Some of the cloths themselves are golden thread
> With silk enwoven, azure, green, or red;
> Some spotted on a ground of different hue,
> As burning stars upon a cloth of blue. . . .[21] (I, 185–94)

The Story of Rimini is sensual and delicately erotic. It creates a world in which the responsibilities of urban industry vanish before the luxuriant freedom of an idyllic Nature, where intellectual concentration melts into the looseness of amatory daydreams, where there is always too much emotion for the easy circumstances of life, where feeling overflows, pours out unstintingly, even as water splashes, gushes, and spills in every natural scene. Yet *Rimini* is melancholy rather than cheerful. Its story of destructive passions is pathetic, and at its conclusion the pageantry of man and the luxuriance of Nature darken to elegiac sombreness.

> and last of all
> Appeared a hearse, hung with an ermined pall,
> And bearing on its top, together set,
> A prince's and princess's coronet.
> Mutely they issued forth, black, slow, dejected.... (IV, 446–50)
>
> There was a fitful, moaning air abroad;
> And ever and anon, over the road,
> The last few leaves came fluttering from the trees,
> Whose trunks now thronged to sight, in dark varieties.
> (IV, 484–87)

This is not an escapist world where everyone lives happily ever after. Here we travel from spring to fall, from happy wedding procession to solemn funeral cortege, from innocent love to desperate suicide. But *Rimini* is far removed from the mechanical pessimism of Crabbe's tales, where the corrosion of time and the necessities of material circumstances wear away emotional vigor. The characters in *Rimini* are destroyed by excessive feeling. Freed from the practical demands of ordinary life, Paolo and Francesca indulge in all the luxuries of sentiment and sensuality. It is Giovanni, the villain of the piece, who busies himself with the administration of his estate and with his warlike occupations. As for his wife, he is

> relieved indeed
> To see another to his place succeed,
> Or rather filling up some trifling hours,
> Better spent elsewhere, and beneath his powers. (III, 328–31)

Paolo and Francesca are idlers and at liberty to develop the full resources of feeling, to pursue, even to disaster, the refined pleasures of art, of Nature, of illicit passion. Hence Hunt can defend the sadness of his story as a source of enduring delight.

> Sorrow, to him who has a true touched ear,
> Is but the discord of a warbling sphere,
> A lurking contrast, which though harsh it be,
> Distils the next note more deliciously.
> E'en tales like this, founded on real woe,
> From bitter seed to balmy fruitage grow:

> The woe was earthly, fugitive, is past;
> The song that sweetens it, may always last. (IV, 17–24)

Seen down the vistas of the centuries, the passion of Paolo and Francesca takes on the color of tender pathos. It is sad, but too distant to be painful; over and done with long ago, it is capable of arousing only the delicious "fruitage" of weak emotions savored and toyed with, not suffered with acute intensity.

There is nothing genuinely historical about *The Story of Rimini.* Hunt makes little effort to recreate the actuality of thirteenth-century life; on the contrary, he stylizes the background of his pathetic story into brightly colored pageantry and fairy-tale-like natural scenes. By simplifying the historical framework of his narrative he is able to concentrate on the inner feelings and personal sensations of his protagonists. He escapes from the hard realities of ordinary life which press into Crabbe's art. Hunt explores and exploits the refinements of private sentiment. Hence the confusion in his language, which wavers among prosaic colloquialisms, quaint archaisms, and linguistic innovations.[22] Most characteristic of *Rimini's* diction is the high proportion of adverbs, a good many of them manufactured by Hunt. Almost any passage will yield words like *grassy, leafy, scattery, mellowly, balmy, glary, gravelly.* This trick of softening substantives and adjectives into vaguely emotionalized adverbial forms helps to blur the harsh outlines of his story, just as the intermixture of archaic and contemporary language helps to transform historical fact into subjective fantasy. While seeming to commit himself to the objectivity of historical events and to the necessities of a social tragedy, Hunt indulges a taste for individualistic, sensual daydreaming. The resultant moral equivocation in *Rimini* becomes apparent as soon as we compare it with Dante's treatment of Paolo and Francesca. The poet in the *Divine Comedy* is so affected by the story of their unhappy love that he falls in a faint—he pays tribute, as it were, to the glamor of their romance. But, as many commentators have pointed out, Paolo and Francesca *are* in Hell, and their vague, drifting, unreal existence there dramatizes both their inexcusable moral irresponsibility and the immaturity of their grand passion. Hunt urges us to enjoy their sin, to gain pleasure from the contemplation of their melancholy love. Yet we must do so clandestinely, so to speak. The convention of punishment visited upon improper behavior is maintained. Hero and heroine die, but both in prayer and with the sympathy of all, even that of the wronged brother.

Though he never says it is his aim, Hunt plainly wishes us to feel that Paolo and Francesca are more sinned against than sinning. They do not for him, as for Dante, illustrate a moral lesson, inculcate a moral doctrine. They are pathetic. They raise the question, is not the world well lost for love?

Hunt would probably not urge us to take the same attitude if his story concerned a middle-class Paul and Frances in early nineteenth-century England. A literary subject and a medieval setting allow for the enjoyment of sensations and feelings which in the context of ordinary bourgeois living would seem inappropriate and un-respectable. This does not mean that Hunt and his readers were self-deceiving hypocrites. A life in which there was no place for fine and refined sentiments, where social conventions never gave way to the pressure of individual passions, and where sensuality was forced always to be regulated "properly" would be scarcely tolerable. There are times when all of us give our sympathy to those who follow their private feelings and indulge in the selfishness of moral irresponsibility, for they enlarge the human capacity for experience. Yet all of us must sooner or later return to the practical necessities of life, to the restrictive but generally successful morality of everyday social intercourse, to the relatively rational planning and judging which visits awkward consequences upon emotional adventuring. A great poet like Dante, or Keats in his last odes, can fashion his art out of the tension created by these contending impulses, but the ordinary poet, particularly at a time when a militantly middle-class morality is beginning to predominate in society, is more likely to disguise his (and his audience's) pleasure in liberated passion beneath the respectable clothing of belletristic romance. Such disguise is artistically enfeebling, and we may find a stern, stiff, pessimistic realism like Crabbe's both more truthful and more interesting than Hunt's pretty romancing. At the same time we cannot deny that Hunt's treatment suggests possibilities both of formal design and of substantive emotion which could never arise from the rationalistic narrowness of Crabbe's view. Both the fresh charm and the dangerous, perhaps fatal, weaknesses of *The Story of Rimini* are signs that Hunt, unlike Crabbe, uses narrative verse to reorient literary interests, concepts, and values in the direction of emotional individuality.

Or, to define Hunt's achievement in the terms we applied to Crabbe's narrative art, reality to Hunt is something more complicated than it appeared to Crabbe.[23] To Hunt the irrational and the illogical loom large. Emotion, with all its contradictions and confusions, is his central concern. He focusses on cause rather than conclusion. His descriptions aim at evocative splendor and are not analytic and enumerative. Finally, although Hunt can scarcely be credited with an organic conception of society, he does see the tensions and difficulties which arise from the clash of the individual's will with the larger will of his society. It is not surprising, therefore, that Hunt's idea of what constitutes poetry differs from Crabbe's. Evocative sensory details and direct appeals to emotion are for Hunt more important than matters of rhyme and meter. It is sometimes hard to remember that he writes in Alexander Pope's favorite form. Hunt's couplets are unpolished, however, not because he is an impatient craftsman but because he conceives of poetry as the total attitude or total feeling expressed by the whole poem. What makes *The Story of Rimini* interesting—in a way that Crabbe's often more powerful, more truthful, more serious poems are not—is Hunt's understanding that poetry is more than a craft and depends less on plotting and planning of details than upon a vital central vision or inspiration. Hence while the technical workmanship of *Rimini* is often faulty, the poem possesses a unity, a wholeness of effect, that, on one side, links it to the more imaginative, more mythical narratives of Hunt's young disciples Shelley and Keats and, on the other side, suggests the combining of personal emotion with real social complexities for purposes other than those of satire and scientific naturalism —a union developed in the adventurous narratives of Byron and Scott.

Although Keats died at the age of twenty-five, his development was so rapid that he had time to outgrow his discipleship to Hunt. It is nearly as surprising that Thomas Hood, born only four years later than Keats, began his career as a disciple of Keats rather than of Hunt.[24] This point is worth making because Hood is now remembered, and dismissed, as a compulsive punster, a popular clown who composed only "whims and oddities." He was in fact a poet not without skill and sensitivity who struggled as vigorously and gaily against his own impoverished circumstances and ill-health as he did against the growing prudery and hypocrisy of "respectable" society. The sardonic, unsparing sincerity of *The Song of the Shirt, The Bridge of Sighs,* and *The Lay of the Labourer,* perhaps Hood's most celebrated poems, is only a later manifestation (all were composed in almost the last year of his life) of the same artistic seriousness which at the beginning of his career attracted Hood to Keats's combination of sensual opulence with serious moral probing and questioning. Hood's *Hero and Leander,* for example, though in the tradition of the Huntian belletristic romance, is built around an original and poignant conception of the old story. Hood tells us that Leander was drowned not by a storm but by a mermaid who had fallen in love with him and who seized him and carried him down to her palace under the sea. Leander dies, of course, but the immortal mermaid at first is unable to comprehend his fate. Her jealous hiding of Leander from her fellow sea-creatures is skillfully described, as is her lonely grief, when, after she has laid Leander's corpse upon the beach in hopes that he will revive in his native element, fishermen carry off the body. Robbed even of Leander's corpse, like Ariadne

> she bows, and bends her gaze
> O'er the eternal waste, as if to sum
> Its waves by weary thousands all her days,
> Dismally doom'd! meanwhile the billows come,
> And coldly dabble with her quiet feet,
> Like any bleaching stones....

Meanwhile the fishermen's report

> Has throng'd the beach with many a curious face,
> That peeps upon her from its hiding place.

Finally a woman, moved by the mermaid's sorrow, goes to her and lays her hand sympathetically on her shoulder. With a shrill scream of terror the mermaid plunges back into the sea, completing the sad cycle of unavailing affection between creatures of incompatible worlds.

The theme of the outsider, the creature not rebellious but excluded by fate or social antipathy from fellowship with others, is predominant in most of Hood's mythological romances. Another early poem, *Lycus, the Centaur,* stresses a human-brute's monstrous alienation and consequent emotional perversion. Again the central scene is one of misunderstood sympathy.

> For the haunters of fields they all shunn'd me by flight,
> The men in their horror, the women in fright;
> None ever remain'd save a child once...
>
> . . . .
>
> He came, with his face of bold wonder, to feel
> The hair of my side, and to lift up my heel,

And question'd my face with wide eyes; but when under
My lids he saw tears,—for I wept at his wonder,
He stroked me, and utter'd such kindliness then,
That the once love of women, the friendship of men
In past sorrow, no kindness e'er came like a kiss
On my heart in its desolate day such as this!
And I yearn'd at his cheeks in my love, and down bent,
And lifted him up in my arms with intent
To kiss him,—but he cruel-kindly, alas!
Held out to my lips a pluck'd handful of grass!
Then I dropt him in horror, but felt as I fled
The stone he indignantly hurl'd at my head....

Lycus and *Hero and Leander,* like several other of Hood's early poems, are superficially like Hunt's *Rimini* in their descriptive lushness and sensual beauty, and in their appeal to pathetic sentiments. But Hood's narrative romances cannot be called escapist,[25] despite their magical or mythological elements. Hood turns to narratives of the strange and the remote not to evade problems of social life but to render unmistakable their enduring essence. The partial humanness of the centaur and the mermaid (like that of the two swans in the poem of that title) dramatizes the difficulties of attaining personal fulfillment in an alien world. Paolo and Francesca suffer from unfortunate circumstances. The mermaid and the centaur, as passionately subjective as Hunt's hero and heroine, are victims not of bad luck but of the hostility of "normal" creatures to that which is different. What to Hunt is unfortunate to Hood is inevitable.

Unlike both Crabbe and Hunt, Hood is a divided soul. The primary sign of his dividedness is his punning. But his puns are less witty than macabre; they turn horror into grotesquerie. We find in *The Carelesse Nurse Mayd,* for example:

I sawe a Mayd sitte on a Bank,
Beguiled by Wooer fayne and fond;
And whiles His flatteryinge Vowes She drank,
Her Nurselynge slipt within a Pond!
All Even Tide they Talkde and Kist,
For She was fayre and He was Kinde;
The Sunne went down before She wist
Another Sonne had sett behinde!

Hood was on the side of the poor and the underprivileged. The great mass of his poetry deals with servants, laborers, drunkards, thieves, and vagabonds. His subject-matter is potentially even grimmer than

Crabbe's, for Hood deals with the lower classes of London at a time when the worst effects of the Industrial Revolution were ravaging the metropolis. But Hood's literary masters were Keats, Shelley, and Coleridge, who celebrated the individual soul in luxuriantly sensual, melodic poetry inappropriate for annals of the urban poor. So Hood compromised. He wrote mythological romances or he turned the real suffering of contemporary London into grotesquely humorous verse palatable to his bourgeois readers, who, in all likelihood, were oblivious to the anti-Chattertonian satire of verses like *The Carelesse Nurse Mayd*. For the radical Hood, unlike the conservative Crabbe, had no patrons. He earned his living, such as it was, with his pen.

But early in his career Hood began developing a new vein, that of the macabre melodrama, which enabled him to unify the contradictions of his art. *The Last Man,* for example, tells of the sole two survivors of a world-wide plague. The narrator becomes the last man when he hangs his one companion, a beggar, partly out of selfish jealousy and partly because the vagabond does not behave in accord with his station. Here again is the theme of isolation, but now carrying overtones of social criticism. And here Hood abandons his neo-Keatsian cadences for a sing-song broadside-ballad rhythm and a colloquial directness of diction that are a satire not merely of Chatterton but of his own mythological narratives.

> 'Twas in the year two thousand and one,
> A pleasant morning of May,
> I sat on the gallows-tree all alone,
> A chaunting a merry lay,—
> To think how the pest had spared my life,
> To sing with the larks that day!

The Last Man is only grotesque. *The Dream of Eugene Aram, the Murderer* (1829) is melodramatic. Hood's picture of one of the most notorious criminals of his time is deliberately simplified and sensationalized, but its emotional impact is authentic. Hood uses simple meter and colloquial language not for ironic mockery but for presentation of dramatic scenes.

> That very night, while gentle sleep
>   The urchin eyelids kiss'd,
> Two stern-faced men set out from Lynn,
>   Through the cold and heavy mist;
> And Eugene Aram walked between,
>   With gyves upon his wrist.

In *Eugene Aram* Hood succeeds in combining the realism and honesty of Crabbe with the imaginative freedom and emotional extravagance of Hunt to produce a new kind of narrative verse which is responsive to the new social realities of English life.

The central focus in *Eugene Aram* is the unique personality and the private suffering of the murderer. He tells one of the boys at the school where he is employed of his "dream" of having killed an old man for his money. The dream of course is a disguised confession. The confession story derives from traditions established by Hood's predecessors. Aram might be called a *déclassé* Manfred or a debased ancient mariner.[26] And, leaving aside such literary ancestry, Hood's interest in the murderer's emotions, not only his feelings at the moment of his crime, but his fears afterward when he tries unsuccessfully to hide the body of his victim, and the gnawing wretchedness which drives him to thrust his disguised confession upon an innocent child, is not unlike Hunt's interest in the emotional travail of Paolo and Francesca. Both Hunt and Hood, as contrasted to Crabbe, are interested in emotion for its own sake, in the inner dynamics of extreme and anti-social experience. The particularized sensory detail which we observed in *Rimini* and in Hood's magical romances is retained in *Eugene Aram* but is now put to the service of horror rather than of beauty.

> Two sudden blows with a ragged stick,
> And one with a heavy stone,
> One hurried gash with a hasty knife,—
> And then the deed was done. . . .

But in *Eugene Aram* the personal experience of the protagonist cannot be separated (as it is in *Rimini*) from the social realities of contemporary life. The main body of the poem concerns a false dream, an unsuccessful effort to escape the context of social existence. So Aram's fate, finally, is not part of a conventional system of rewards and punishments, such as we find in *Rimini*. His doom is the result of society's reaction to the aberration of the individual. Francesca passes away peacefully—and inexplicably—with her hands joined in prayer as she lies on her bed. The conventionality of her pose reveals the conventionality of her fate. Aram, walking between the "stern-faced men . . . with gyves upon his wrist," is last seen also in a position hallowed by tradition, but a tradition derived from the harsh truth of real life.

On the other hand, the difference between *Eugene Aram* and

Crabbe's stories is just as striking. Hood is not objective, descriptive, and logical. He condenses, simplifies, and exaggerates. Aram, as compared to Peter Grimes, appears more than life size, monstrous, gigantic. The figure of Hood's murderer towers above the society that punishes him. Crabbe's protagonists are always weaker and smaller than their social environment. Because to Crabbe society is an aggregation rather than an organism, no one individual seems to him enormously impressive or enormously effective. The monster is a product of an organic system. Paradoxically, Hood's exaggeration or enlargement of the individual implies a deepening sense of the organic coherence of society. This is not, perhaps, fully apparent in *Eugene Aram,* in which, except for the last scene and for the innocent schoolboy life into which Aram's dream intrudes, the social context of his crime is mostly remote. It is manifest, however, in Hood's longest and most substantial poem, *Miss Kilmansegg and Her Precious Leg.*

Miss Kilmansegg is the daughter and heir of a rich middle-class family. Their power and prominence depend on their money, which has been amassed by profiteering, usury, and sharp practice, and they use every opportunity to display this wealth and with it to trample under their financial inferiors. Miss Kilmansegg absorbs these ideals of conduct and behavior, and when she is thrown from a horse and has to have her leg amputated she demands and receives an artificial limb of solid gold. This "branch of the family bank" draws to her a crowd of suitors. Unfortunately for herself, she chooses the worst, a penniless adventurer from the Continent who calls himself a count but who has no true claim to that title. Their marriage disintegrates into unhappiness and hatred. Before long the count has run through Miss Kilmansegg's money and begins to eye her leg longingly. She, however, has made sure that—legally—she is sole owner of the leg. But she removes it when she retires to bed. One night the count slips into her room, steals the leg, smashes in her skull with it, and runs off. A coroner's jury returns a verdict of suicide, for she was killed by her own leg.

As a satiric portrait of the mores of the *nouveaux riches Miss Kilmansegg* is as mordantly devastating as any of Crabbe's bitter studies. But Hood's satire is melodramatic. Miss Kilmansegg is a gigantic grotesque whose fatal devotion to "gold! gold! gold!" reveals in all its monstrosity the corruption of her society. She is a distorted caricature endowed with the vitality of her author's insight into the moral deformities of his age. Miss Kilmansegg is not aberrant; she is the essence of the normal in an aberrant society. Her unmitigated ostentation and acquisitiveness are the characteristics of her society, with their disguises ripped off. Hence the superficial exaggerations of *Miss Kilmansegg* enable Hood to penetrate to a level of reality, sociological reality we may call it, far beyond the accurate surface representations of Crabbe. And Hood's poetic form undergoes a corresponding change. He discards not only Crabbe's stiff regularity but also Hunt's loose sensuousness and turns his verse into a vivacious expression of pell-mell excitement and humor. The poetry of *Miss Kilmansegg* lies solely in the energy of Hood's central conception and in his imaginative enthusiasm, which endows even inanimate objects with life, as when Miss Kilmansegg's horse shies from a beggar and runs away with her:

> Sick with horror she shuts her eyes,
> But the very stones seem uttering cries,
>
> . . . .
>
> "Batter her! shatter her!
> Throw and scatter her!"
> Shouts each stony-hearted chatterer!
> "Dash at the heavy Dover!
> Spill her! kill her! tear and tatter her!
> Smash her! crash her!" (the stones didn't flatter her!)

Enough has been said, perhaps, to suggest that the real successor to Miss Kilmansegg is Mr. Pecksniff. Dickens is, in fact, the principal beneficiary of the verse narrative evolution we have been tracing. We have compared Hood's satire to Crabbe's, but the truth is that *Miss Kilmansegg* is closer to comedy than to satire.[27] Hood makes clear his distaste for a society that worships a "golden calf," but his delight in portraying a particularly obscene calf runs away with him. He makes the golden leg so much livelier than any real leg, so grotesquely uproarious, that we forget what it condemns. We lose ourselves in his helter-skelter vitality of macabre caricatures, forget the social reality being criticized, and enjoy the absurd coherence of a world of poetic comedy. Mr. Pecksniff likewise, though he may have originated in Dickens' hatred for the hypocrisy of his society, rapidly transcends his satiric function. Indeed, one wonders if a world without hypocrisy is to be preferred to a world without Mr. Pecksniff.

Henry Fielding hated hypocrisy, too. But when Fielding created a hypocrite, Blifil, for example, he took care not to let that character transcend his function. Fielding's practice is typical of that of all the Augustan novelists, who operated so marvellously within the limits we are here defining. There is nothing poetic about Augustan fiction. Fielding, Richardson, and Smollett are wise and witty, skillful commentators, and perceptive observers. They are masters of prose; they never attempt the fine frenzy of poetry. Now it is precisely the sixty-five years between Smollett's death and the appearance of Dickens' *Pickwick Papers* in which the verse narratives we have been considering flourished. The chronology, we suggest, is not accidental. There were some truths that the eighteenth-century novelists were not interested in, not merely the truth, for example, of Dickens' Mr. Toots, who, as Chesterton says, "reveals the great paradox of all spiritual things, that the inside is always larger than the outside,"[28] but also the truth of Emily Brontë's mythopoetic Heathcliff and of her sister's existentialist sufferer Lucy Snowe. Truths like these found their way into prose fiction, in part at least, through verse narratives.

The development we have traced in this chapter we may summarize as follows. Crabbe strove for literal, surface realism, treated society as a mechanical aggregation of separate parts, and tended to regard poetry merely as form. To Hunt poetry became more closely identified with the expression of sentiment, and his efforts in verse narrative were devoted to the evocation of personal emotions established and defined by their inherent antagonism to the social system within which they exist. Hood, like Hunt, concentrated on extreme emotions in the individual but went further, making the individual's emotional experience representative of disorders in the social organism. What to Hunt had been escape to Hood became the means to a more dramatic rendering of sociological reality; and consequently, he tended to move away from the loose, sensuous, and evocative style of Hunt toward one more energetically and racily colloquial.[29] Such development points toward those enrichments and transformations of both the subject and the structure of prose fiction which are characteristic of the early years of the nineteenth century. This is not to deny that during the same period the novel itself was evolving as an art form—one thinks at once of experiments in Gothic fiction. Our suggestion is that Romantic verse narrative also had a contribution to make to that evolution. The artistic progress of Scott, who began his career writing balladic lyrics, advanced to long narrative poems, and finally turned to the novel, in itself illustrates the intimate connection between verse and prose storytelling which we have endeavored to emphasize.[30] And, as we shall try to show in the following chapter, the same pattern can be discerned in Lord Byron's career.[31]

Chapter VIII

*

BYRON: THE ADVENTUROUS NARRATIVE

Byron's first published work, *Hours of Idleness,* was a collection of lyrics which, as much for the superciliousness of its preface as for the rhetorical sentimentality of its verses, received a critical trouncing. The attacks it aroused in turn provoked Byron to write his first significant poem, *English Bards and Scotch Reviewers* (1809), a slashing satire upon almost all contemporary poets and critics. The history of Byron's later poetic development was to consist of his search for a means of uniting the fervid emotionalism which animates the lyrics in *Hours of Idleness* with the spirit of sardonic satire which *English Bards and Scotch Reviewers* expresses. The latter poem, though often sharp and sometimes quite funny, is not up to the level of the satiric masterpieces of Dryden and Pope with which it is frequently compared. It is too disorganized, too random in its attacks, too ostentatiously abusive to be truly critical. It lacks the emotional coherence of *The Dunciad,* for example; it expresses only transient private pique, no deep or long-cherished feelings.

On the other hand, in *The Vision of Judgment,* which Byron wrote some twelve years later and after he had begun *Don Juan,* we find strong feelings strongly controlled. The instrument of control is narrative structure. *The Vision of Judgment* is perhaps the most lively and readable of English satires because its criticism is embodied in a first-rate story. Here Byron replaces the vehement but disorganized abusiveness of *English Bards and Scotch Reviewers* with the increasing concentration of evolving narrative. In the first poem Southey, for example, is harshly pilloried.

> With eagle pinion soaring to the skies,
> Behold the Ballad-monger Southey rise!

> To him let Camoëns, Milton, Tasso yield,
> Whose annual strains, like armies, take the field.
>
> . . . .
>
> Next see tremendous Thalaba come on,
>
> . . . .
>
> Domdaniel's dread destroyer, who o'erthrew
> More mad magicians than the world e'er knew.
> Immortal hero! all thy foes o'ercome,
> For ever reign—the rival of Tom Thumb!
> Since startled Metre fled before thy face,
> Well wert thou doomed the last of all thy race!
> Well might triumphant Genii bear thee hence,
> Illustrious conqueror of common sense!
>
> . . . .
>
> Oh! Southey, Southey! cease thy varied song!
> A bard may chaunt too often and too long. . . .[1]

In the later poem Byron's assault on Southey is more devastating because subtler. In *The Vision of Judgment* Southey appears only at the climax as a dramatic character, who speaks and reads for himself and whose vicious puerility, quite by chance, solves the fundamental problem of the poem: does George III belong in Heaven or Hell? Not so much Southey but all that Southey represents is made the focal point of a story which expresses dramatically what Byron hates and disdains. In *The Vision of Judgment* (which is, of course, as a whole a burlesque of Southey's pompous *A Vision of Judgment* in praise of George III) Southey the narrative *persona* is self-revealing. The ridiculousness of his lame verse and the nastiness of his hypocritical posturing are exposed by his own unconscious display of moral ugliness and triviality. The historical person Robert Southey submerges or fuses into the more enduring and broadly significant outlines of narrative characterization. So one need know nothing of English kings or laureates (or of Southey's verse—a real blessing) to relish the triply characterizing exclamation of George III when Southey begins to read: "The Monarch, mute till then, exclaim'd, "What! what!/"*Pye* come again? No more—no more of that!" The superiority of *The Vision of Judgment* to *English Bards and Scotch Reviewers* derives primarily from the narrative conception of the later poem. Byron's artistic maturing is to be defined, we suggest, as the progress of his control of the narrative mode. That progress is toward novel-like narrative. Byron's development is unlike Wordsworth's. Byron moves from simple narrative organization toward narrative arrangements more like those of the *Waverley* novels than those of *The Excursion.*

Childe Harold, begun in 1812 but not finished until 1818, is Byron's first attempt at sustained narrative. The story element is in itself slight, but what story there is links lyric meditations or descriptions with satiric commentaries, connects Byron's realistic sense of hard fact to his surging emotionalism. *Childe Harold* is the first Byronic poem, if by that adjective one means the union through narrative of grandiose emotionalizing with sardonically realistic irony.[2]

Because *Childe Harold* overlaps many of Byron's other narratives it cannot be fitted into our treatment of his works in their chronological order, and we digress slightly here to discuss its principal characteristics. It belongs to the category of the Romantic journey poem and is in several ways like Wordsworth's *Prelude. Childe Harold,* though less significant and less powerful than Wordsworth's masterpiece, has much the same theme—the individual, alienated from his civilization, tries to find peace and security within himself. But Byron appears half a poetic generation later than Wordsworth. The exultation, however transitory, which Wordsworth and his contemporaries had felt at the beginning of the French Revolution is not a part of Byron's experience. Byron stands, literally and figuratively, among ruins and monuments, and his mood is elegiac, ironic, disenchanted. Compared to *Childe Harold, The Prelude* seems almost a psychological *Iliad;* Byron's poem is the mournful *Odyssey* of a more modern ego.

For all his adolescent posturing and theatrical melancholy Byron conveys his disenchantment with astonishing impact. *Childe Harold* is still readable, partly because Byron is honest about the fundamental issues, and partly because he finds in the figure of the heroic tourist an embodiment for his elegiac mood which transforms trivial sentimentality to genuine pathos.

Byron is honest in his shrewd, realistic, and sardonic descriptions of places and persons. Portugal is beautiful from a distance; at close range the country is seen to seethe with the evil effects of poverty, disease, and ignorance. Yet Portugal's dirty people and rotten social structure are undeniably enveloped in the lovely tranquillity of their geographic surroundings. Both facts are presented, but no choice is forced on the reader.[3] In Spain Byron finds the symbol for that nation's contradictions in the bullfight,[4] where Spanish bravery, too much involved with empty forms of honor, disintegrates into brutality, as did Pizarro's magnificent conquest of Peru.[5] In the bullfight the Spaniards' almost ascetic independence, frustrated by the oppressiveness of a feudal society, corrupts into the covert sensuality of spectacle.[6] Byron's characterizations are penetrating and just. His portrait of Napoleon is still one of the most convincing judgments of that enigmatic personality, because in Byron's analysis admiration and dislike are maintained in balance.[7] Byron's sketch of the Albanians—admirable but bestial—is likewise neither mere praise of noble savagery nor the mere ironic disdain of a cultivated gentleman, but encompasses both attitudes.[8]

Byron is equally honest in portraying his own spiritual condition. There is for him no comfort, faith, or honor in his civilization, and he rejects it. But he recognizes that that rejection destroys him, leaves him at home only with those manifestations of Nature most hostile to humanity in the indifference of their grandeur and power. The rhetoric of isolated passages, particularly the closing apostrophe to the ocean, should not be allowed to obscure the repeatedly emphasized parallel he draws between the wanderings of Harold (Byron) and the damned, restless, despairing journeys of Cain and the Wandering Jew.[9] Byron sees that a man may reject his civilization but cannot reject his humanity. His dramatization of his own suffering is undercut by self-irony. When he concludes the Curse of Forgiveness upon mankind by insisting "But I have lived, and have not lived in vain" (IV, 137), he at once exposes this false self-dramatization with the theatrical *ekphrasis* of the dying gladiator.

> What matter where we fall to fill the maws
> Of worms—on battle-plains or listed spot?
> Both are but theaters—where the chief actors rot. (IV, 139)

My heroic posturing, he implies, is merely a form of self-butchery "to make a Roman holiday." Here, and throughout *Childe Harold,* the falsity of melodramatic posture is made to illuminate the traveller's spiritual emptiness.

Yet even this honesty (which allows Byron to be the first critic of the Byronic pose) would not be so impressive were it not given such magnificent organization in the form of the grandest of Grand Tours, which is, of course, the most formless of all formal expeditions. The scenery and monuments which evoke the ravages of time and the ruin of men's aspirations are not merely illustrative of *sic transit gloria mundi.* They are, rather, symbolic of the contemporary spiritual condition. The past has been overthrown—"why deceive ourselves?" Yet out of its ruins have been created only new oppression and new despair. In the tourist Byron strikes upon the appropriate protagonist for his modern epic of disillusion, his autobiographic journey into despair. It is the tourist, bent on the pursuit of pleasure, yet somehow obscurely yearning for a discovery of his spiritual origins, strangely attracted to a past he is committed to regarding as alien, caught by the fact of his tour in the unreal temporal worlds of travel and of history, whose psychological odyssey perhaps best symbolizes the essential uncertainties and essential desires of Byron's era—and possibly of our own.

Byron's Oriental tales, with which he supplanted Scott as England's most popular narrative poet, have in recent years received high praise from critics as different as Mr. Eliot and M. Escarpit.[10] We cannot deny, however, that these stories are crudely fabricated and that their characterizations tend to be simple-minded. Still their depictions of the sensual, passionate (according to Byron) life of the Eastern Mediterranean are colorful, even if too melodramatic for modern taste. The alternation of cut-and-slash heroics with rhetorical enunciations of extravagantly violent feelings never becomes tedious. And Byron's verse is more supple and evocative than that of most of the adventurous tales of his time. In some scenes, the ambush of Selim in *The Bride of Abydos,* for example, Byron manages a large cast of characters with admirable skill.[11]

The first of these tales, *The Giaour* (1813), despite its patronizing accolade from Mr. Eliot, is a silly story, as Byron himself recognized. "*The Giaour* I have added to a good deal, but still in foolish fragments," he wrote to Moore (September 1, 1813). Had Byron narrated the events in a straightforward, chronological order, instead of mixing them up in a network of befuddling flashbacks, the unreality of the Greek's sentiments (he is even made to feel remorse at killing a Turk) and the improbability of the sequence of occurrences would be glaringly apparent.[12] But it is precisely this fakery, or disguise to use a kinder term, which carries the promise of Byron's later skill and which at once identifies him as potentially a better storytelling poet than Scott. Byron manipulates and distorts the order of events because he is interested in poetic effects. He does not appeal merely to the curiosity or the rational understanding of his reader. He recognizes that in verse sustained sentiment aided by the systematic progression of compressed, rhythmic language can be relied upon to produce a coherence of effect that could be attained in prose only through careful analysis and thorough description. And even in this first narrative Byron gropes toward the principle that the effect of a poetic story is determined by the character of its narrator. As we have seen before, in Romantic verse narrative the system of expectations and fulfillments derives from the incidents rather than from the protagonist. The aspect under which events are presented to us determines what form our hopeful or fearful envisagements will take. Byron tries to charge the relatively simple sequence of incidents in *The Giaour* with fearful emotions by recounting it through different narrators whose observation is limited or whose understanding of the events is partial. The result, however, is bewilderment rather than suspense. The reader tends to be puzzled more by the character and circumstances of the narrators than by the fateful order of events. The poem begins with a generalized description of and meditation on the history and landscape of the Eastern Mediterranean by the "author" (ll. 1–179). Then a Turkish fisherman, who has observed or participated in most of the events of the story, tells what he knows (ll. 180–797). Next we shift to a dialogue between the author and the monk at whose monastery the giaour has been living since the occurrences described by the fisherman (ll. 798–970). The last part of the poem consists of the giaour's confession and explanation of his deeds (ll. 971–1334). These many changes, all of which occur with unnerving abruptness, make for confusion instead of enlightenment because the action out of which they grow is conceived of as schematically sensational. Multiple narrators are perhaps most useful when the intricacy of events is being explored, as in *The Ring and the Book*. But Byron, while devoting more and more attention to such intricacies, never again attempted multiple narration. Instead he worked to simplify his narrative perspective until in *Don Juan* we find him discussing in his own person the complicated motives and consequences of apparently trivial occurrences. This does not mean that Byron grew into a garrulously satiric commentator. On the contrary, he became a better and better narrative poet, one who without (like Browning) becoming almost exclusively concerned with motive was able to comprehend and to express the inner dynamics of human behavior. In fine, the incoherence of *The Giaour,* as M. Escarpit has suggested,[13] springs from Byron's original conception of his action as a series of fixed, sensational scenes, and, as we shall try to show later, his success in *Don Juan* is in part due to his ability to render the developing movements concealed within apparently static situations.

In *The Bride of Abydos* (1813) we find something of the same scenic conception which mars *The Giaour. The Bride of Abydos,* like its predecessor, is based on an anecdote rather than on a complete story. But its narration is simplified; it is told by an omniscient author. Variety in pace and shifts in perspective are provided now by lyrical interruptions, long passages of dialogue, and by some rather surprising changes in meter.[14] This last is important, for it represents the introduction in crude form of a device which is beautifully manipulated in *Don Juan*. There variety in language, rhythm, and tone occurs within the fixed pattern of the *ottava rima.* In *The Bride of Abydos* Byron is still committed to the traditional couplet form of narrative poetry, and he can shift his tone and mood only by abruptly wrenching his regular tetrameters into pentameters or switching to cross-rhymes. Such changes are too obvious to be effective, though we must give Byron credit for being the first poet of his time to realize that sustained adventurous narrative permits, even demands, changing contrasts in form as well as in subject. One further point deserves attention. The story of *The Bride of Abydos* turns on a situation of supposed incest. Our purpose is not to suggest biographical implications in this circumstance but to observe that it urges more intensive focussing upon the individuality of the characters. Byron's characterizations of fierce old Giaffir, heroic Selim, and lovely Zuleika are melodramatically stylized, but they are more complex than those of *The Giaour,* and the tragic complications of the story arise in part from divisions within the protagonists' personalities, not, as in *The Giaour,* solely from the monomaniac consistency of their dispositions.

The Corsair (1814), the third of Byron's Oriental tales, develops this concern with characterization. Here we find the first example of what M. Escarpit calls the *portrait intérieur,* an "historical" analysis of the protagonist's complex personality.

> Warp'd by the world in Disappointment's school,
> In words too wise—in conduct *there* a fool;
> Too firm to yield, and far too proud to stoop,
> Doomed by his very virtues for a dupe,
> He cursed those virtues as the cause of ill,
> And not the traitors who betrayed him still;
> Nor deemed that gifts bestowed on better men
> Had left him joy, and means to give again.

> Feared—shunned—belied—ere Youth had lost her force,
> He hated Man too much to feel remorse,
> And thought the voice of Wrath a sacred call,
> To pay the injuries of some on all.
> He knew himself a villain—but he deemed
> The rest no better than the thing he seemed. . . . (*Corsair,* I, xi)

The Corsair suffers from Byron's interest in the nature of his hero Conrad, for, unlike the earlier stories, it possesses a genuine plot, but one which both poet and reader tend to lose sight of in the pursuit of Conrad's reactions to the vicissitudes of his fortune. Even the heroine, Gulnare, who is made to illustrate the position of women in a society ruled by and for men, lacks the vividness of Zuleika in *The Bride,* although the conception of Gulnare herself and of the difficulties of her situation is more realistic and poignant. This same tendency to sacrifice plot coherence to characterization appears in the last and most interesting of Byron's early verse stories, *Lara* (1814). The poem is a kind of continuation of *The Corsair,* Lara being Conrad, and Kaled his mysterious page being Gulnare in disguise. But in *Lara* Byron abandons his Aegean seascapes for a vaguely medieval milieu, suggestive of Spain. Byron himself said, "The name only is Spanish; the country is not Spain, but the Moon." [15] The indefiniteness of time and locale weakens what might have been a powerful narrative. Both the character of Lara and the action in which he is involved, though sensational, carry "the sentiment of reality." Lara is not so much an outcast from humanity, a Satan, a Cain, or a Conrad, as an outcast from one segment of a particular society. He is the proudest and haughtiest of a group of proud and haughty barons, whose hostility drives him to espouse, unsuccessfully, the cause of popular liberty. Lara's private quarrels and his personal incompatibility with his peers are treated as symptomatic of dislocations within his society. But Byron's unfortunate decision to make that society timeless and placeless renders this interpenetration of the personal and the social virtually meaningless. Nevertheless, by locating his melodramatic protagonist within some kind of network of social relationships Byron has taken a long step toward *Don Juan,* in which the hero's behavior, for good or ill, always interacts with the social group within which he functions. *Lara,* in other words, shows a considerable advance beyond the schematic, scenic conception of *The Giaour* and the psychological portraiture of *The Bride* and of *The Corsair,* which is bold but flat, the individual's personality being dramatized at the expense of all normal social responsibilities and relationships.

These four early adventurous tales exhibit kinship to Hunt's *Story of Rimini.*[16] In each poem the focus of interest is strong, individual emotion, in fact or by implication anti-social. Description abounds, and the lush, the exotic, and the picturesque are favored over accurate observation of the commonplace. Byron's characters tend to be simplified in the same way that Hunt's are. They are particularized by one tragic, overwhelming sentiment. The Byronic hero is a victim of passion rather than its master. Despite the violence of the events in which he becomes involved he gives the impression of passivity, even as Hunt's feebler Paolo and Francesca do. Byron, on the other hand, shows a far more independent and vital mind than Hunt, who is bourgeois in attitude and becomes entangled in moral equivocations when he tells the story of romantically illicit love. Byron is not bourgeois and in no way equivocates. His tales are, one might say, sincerely melodramatic; there is no falseness, no coyness, no apology in his presentation of extravagant emotion. His enthusiastic concentration in these narratives seems analogous to the absorbed intensity of a child at play. His occupation may not belong to the serious business of life, but one respects the capacity to become totally engrossed. But perhaps the most important difference between Byron's tales and Hunt's *Rimini* lies in the poets' skill as versifiers. At its best Hunt's verse is only weakly sensuous. Byron's verse is rapid and keen, and if sometimes flashy rather than brilliant, rhetorical rather than evocative, it never becomes pedestrian or uncouth. The one significant flaw in his early narrative verse is its lack of depth; it possesses verve but never that density of the finest poetry, wherein contrasting emotions and related but disparate ideas find unity in lucid but complex expression. We have commented on the separation of the different meters in *The Bride of Abydos,* and in all these early tales Byron tends to separate in this fashion or by similar, essentially rhetorical devices different moods and different attitudes. Passages of description he clearly sets off from passages of meditation, narration from characterization, and so on. The art of these early adventure stories, in short, is an art of contrasting surfaces.

Lara was Byron's last full-scale narrative until he began *Don Juan* in 1818. Between 1814 and 1818 his narrative verse consisted of experiments, none of which is completely successful, perhaps, but all of which are interesting and illuminating as to the direction in which he was working. All of these poems, most notably *The Siege of Corinth* (1815), *Parisina* (1815), *The Prisoner of Chillon* (1816), and *Mazeppa* (1818), unlike *The Corsair* and *Lara* and like *The Giaour,* are in essence anecdotes. But each of the later tales has a genuine historical basis, and in each Byron tries to render the time and place of the occurrence with solid factuality and to show the characters as conditioned by their particular social milieu. By restricting himself to limited actions Byron is able to concentrate on blending realistic characterization with plot development. The principal figures of these later stories have an autonomous vitality which Conrad and Lara lack. *The Prisoner of Chillon* illustrates this point. Bonivard, a chained prisoner, is without that freedom of action which is the central fact of Conrad's or Lara's life. Bonivard's story is the story of the change in his mind created by his long incarceration. Physically passive, Bonivard is psychically active, whereas Conrad and Lara though physically rambunctious are psychically monolithic and inert. Despair induced by isolation is possibly Byron's commonest motif in his early tales, but in *Chillon* he portrays the growth of that emotion meticulously and in detail. His descriptions become functional to his characterization. His attention has turned to detailing the process by which events occur. Not merely *what* happened but *how* it happened is increasingly his preoccupation.

This change is observable in the quality of Byron's verse, which is, on the whole, richer in texture, more reflective, and more controlled than that of the earlier tales. Byron tends now to avoid the striking but superficial contrasts which characterize his first narratives and to strive for a more flowing manner. Moreover, in *The Prisoner of Chillon* for the first time, if we disregard the autobiographical *Childe Harold,* he makes his protagonist the narrator, thereby rendering it easy to intermingle description with developing characterization and to steep objective drama in subjective emotion. A conflict between objective and subjective viewpoints, between what we have called the lyrical and the satirical impulses, is probably the most significant characteristic of Byron's art until the last cantos of *Don Juan,* wherein the conflict is resolved through the use of novel-like narrative. The direction of movement is illustrated by *Childe Harold,* in the later cantos of which the original Byron-Harold schizophrenia is resolved in Byron's favor. We find a protagonist-narrator in *Mazeppa,* also, although in this later poem Byron begins and ends with objective narration.

Mazeppa, which was written after Byron had begun *Don Juan,* is in fact one of his most fascinating experiments. Although the major incident, Mazeppa tied to the back of a terrified horse being carried on a frantic ride through wild scenery, seems as sensational as the most romantic of Byron's earlier tales, the poet's treatment makes the story believable, almost realistic, without in any way diminishing the excitement of the gallop itself. Byron blends together romance and realism, in part through the characterization of Mazeppa himself, an experienced veteran recollecting his riotous youth half-humorously and half-nostalgically and applying to his early adventures the wisdom of a long and active life. Lightly, almost casually, too, Byron suggests without emphasizing the symbolic significance of Mazeppa's story.[17] And by making the scene of Mazeppa's recitation the discouraged camp of Charles the Twelfth's few frightened followers after the disaster of Poltava, Byron confines the thundering energy of Mazeppa's adventures within an atmosphere of discouragement, weariness, and despair, an atmosphere which in its turn is lightened by touches of realistic humor, as when at the end of his narrative Mazeppa discovers that for an hour the King has been asleep. All these devices, especially the penetration of sardonic humor into exotic adventure, are essential to the manner of *Don Juan,* and *Mazeppa* might almost be regarded as an offshoot of the longer poem did it not lack two of the most important features of *Don Juan:* the *ottava rima* stanza and the pervasive presence of Byron's own personality.

These features appear together in *Beppo* (1818), which served as a kind of trial run for *Don Juan* but is a minor masterpiece in its own right. By taking over the role of narrator Byron was able to keep constantly in operation both his naturalistic irony and his delight in extravagant occurrences, both his mordant factuality and his flamboyant emotionalism. The Byron who narrates the story of *Beppo* and later of *Don Juan* is no fictive being, no literary mask, but the real man, complex, contradictory, amusing, and exasperating. Hence the complete believability and the amazing suspense of these later stories, even when they treat of improbable or absurd events. Suspense, after all, is a function of realism. Wherever a literary work is invested with any aspects of authentic experience its development becomes tinged with those uncertainties and unexpected imbalances which provide actual existence with an ever-doubtful future. Byron as narrator, moreover, can force us to see his hero as part of the complex interrelationships that make up his society with an objectivity which a protagonist-narrator could not attain. In *Beppo* that relationship between the individual and his social milieu has become Byron's central preoccupation. The story of *Beppo* appears to be scarcely an anecdote. As a reviewer of *Blackwood's* observed:

> The story that's in it
> May be told in a minute;
> But *par parenthèse* chatting
> Of this thing and that thing,
> Keeps the shuttlecock flying
> And attention from dying.[18]

We may remark, *par parenthèse,* that there is more balance in *Don Juan,* where, despite Byron's persistent digressing, the pressure of a strong narrative impulse is constantly exerted. But in *Beppo* it is the satiric portrayal of the grotesque vagaries of Venetian etiquette which holds our attention, not the tale of Laura, her *cavalier servente,* and her long-lost husband. *Beppo* is almost an upside-down version of one of Byron's early tales. Beppo's adventures, including kidnapping, slavery, change of faith, and piracy, might serve as the basis for another *Lara;* but his escapades seem trivial and absurd because they are seen through the wrong end of the telescope, not as splendid displays of liberated passion in isolation, but as an odd illustration of the strength of vulgar, commercial, artificial Venetian society. We are not suggesting that *Beppo* is self-parody, but only that in it Byron does to earlier tales of heroic adventure what Pulci, Boiardo, and Ariosto had done to the traditional stories of Roland, whose heroic prowess, instead of being allowed to operate freely in the grandly simplified world of popular saga, they entangled in the sophisticated intricacies of a highly articulated and complex civilization.

That is why Byron's adoption of the *ottava rima,* the stanza of Italian Renaissance epic, is appropriate in *Beppo* and *Don Juan.* The verse unit of heroic narrative is almost always simple, usually the single line.[19] The complexity of Pulci's and Ariosto's stanza expresses the complexity into which these authors projected their simple, physically powerful heroes of popular epic with such entertainingly incongruous results. Byron uses the *ottava rima* in analogous fashion, particularly in *Don Juan,* where romantic and exotic adventures and fierce, overwhelming passions become enmeshed in a network of crossed rhymes and interwoven sentence patterns that convert titanic self-assertion into absurdity. But Byron's *ottava rima* is no mere copy of that of the Italian epic writers. For one thing, he treats it more colloquially, relying on the rigidity and artificiality of the stanza in English to provide order and structure for the conversational inchoateness of his tone and language. At the conclusion of *Beppo,* Laura's recognition of her long-absent husband, the ludicrous anticlimax of the heroine's reaction is reinforced by the ludicrous fashion in which a natural rendering of a silly woman's chatter is fitted to the formalistic stanza requirements.

> "And are you *really, truly,* now a Turk?
> With any other women did you wive?
> Is't true they use their fingers for a fork?
> Well, that's the prettiest Shawl—as I'm alive!
> You'll give it me? They say you eat no pork.
> And how so many years did you contrive
> To—Bless me! did I ever? No, I never
> Saw a man grown so yellow! How's your liver?"

Byron strives, furthermore, to keep us aware of how difficult it is to write *ottava rima.* He puns, distorts the rules of grammar, and palms off rhymes such as "fellows-jealous," and then, to make sure we get the point, he apologizes or complains or promises to become serious:

> I've half a mind to tumble down to prose,
> But verse is more in fashion—so here goes.

By calling our attention to the artificiality of his verse form Byron creates a separation between it and his ostensible subject. We see the action of *Beppo* and *Don Juan,* as it were, through the screen of the *ottava rima.* Or, more precisely, though the actions Byron narrates exist in the past, his verse form exists in the present, always available and suitable for comment or digression in the present tense. Byron, one might suggest, identifies his stanzaic form with his own personality. The presence of the *ottava rima* recalls him even in passages of objective narration. In both *Beppo* and *Don Juan* the usual sense of pastness or completedness created by the narrative mode is converted by the continuous existence of the narrator's form into a sense of presentness and suspenseful incompleteness. The separation of story from narrator-form is also exploited by the poet to create in the reader's mind simultaneous awareness of individual characters both as free agents and as people controlled and conditioned by their environment, a double consciousness which is supported by the poet's perpetual intermingling of dramatic action—swift, straightforward narration or dialogue—with social commentary—remarks in his own person on the limiting complexities of natural life and of civilization. And that double consciousness, which appears to be a central characteristic of the novelistic vision,[20] becomes increasingly the chief concern of Byron's art.

Our discussion of Byron's *ottava rima* has carried us rather abruptly into consideration of *Don Juan*. Before engaging ourselves with details of that masterpiece, however, we must describe the kind of poem it is. There has always been a tendency to call the poem an epic, and even Guy Steffan's extended critique in the recent "variorum" edition treats it as an "epic carnival." [21] Here as elsewhere, however, "epic" is applied to *Don Juan* only in a vaguely laudatory sense; no evidence is provided to show that the poem is epic in any exact sense of that term. It is a long narrative in verse, but so are many other poems that no critic would for a minute consider as epic.[22] And, except for his ironic assertions—"My poem's epic"—Byron regularly insisted that he had no intention of writing an epic.[23] Much more persuasive is the tendency of modern critics to describe *Don Juan* as a novel. Miss Elizabeth Boyd, for example, states flatly that it "must be judged as a novel . . . if we care to understand what Byron has to say through it." [24] And she draws attention to Byron's abortive effort to write prose novels, to Wordsworth's recognition of the "metrical Novel" as a favorite species of narrative poetry in his day, and to the fact that many spurious continuations of *Don Juan* were novelistic in character.[25] We have already stressed the way in which much narrative poetry of the early nineteenth century led into novelistic conceptions and techniques. We are committed to viewing *Don Juan* as a novel in verse, but we offer one modification of the contemporary view. All critics who have regarded the poem as a novel have looked backward rather than forward and have discussed it as a picaresque novel that is to be understood as a slap-happy successor to *Tom Jones*.[26] No doubt Byron knew and admired Fielding's work. But our position, already expressed in the preceding chapter and to be restated in the succeeding one, is that the narrative poems of the end of the eighteenth century and the beginning of the nineteenth operated to transform both the subject and the form of the Augustan novel, worked to enrich its contents and to enlarge the range of its techniques. *Don Juan,* we propose, belongs to that development and will be understood best if treated not as a belated contribution to the Augustan novel but as a precursor of a new kind of novel writing. Surely no one would deny that the novels of Scott initiate nineteenth-century developments in fiction rather than conclude the evolution of eighteenth-century forms. *Don Juan* likewise anticipates later novels rather than reworks earlier models. Russian literature provides evidence of this. The most significant poetic successor to *Don Juan* in European literature is Pushkin's *Eugene Onegin,* and *Onegin* becomes the starting point for the magnificent florescence of nineteenth-century Russian prose fiction.[27]

Don Juan, however, is not of a piece. It changes and develops. Only in the final cantos does Byron fully adumbrate a new style in the novel form. The poem begins, as Byron himself did, in an eighteenth-century manner and only gradually becomes an anticipation of nineteenth-century fiction. Canto I is very much in the vein of the picaresque novel. In the first episodes Juan is like Tom Jones, a young gallant whose spirit and virility lead him into an escapade the excitingly bawdy nature of which provides us with farcical entertainment. Juan hiding in the bedclothes and wrestling naked in the dark with Don Alfonso are straight Fielding. But even in this opening canto there are suggestions of non-picaresque elements and of attitudes alien to Fielding's spirit. The first four words of the poem—"I want a hero"—which seem to recall Fielding's conception of the novel as a comic epic, actually imply something different. Joseph Andrews, for example, is a burlesque hero, a figure who parodies the heroic chastity of Richardson's Pamela. Tom Jones is a burlesque hero of a more generalized kind—his naturalness (animal vitality and only average intelligence) parodies the superhuman virtue and rich mental endowments of all the protagonists of heroic literature. But Fielding has no trouble finding a hero—almost any honest, unspoiled English lad will do—nor has he any doubt of his protagonist's heroism in his sense of the term. Joseph's chastity and Tom's naturalness are most impressive. *Don Juan,* on the contrary, is a search for a hero; it attempts to discover what true heroism consists of in the modern world. Byron's "I want a hero" is, in fact, akin to the spirit of Jane Austen's *Northanger Abbey,* which begins, "No one who had ever seen Catherine Morland in her infancy, would have supposed her born to be an heroine," and goes on to explore through a burlesque of the novels of terror and sentiment the nature of heroism in the circumstances of real life. Catherine and Juan are very different people who undergo very different experiences, but they are alike in working toward heroic stature, rather than being innately endowed with an heroic nature, and in progressing toward heroism through increased self-understanding and more sophisticated perception of the falsity and the genuineness of their society. Catherine and Juan, unlike Tom Jones or any of the heroes of picaresque literature, move from naturalness toward a sophistication that enables them to retain and to express natural feelings within the restrictions of a necessarily artificial society. To Byron and Jane Austen naturalness *per se* is a virtue which must be outgrown. "I have *learned* to love a hyacinth," exclaims Catherine, who must also learn to distinguish between the formal excellence of General Tilney's manners, which disguise poverty and meanness of spirit, and those of his son, which are the social expression of his warm and generous heart. Juan, similarly, must learn to maintain the proper balance between Nature and civilization, to make the artifice of social intercourse a more intense expression of natural virtues rather than a negation or deformation of them.

If we examine the principal episode of Canto I we find that, despite its Fieldingesque qualities, it hints also of a new conception of the individual's relation to his society. Juan is victimized as much by a complicated network of social relationships of which he has no knowledge and which do not directly concern him as by the upsurge of his sensual appetite. He is brought into contact with Julia through his mother's offices.

> Julia was—yet I never could see why—
> With Donna Inez quite a favourite friend;
> Between their tastes there was small sympathy,
> For not a line had Julia ever penn'd:
> Some people whisper (but, no doubt, they lie,
> For malice still imputes some private end)
> That Inez had, ere Don Alfonso's marriage,
> Forgot with him her very prudent carriage.... (I, 66)

And Byron is careful to make Julia's motives ambiguous (I, 68). Both lust and jealousy of Donna Inez's relation with her husband seem to contribute. And as the passion between Juan and Julia begins to intensify, Donna Inez contributes to its development by her passivity.

But Inez was so anxious, and so clear
  Of sight, that I must think, on this occasion,
She had some other motive much more near
  For leaving Juan to this new temptation;
But what that motive was, I sha'n't say here;
  Perhaps to finish Juan's education,
Perhaps to open Don Alfonso's eyes,
In case he thought his wife too great a prize. (I, 101)

No hero of Fielding's is ever victimized by this kind of complex, ambiguous interaction of distant and doubtful motives. Nor is the conclusion of this first episode of *Don Juan* at all in keeping with the traditions of the eighteenth-century novel. Julia's letter to Juan (I, 192–97) casts the farcical ribaldry of the adventure into the sombre though non-tragic perspective of realistic social vision. The letter forces us to regard the amorous escapade as an unpleasant affair which, without killing Julia, causes her much anguish and which drives Juan away from his home. The realistic ambiguity of Byron's final view of an incident that to Fielding, Smollett, or Sterne would have been purely comic, and to Richardson perhaps tragic, is illustrated by the stanza which follows the quotation of Julia's letter.

This note was written upon gilt-edged paper
  With a neat little crow-quill, slight and new;
Her small white hand could hardly reach the taper,
  It trembled as magnetic needles do,
And yet she did not let one tear escape her;
  The seal a sunflower; *"Elle vous suit partout,"*
The motto, cut upon a white cornelian;
The wax was superfine, its hue vermillion. (I, 198)

Here the factuality of the description makes us feel both the pity of Julia's position and its absurdity. Her fortitude is admirable, her motto poignant, yet the notepaper is "gilt-edged" and the wax "superfine." Thackeray may have learned much from Fielding, but he also picked up a trick or two from Byron.

But Byron could not free himself at once from the idea of the comic epic or from the influence of the picaresque tradition. The shipwreck episode of Canto II, though justly admired by many critics, fails as a whole because Byron's treatment of the situation is inconsistent. His attitude is divided instead of complexly integrated. In general his presentation of the storm, the wreck, and the trials of the survivors is naturalistic and objective. But instead of consistently developing humor out of realism, as he does, for example, when Pedrillo in his fright damns the sailor asking for absolution (II, 44), Byron too frequently tries to raise a laugh by ironic comments detached from the naturalism of the scene, i.e., the murder of Pedrillo (II, 75–82). By so detaching the reader's mind from realistic involvement in the situation Byron renders his descents into compassionate tenderness mawkish and forced. The reader is more repelled than moved, for example, by the sudden introduction of the incident of the father and his two dying children (II, 88–90), for he is driven to contemplate the separateness of humorous and pathetic sentiments, the difference between realism and romance, instead of the mutual interdependence and interaction of these contraries.

From these inconsistencies Byron escapes by flinging Juan on to the shores of Haidée's island. The Haidée episode is deservedly famous, but little attention has been paid either to its position in the economy of *Don Juan* as a whole or to the reasons why this island idyl is so much more effective than Byron's earlier Oriental tales, of which it is reminiscent in length, theme, and structure. As to the place of the episode in *Don Juan's* economy, Steffan has observed that the second canto is divided into two "sensational" extremes: "its two halves represent two states of nature that are utterly incongruous to each other. Man is stripped of civilization both in the shipwreck and on the island, but with what different results!" And he points out that the sensuous beauty of the island experience operates as a foil to the horrors of the shipwreck, as well as to the artificial life of Canto I.[28] All this is true and deserves emphasis. But we must not let our preconceptions about Byron's sympathy for innocence and naturalness confuse our understanding of his methods and purposes. He does stress Juan's and Haidée's innocent naturalness, but never in a Rousseauistic fashion. Juan and Haidée are no more like savages than Adam and Eve. That comparison is Byron's, not ours. From the beginning to the end of the episode he uses images, allusions, and comparisons to remind us of Paradise and the Fall.[29] The innocence of this idyl is more profound and complicated and perhaps more symbolically significant than commentators like Steffan have admitted. The naturalness of Haidée, furthermore, has been exaggerated by critics. Almost the first thing we are told about her is that

> . . . in her air
> There was a something which bespoke command,
> As one who was a lady in the land. (II, 116)

And we learn that she is neither a child nor inexperienced:

> She grew to womanhood, and between whiles
> Rejected several suitors, just to learn
> How to accept a better in his turn. (II, 128)

Juan, too, can scarcely be called an innocent or a child of Nature. His experience on Haidée's island occurs after his introduction to sex and society in Canto I and his travail in the shipwreck of Canto II. Though still a stripling when he lands on the island he has undergone enough to have attained reasonable maturity. His maturity and Haidée's, along with their aristocratic upbringing (neatly brought into relief by the coarse simplicity of Zoe and the other islanders), accounts for our acceptance of their passion as authentic. One does not doubt that they are genuinely in love. Love is probably too complex an emotion to be experienced fully by the immature. Julia is as necessary a precursor to Juan's affection for Haidée as Rosalind is to Romeo's love for Juliet, just as through the killing of Tybalt and the shipwreck Romeo and Juan, respectively, are enabled to participate in a love affair more intense than they could have appreciated "unblooded."

The maturity of Juan and Haidée distinguishes their story from that of the heroes and heroines of Byron's earlier tales, who, though older, seem to us like retarded adolescents. The passionateness of Lara or Conrad exists only by virtue of its isolation from the trivial but obstinate intractability of the circumstances of ordinary living. Their grandeur springs from the illusory magnification of a dream world. They are as remote from the practical limitations of ordinary experience as Keats's Endymion. Juan and Haidée, on the contrary, operate within an environment of actuality. Juan arrives on the island not decently clad but "shockingly" naked. When he does not awake and Haidée refuses to arouse him, Zoe's breakfast, to her disgust, is spoiled. To make her visits to Juan's cave Haidée has to be stirring early, and this upsets the servants' routines and makes them grumble. After his morning swim Juan returns to "coffee and Haidée." Details like these —supported by the commercial practicality of Lambro, whose presence either in foreground or background constantly influences the mood of the idyl, and buttressed by Byron's own cynically sardonic comments and digressions—force the reader to respond to the story in a complex fashion. They arouse various and conflicting thoughts and ideas, whereas Byron's earlier tales had appealed to a single sentiment. Hence the action of the Haidée episode is not a series of melodramatic incidents but the slow unfolding of Juan's and Haidée's intensifying love. Even the most sensational event of this story within a story, Lambro's unexpected return, is presented with restraint and always in the perspective of his harsh and fierce but not unsympathetic character. Byron makes us anticipate Lambro's mobilization of his forces for a counterattack by showing in full, and funny, detail the old man's reaction to what has happened to his island kingdom during his absence. The actual gathering of his companions and their entrance into the palace is omitted, so that the climactic scene in which Lambro suddenly confronts Juan and Haidée focusses on the opposition of father and daughter, so alike in character and so contrary in purpose that their reunion can only produce catastrophe.

Yet the Haidée episode is still simple narrative in much the same way that the Oriental tales are. Neither Juan nor Haidée, nor even Lambro, is individualized fully. Juan and Haidée are idealized: in large measure they are the embodiment of young love. The difference between their experience and that of Conrad and Gulnar, say, is that it transcends without denying all those elements in human life which resist the growth and continuance of intense passions. The ideality of Juan's and Haidée's love is conditioned, as the experience of Conrad and Gulnare is not, by the large realistic fact of the shipwreck and the small realistic fact of Zoe's spoiled breakfast. We believe in the ideal beauty of Haidée's island not because it is more naturalistically described than the "gardens of Gul" but because Byron has shown us in the first half of Canto II the savage and ugly aspect of Nature. We believe that Juan loves Haidée because we have seen him in the first canto experiencing mere adolescent sexuality, and not because his later emotion is presented more naturalistically. What Byron does, in fact, in the island episode is to insert a narrative of idealized emotions into a context of tough naturalistic detail.[30]

It has been observed that Byron's conception of the Don Juan story may owe something to Coleridge's discussion of the traditional Don Juan figure in the twenty-third chapter of the *Biographia Literaria*.[31] The whole of Coleridge's analysis is fascinating, but for our purposes the following passage is most significant.

It is not the *wickedness* of *Don Juan,* therefore, which constitutes the character an *abstraction,* and removes it from the rules of probability; but the rapid succession of the correspondent acts and incidents, his intellectual superiority, and the splendid accumulation of his gifts and desirable qualities, as co-existent with entire wickedness in one and the same person. But this likewise is the very circumstance which gives to this strange play its charm and universal interest. *Don Juan* is, from beginning to end, an *intelligible* character: as much so as the *Satan* of Milton. The poet asks only of the reader, what, as a poet, he is privileged to ask: namely, that sort of negative faith in the existence of such a being, which we willingly give to productions *professedly ideal,* and a disposition to the same state of feeling, as that with which we contemplate the *idealized* figures of the Apollo Belvedere and the Farnese Hercules. What the Hercules is to the *eye* in *corporeal* strength, *Don Juan* is to the *mind* in strength of *character.* The ideal consists in the happy balance of the generic with the individual. The former makes the character representative and symbolical, therefore instructive; because, *mutatis mutandis,* it is applicable to whole classes of men. The latter gives it *living* interest; for nothing *lives* or is *real,* but as definite and individual.[32]

Coleridge's remarks illuminate how little Byron's Don Juan owes to the traditional figure of the irresponsible libertine. An easy inference is that Byron modelled his protagonist upon picaresque heroes like Tom Jones and paid no attention to the conventional Don Juan. But that inference evades the problem that Coleridge's discussion raises for us. Why should Byron, as some critics have suggested he has done,[33] transform the traditional character of Don Juan from that of heartless seducer to its opposite—a helpless prey of women? Why choose a protagonist whose character is fixed by convention as opposed to that which one wishes to create? Who would write a novel about an Odysseus who never left home? One might say that Byron's aim was satiric, but then one is forced to ask, what does the love of Juan and Haidée satirize? It may be more fruitful to consider if Byron's conception of Don Juan owes anything positive to Coleridge's critique. Coleridge's observation that "the ideal consists in the happy balance of the generic with the individual" could be applied quite appropriately both to Juan's character and to his adventure with Haidée. Coleridge assumes, however, that the dramatic version adheres to his precept that poetry depends on "the willing suspension of disbelief." To that negative principle, surely one of Coleridge's least happily phrased intuitions, Byron makes no appeal. He aims to create belief in his idealization, not the suspension of disbelief in it. That is why his Don Juan differs from the legendary figure Coleridge describes. Byron, in effect, accepts Coleridge's analysis of the traditional Don Juan and his definition of what constitutes the ideal in art but then twists that formula into a means for dramatizing an idealized character within a realistic context. By putting the ideal within the real Byron makes any suspension of disbelief unnecessary, for the realistic environment, as it were, authenticates our vision of the idealized character.

When we refer to Byron's characterization of Juan as ideal in the Coleridgean sense and when we say that Byron's Juan differs from the conventional prototype because his character does not require suspension of disbelief, we do not mean to suggest that Byron consciously thought out these matters. Rather we suggest that Coleridge touches points so fundamental to the Don Juan legend that Byron could not have escaped them. Coleridge observes that our belief or pleasure in characters like Milton's Satan or the traditional Don Juan is of a different kind from our belief or delight in a character such as Tom Jones. Plainly this is true. Byron's transformations of the conventional Don Juan figure can be understood as the result of his having removed the ideal Don Juan from his traditional, stylized world of legend to place him within the naturalistic world of the novel. But let us emphasize that Byron's Juan is not turned into a realistic picaro of the Roderick Random or the Tom Jones type; he remains Don Juan, that is, an idealized figure. But because his artistic environment, so to speak, has been altered from one of legendary simplicity to one of realistic complexity both his function and our attitude toward him become much more complicated, and, as a consequence, he can serve as the focus for a new kind of vision of human life. This vision of the ideal within the real obviously derives from the totally realistic vision of the Augustan novel but advances beyond the earlier tradition.

More specifically, in Byron's view, as revealed by the Haidée episode, individual desire is inimical to the purposes of social life. Lambro (technically a freebooter but actually representative of *laissez-faire* businessmen) poses a perpetual threat to Juan's idyllic love. By bringing Lambro privately into the palace in stanza 61 of Canto II and then not reintroducing him until Haidée awakens from her dream in stanza 35 of Canto IV, Byron surrounds his richest description of the lovers' passion in the intervening stanzas with the malign if unseen influence of the threat of Haidée's father. If the islanders forget Lambro, the reader does not. When at last Lambro strikes, he is ruthlessly efficient in destroying Juan's love. Yet Juan is equally destructive of what Lambro cherishes. When Juan is washed ashore the society of the island is happy and prosperous. In our last view, however,

That isle is now all desolate and bare,
  Its dwellings down, its tenants past away;
None but her own and father's grave is there,
  And nothing outward tells of human clay;
Ye could not know where lies a thing so fair,
  No stone is there to show, no tongue to say
What was; no dirge, except the hollow sea's,
Mourns o'er the beauty of the Cyclades. (IV, 72)

It is this fierce hostility between individual passion and a repressive society which links the Haidée episode, on the one hand, with Byron's earlier tales and separates it, on the other hand, from the last cantos of *Don Juan,* in which Byron is concerned with the expression of individual passion through the forms of social intercourse. But the episode is endowed with an ambiguity which, paradoxically, detaches it from Byron's earlier narratives and establishes it as a forerunner to Juan's later adventures. We have commented on the many allusions in these cantos to Adam and Eve in Paradise. But the accumulation of these allusions does not create a single, unified emotional bias in the reader. The island is a kind of Eden, but no one-to-one correspondence can be established between the other elements in the myth of the Fall and the characters in Byron's narrative. Again legendary simplicity has been complicated by naturalism. Juan is both victim, the man expelled from his paradise, and the intruder who wrecks the happy garden of love. Lambro is made a complex foil to this double role of Juan's. Though the evil opponent of Juan's love, he drives out a destructive intruder. It is, after all, Lambro's paradise which Juan desecrates. Byron compares Lambro on his return to an unwanted Odysseus, for it is not so much Lambro's power that Juan has detroyed as his love.

He enter'd in the house—his home no more,
  For without hearts there is no home; . . . (III, 52)

Lambro is not merely well characterized, then, but presented in a way that prevents us from responding simply to the plight of the lovers. We are made to feel, for example, not only Lambro's outrage as a father but his obscure sense that Juan's "theft" of his daughter is representative in miniature of how dishonest foreigners have raped his Grecian motherland (III, 53–55). This complicating of a simple story is new to Byron's art, as is his purpose of playing off ideality with naturalism and romantic passion with realism to the advantage of both contraries. Previously he had tended to oversimplify intricate situations and to revel in the negativism of contradictory attitudes.

This new creative equilibrium of Byron's art is maintained in the harem episode of Cantos V and VI,[34] which is not, as most commentators assume, a return to the manner and the attitude of the first canto. True, the harem scene is filled with joyously ribald farce, but now the comic dilemmas arise not from the opposition of the individual's natural appetite to the conventions of society but from the effort of the individual to subvert social conventions by seeming to adhere to their requirements. Instead of the superficial, schematic conflict between Nature and civilization which dominates Canto I, we find in the harem adventure the comic complexities created by confusions between appearance and reality—illustrated by Juan's being dressed as a girl. Whereas Juan and Julia naturally and easily disrupted the regulations of Spanish society, it requires an elaborate plot (hence one vulnerable to all sorts of secondary comic mishaps) by Gulbeyaz to violate the Turkish code. The characterizations are also richer in the harem episode. Gulbeyaz, Baba, and Dudu are conceived of as genuine individuals in a way in which Julia, Alfonso, and Inez are not, for the Turkish characters are dramatized by the interactions of their personalities with the requirements of their special social positions. Inez is really nothing more than a hypocritical, sanctimonious bluestocking; Julia is defined by her situation—the lively young wife of an old bore. In the Turkish court, on the contrary, what amuses and intrigues us is the incongruity between the personal inclinations of the characters and the public attitudes they are required to display. Nothing could better illustrate this than Baba's speech to Gulbeyaz when he bursts into the room where the sultana has been reduced to tears by Juan's unexpected rejection of her passion.

> "Bride of the Sun! and Sister of the Moon!"
> ('Twas thus he spake), "and Empress of the Earth!
> Whose frown would put the spheres all out of tune,
> Whose smile makes all the planets dance with mirth,
> Your slave brings tidings—he hopes not too soon—
> Which your sublime attention may be worth:
> The Sun himself has sent me like a ray
> To hint that he is coming up this way." (V, 144)

But the battle scenes of Cantos VII and VIII are the real turning point of *Don Juan*. Up to the siege of Ismail Byron conceives his action and presents it to the reader as biography. Through the first six cantos Juan is not only the center of attention but the primary agent of the action. From Canto VII on he participates in events of which he is not the prime mover, in which he is only peripherally or accidentally concerned. Juan loses all resemblance to a picaro. He becomes something like a Jamesian "central intelligence," a lens for focussing and illuminating the actions of others. He becomes what the Russians call the superfluous man, a character not completely part of the society within which he moves, and hence an excellent means of dramatizing its configurations and commenting upon them. Because he is superfluous to the order and organization of society, moreover, such a character is in a more subtle and complex way than the traditional picaro a potential source of disruption and destruction. The picaro introduces physical confusion, the superfluous man moral crisis.

Juan does not fully adopt this latter role until the last cantos of the poem. But the outline of his new character begins to take shape in the battle scenes. He is no longer the nexus of action. He is only a single participant, although a leading one, in an event the vastness of which overshadows all personalities, even that of its architect, the brilliantly characterized Suwarrow (VII, 52–56). Hence the anti-epical quality of Byron's narration of the siege.[35] The conflict is too big to be the expression of individual heroism, so the individual, here particularly Juan, becomes a means for making us understand its massive, impersonal brutality and destructiveness. Juan's principal heroism consists in his dramatizing the rarity of old-fashioned heroism in modern war.

The impressiveness of these battle cantos springs from this new, almost modern viewpoint. It is not alone the realism of Byron's descriptions of fighting on a large scale which makes these cantos so powerful.[36] It is, rather, the almost Tolstoyan insight into the meaning or meaninglessness of modern mass warfare which Byron's new attitude toward his protagonist permits him to display. Freed from the necessity of subordinating the bloody siege to the personal experiences of his hero, he can portray the moral distortion forced upon ordinary, decent people when they are encouraged by politicians to glory in destruction.[37] He can point out the ironic persistence of habit under conditions inappropriate to ordinary behavior.[38] He can explain the disparity between the reported heroism of modern war and the subhuman bestiality which in fact it provokes.[39] And Byron, like Tolstoy, can understand that behind all the statistics and logistics the significance and ultimate decision of modern battle rest upon the character of the insignificant individuals who are engaged in it.[40]

Cantos IX through XII are narratively the weakest in *Don Juan.* This may be because Byron still felt committed to a picaresque form, although his conception of his protagonist's role had changed. Then, too, because Byron really knew nothing about Russia, he fell easily into a mode of detached satiric comment in the scenes at the Petersburg court. And the temptation to ridicule in his own person English manners and customs when Juan first arrives in England may have been irresistible to a half-willing expatriate. The fact remains that Byron's inventiveness lapses in these cantos, though his irony and satire are unimpaired. And while his narrative impulse weakens, his linguistic and prosodic skill continues to develop. In these cantos Byron becomes a master of the *ottava rima,* whose fluency and subtlety make the early cantos seem almost stiff. T. S. Eliot has called attention, for example, to the dramatic originality of the dying highwayman's last words:

> But ere they could perform this pious duty,
> The dying man cried, "Hold! I've got my gruel!
> Oh! for a glass of *max!* We've missed our booty—
> Let me die where I am!" And as the fuel
> Of life shrunk in his heart, and thick and sooty
> The drops fell from his death-wound, and he drew ill
> His breath,—he from his swelling throat untied
> A kerchief, crying "Give Sal that!"—and died. (XI, 16)

That the final episode of the poem, the gathering of socialites at Lord Henry's Abbey is artistically the most rewarding in *Don Juan* is largely due to Byron's mastery of all the potentialities of his stanzaic form, a mastery confirmed by the poetry of Cantos IX through XII.

In the last episode Byron employs the same comic technique he had developed in the harem scenes of Cantos V and VI, that of characterizing by exploring the inconsistency between the individual's inclinations and the demands of his social role. But English society, unlike Turkish society, is flexible and mobile. At Lord Henry's Abbey we are more intrigued by the complexity of the different characters' adjustments to their more doubtful roles than amused, as we were at the Sultan's court, by static incongruities. The comic confusions of appearance and reality are much more intricate and provocative in the English scenes. We understand Gulbeyaz. But, we wonder with Juan, to what degree is Adeline Amundeville "real"? Is Aurora Raby a girl of spiritual intensity or only a frigid prude?

The sociological focus in these final cantos is the English *beau monde,* but the *beau monde,* in the country at least, includes for Byron a wider range of social types than it did for most of the eighteenth-century novelists. The variety of people that Lord Henry and Adeline entertain at the Abbey and the diversity of talents they need to maintain their position there is considerable. Not only is the society which Byron depicts more interdependent than that portrayed by Augustan fiction, but the relation of the individual personality to society is more subtle. The difference between Tom Jones and Blifil is essentially defined by the fact that Blifil is socially acceptable (because legitimate) but is in personality a bastard, whereas Tom, legally a bastard, is personally acceptable and attractive. The dramatic difference between Adeline and Aurora Raby does not consist merely in their different personalities or their different social positions. They are distinguished by the different relation the personality of each bears to the demands of her particular station. Nor is this solely a distinction of sincerity, of genuineness, or of good nature. The more complex personality of Adeline would be falsified if she adopted the attitude of scornful superiority to the values of her society which characterizes Aurora. Conversely, Aurora's austere honesty, based as it is on her youth, her Catholicism, and her lack of responsibilities,[41] would become a pose were she to assume a position in society equivalent to Adeline's. Aurora, Byron is careful to point out, resembles Haidée, but

> ... the difference in them
> Was such as lies between a flower and gem. (XV, 58)

Aurora, like Adeline, is "artificial" rather than "natural." What Haidée is she appears to be; her charm lies in her impulsive directness. Aurora's charm resides in the mystery which surrounds her personality. In her own way Aurora is as puzzling as Adeline, whose courtesy and formal good manners appear to conceal a passionate and jealous nature. We are led to suspect that Aurora's aloofness (a hardness suggested by the gem image) and seeming lack of vitality disguise ardent if more spiritualized emotions. Characterization has become for Byron the depiction of that uneasy adjustment between one's natural propensities and the accommodation one makes to the inevitable demands of one's society.

To embody such complexities Byron needs narrative and verse techniques of flexible subtlety. In these last cantos we find his irony to be no longer merely a weapon of attack but also a means of illuminating. His satire is no longer abusiveness; it becomes a means of evaluation. Nor is his desire to express passion any longer satisfied by a theatrical posture of splendid melancholy. True feeling is as always important to Byron, but he seeks it now in the artifices of a conventional society rather than in the melodramatic isolation of an exotic landscape (which implies that social intercourse dooms any genuine feeling to falsity or extinction). From the first there is apparent in Byron's poetry, as there is not always in that of Shelley and Wordsworth, for example, a strong regard for the traditional and the conventional, which regard, indeed, is partly responsible for his satiric bent, and which in the final section of *Don Juan* Byron utilizes in positive fashion. He directs his attention to extricating those elements of social intercourse animated by genuine feeling from those which are solely artificial. In so doing he transforms satire into something like a novel.

How completely novelistic Byron's narrative verse has become can be illustrated best by comparing a passage from *Don Juan* with a similar passage from one of his earlier narratives. Let us take, for example, the social gathering in *Lara*.[42]

> There is a festival, where knights and dames,
> And aught that wealth or lofty lineage claims,
> Appear—a high-born and a welcome guest
> To Otho's hall came Lara with the rest.
> The long carousal shakes the illumined hall,
> Well speeds alike the banquet and the ball;
> And the gay dance of bounding Beauty's train
> Links grace and harmony in happiest chain:
>
> . . . .
>
> And Lara gazed on these, sedately glad,
> His brow belied him if his soul was sad;
> And his glance followed fast each fluttering fair,
> Whose steps of lightness woke no echo there:
> He lean'd against the lofty pillar nigh,
> With folded arms and long attentive eye,
> Nor marked a glance so sternly fixed on his—
> Ill brooked high Lara scrutiny like this:

At length he caught it, 'tis a face unknown,
But seems as searching his, and his alone;

. . . .

" 'Tis he!" the stranger cried,

. . . .

And drawing nigh, exclaim'd, with haughty sneer,
" 'Tis he! how came he thence?—what doth he here?"

. . . .

"My name is Lara!

. . . .

I shun no question, and I wear no mask."

"Thou *shunn'st* no question! Ponder—is there none
Thy heart must answer, though thine ear would shun? . . ."

. . . .

He deign'd no answer, but his head he shook,
And half contemptuous turned to pass away;

. . . .

The words of many, the eyes of all
That there were gathered, seem'd on him to fall;
But his were silent, his appeared to stray
In far forgetfulness away—away—
Alas! that heedlessness of all around
Bespoke remembrance only too profound. (*Lara,* I, xx–xxiii)

In the sixteenth canto of *Don Juan* Byron describes some of the problems faced by Lord Henry when in residence at his country estate. He is occupied with the purchase of an art work, the remodelling of his Abbey, a lawsuit, a prize pig, and because he is a justice, with two poachers and one pregnant but unmarried village girl. All this Byron describes in detail. No wonder Lord Henry lacks Lara's imperial misanthropy. He has, however, still another ordeal to face.

But once a week or fortnight, *un*invited
  (Thus we translate a *general invitation*)
All country gentlemen, esquired or knighted,
  May drop in without cards, and take their station
At the full board, and sit alike delighted
  With fashionable wines and conversation;
And as the Isthmus of the grand connection,
Talk o'er themselves, the past and next election. (XVI, 69)

The banquet itself is charged with more complicated social tensions than Otho's party.

The squires familiarly formal, and
  My lords and ladies proudly condescending;
The very servants puzzling how to hand
  Their plates—without it might be too much bending
From their high places by the sideboard's stand—
  Yet like their masters fearful of offending.
For any deviation from the graces
Might cost both men and master too—their *places.* (XVI, 79)

Then, after a description of the guests, Byron describes the hostess.

But Adeline was occupied by fame
  This day; and watching, witching, condescending
To the consumers of fish, fowl and game,
  And dignity with courtesy so blending,
As all must blend whose part it is to aim
  (Especially as the sixth year is ending)
At their lord's, son's, or similar connection's
Safe conduct through the rocks of re-elections.

Though this was most expedient on the whole,
  And usual—Juan, when he cast a glance
On Adeline while playing her grand role,
  Which she went through as though it were a dance,
(Betraying only now and then her soul
  By a look scarce perceptibly askance
Of weariness or scorn) began to feel
Some doubt how much of Adeline was *real*. . . . (XVI, 95–96)

In most ways this lengthy comparison speaks for itself. In *Lara* Byron is interested in the outline of action, in *Don Juan* in the dynamics of action. Hence the character of Lara is passive, fixed in the rigidity of melodramatic stance, whereas Adeline is all "mobility" (XVI, 97). In *Lara* the forms of society create a dramatic background; in *Don Juan* the complexities of social forms are Byron's primary concern. In *Lara* feeling is treated as most fascinating in its isolation from or antagonism to manners. In *Don Juan* feeling as exhibited or disguised in social behavior appears more intriguing. These differences in subject are reinforced by differences in verse form and point of view. In *Lara* we see the action directly: it is recounted with the bold simplicity of dramatic narrative. In the last cantos of *Don Juan* our vision is double. In large measure we see through Juan's eyes and judge as he judges, for he is, as the passages quoted above illustrate, relatively detached. But gradually he is drawn into the situation, until we leave him, alas forever, with his hand upon the palpitating bosom of Her Grace Fitz-Fulke. It is the self-preserving instinct of a social group, one might say, to capture free elements and to bring them under the sway of its system, just as it is the individual's instinct to resist such domination. The poet, however, remains to provide us with an always objective vision. Increasingly in the final cantos Byron poses as a scrupulously fair-minded reporter, but of course the more judiciously sympathetic he pretends to be, the deeper his irony cuts and the more we are driven to question the meaning of all social actions and the validity of all motives.

This is why in the final cantos of *Don Juan* the colloquial mode of Byron's *ottava rima* attains its most effective development, becoming as we have said virtually novelistic in character.[43] His colloquialism is the expression of Byron's actual personality, with all its real inconsistencies and complexities. Byron, as Francis Jeffrey observed, is never witty in the way that Pope is, for Pope's wit is a function of the artificiality of his form, the polished perfection of his relatively impersonal manner. The puns, forced rhymes, and grammatical ellipses which play such a positive role in creating the character of Byron's *ottava rima* (the form of his personality in the poem) would be catastrophic in Pope's couplets. The grotesqueness, if one wishes to call it that, of Byron's art testifies that it is not *the* poet who speaks but *a* man. And Byron speaks not as a man applying traditional moral precepts to a fixed, hierarchical society, but as a man developing out of his consciousness of the individual's double role—that of a free agent and that of a creature conditioned by the shifting pressures of his society—new insights into the complexities and confusions of moral behavior. Byron's mode, consequently, is not merely colloquial but narrative too, and looks forward to that style of ironically colloquial narration which plays such a large part in nineteenth-century fiction.

Possibly the best way to make clear the nature of Byron's colloquial narrative is to contrast it with the non-narrative, formalized colloquialism of Pope's wonderful biography of Sir Balaam.

> There dwelt a Citizen of sober fame,
> A plain good man, and Balaam was his name;
> Religious, punctual, frugal, and so forth;
> His word would pass for more than he was worth.
> One solid dish his week-day meal affords,
> An added pudding solemniz'd the Lord's;
> Constant at Church, and Change;
>
> . . . .

Rouz'd by the Prince of Air, the whirlwinds sweep
The surge, and plunge his Father in the deep;
Then full against his Cornish lands they roar,
And two rich ship-wrecks bless the lucky shore.
Sir Balaam now, he lives like other folks,

. . . .

And lo! two puddings smoak'd upon the board.

. . . .

The Tempter saw his time; the work he ply'd
Stocks and Subscriptions pour on ev'ry side,

. . . .

Behold Sir Balaam, now a man of spirit,
Ascribes his gettings to his parts and merit,

. . . .

Things change their titles, as our manners turn:
His Compting-house employ'd the Sunday-morn:
Seldom at Church ('twas such a busy life)
But duly sent his family and wife.
There (so the Dev'l ordain'd) one Christmas-tide
My good old Lady catch'd a cold, and dy'd.
A Nymph of Quality admires our Knight,
He marries, bows at Court, and grows polite:
Leaves the dull Cits, and joins (to please the fair)
The well-bred cuckolds in St. James's air:
First, for his Son a gay Commission buys,
Who drinks, whores, fights, and in a duel dies:
His daughter flaunts a Viscount's tawdry wife;
She bears a Coronet and P-x for life.
In Britain's Senate he a seat obtains,
And one more Pensioner St. Stephen gains.
My Lady falls to play; so bad her chance,
He must repair it; takes a bribe from France;
The House impeach him; Coningsby harangues;
The Court forsake him, and Sir Balaam hangs. . . . [44]

The rapidity of this passage rests upon Pope's faultless skill at selection. What he omits is as important as what he includes. He uses no unnecessary details but speeds from essential to essential. The history of Sir Balaam, like that of Hogarth's Rake, is recounted decisively; each cause produces a precisely defined effect. One feels that nothing significant about Sir Balaam has been left out. In sixty lines Pope creates a complete portrait.

But Pope does not tell a story. Whatever a story may be, it cannot consist of cause *A* immediately and inevitably producing effect *Z*. A story tells how cause *A* produced effect *Z* by way of *M* rather than *N*. The details which Pope omits are exactly those which a narrative poet must dwell upon, out of which he will create his story. Pope's biography of Sir Balaam is analytical and reductive; it achieves swift precision by suppressing the narrative possibilities of the subject. Byron in the final cantos of *Don Juan* attacks from the opposite direction, stresses narrative, and operates synthetically. Hence his poetry, although continuing to share with the verse of Neo-classic poets like Pope the prosaic virtues of clarity, factuality, and rational preciseness, can anticipate—as Neo-classic poetry never could—the highly personalized and tonally flexible prose of the nineteenth-century novel.

The evolution of Byron's art which concludes in the union through narrative of lyric impetuosity with social criticism is exemplary. It helps to explain the struggles of Crabbe, Hunt, and Hood and the progress of Scott from ballads through extended narrative verse to the novel. Byron was not unique but typically Romantic in his desire to enrich serious art with exotic scenes and sensational events. Typical, too, was his interest in the subjective, emotional aspects of human life in conjunction with his perception of society as mobile, shifting, alive, and his concern with the problems of individual personality functioning as part of such an organic society. Since neither objective satire nor subjective lyricism permitted the satisfactory expression of these perceptions and interests, he turned to narrative verse. But simple narrative was an inadequate instrument, and gradually Byron developed a more complex form of verse story which finally became novel-like in character. Yet this novelistic quality of his later verse does not relate back to eighteenth-century fiction so much as it reaches forward to later nineteenth-century prose fiction.[45]

Chapter IX

*

THE NARRATIVE PATTERN OF SCOTT

"How do you like *The Lady of the Lake?*" one of Sir Walter Scott's daughters was asked. "Oh," she replied, "I have not read it! Papa says there's nothing so bad for young people as reading bad poetry." [1] Later Mrs. Scott is reported to have apologized to a visitor for a worn carpet: "I am ashamed of it. I must get Scott to write some more of his nonsense books and buy me a new one." [2] And Sir Walter himself confessed that he wrote so rapidly and published so hastily "that it is no wonder I am sometimes puzzled to explain my own meaning." Only by accepting Scott's own cavalier attitude toward his art and by acknowledging that none of his writing bears the impress of intense artistry can we understand his enormous importance in the history of European literature. His importance is not limited to the almost unbelievable popularity of his writings during his own lifetime, a popularity suggested by a French traveller's remark: "As Scott was not at home, I only saw Scotland." So perceptive a scholar as G. M. Young in his Sir Walter Scott Memorial Lecture at the University of Edinburgh in 1946 observed that "we are . . . accustomed to regard Scott as the central figure in the Romantic Movement" and that "if you think of it as a European movement . . . the word 'central' is justified." [3] Scott's central position is, in a way, the result of his casual attitude toward his writing. He was, as we say, a born storyteller, and he let his natural talent have free rein. Perhaps no gifted writer since Shakespeare had done that. At any rate, Scott contributed to literature neither technical skill nor revolutionary ideas but rather a new sensibility and a way of confronting human experience. That Scott himself had much to do with the transformation in men's dress which coincides with the period of his greatest popularity we can not assert, but the shift from silk to wool, from the ideal of the powdered gentleman dressed in sleek, fitted garments to the casual gentleman in baggy tweeds illustrates the kind of large change that he wrought in the European consciousness. Such a transformation cannot be created by any single literary production. Indeed, had Scott written even one novel or poem of complete artistic excellence the total impact of his work might have been less. For what one gains from the corpus of his writing is not so much any special enrichment of one's aesthetic experience as a broadening and deepening of one's responsiveness to all of life. "The Waverley Novels," said Hazlitt, "are like a new edition of human nature." In them, in fact, are embodied in simple form all the most positive and durable virtues of the intellectual, political, and social revolutions of the late eighteenth century.

Large effects take shape in simple forms, and narrative, the simplest of the literary modes, is the dominant force in all of Scott's writing. One might say that he always thought narratively, just as Shakespeare always thought dramatically. What Young describes as Scott's central position in the Romantic Movement is determined by his persisting inclination toward simple narrative, an inclination which encompasses both his creative strengths and weaknesses. Scott's long poems have sometimes been called epics, or epic-like. They are neither. They are simple stories of romance and adventure. If they are naïve, or even childish, that is because they do not make the worse mistake of pretending to be great poetry. The antiquarian lore in which the poems are steeped may suggest the epic,[4] but, in general, historical circumstances serve only as a backdrop or stage setting for private, domestic events. In *The Lord of the Isles,* the only poem in which an important historical occurrence—the return of Robert Bruce—is an essential spring to the narrative's action, Scott's emphasis falls not upon the story of Bruce but upon the romantic difficulties of Randal and Edith. Scott, like Byron, always went out of his way to deny epic pretensions for his narratives. He called them lays or romances and refused to claim for them profound or serious intent.[5]

But Scott's narratives cannot be dismissed as mere best-selling potboilers that appealed to the antiquarian taste of his day. Scott was an antiquary, to be sure, but his desire to tell stories sprang from the essence of his personality. For all his antiquarianism, he was an historian, and to him history was process. He was the first artist to conceive of history as the organic evolution of competing styles of life. His antiquarianism he could express in ballad-collecting and ballad-imitating. But his instinctive apprehension of life as historical process demanded a more comprehensive form, specifically the long poetic narrative.

Scott's understanding of history, however, was in some ways ill-suited to verse story treatment. Because he saw history as social development (the progress achieved through the competition of different societies) rather than as a series of personal exploits, he had difficulty in writing poems which were humanly interesting, which did not divide into separate fragments of melodramatic action and picturesque description. The unreality of his heroic protagonists often arises from their antagonism to his own understanding of what really matters. An example is Ronald Graeme in *The Lady of the Lake*. Graeme is essential to the personal story of James and Ellen, but he has no role in the conflict of competing civilizations which underlies and informs the private plot. The simple verse story was inadequate to Scott's needs. He finally found a new sort of narrative in which the simple, almost primitive but always interesting stories for which he had a natural genius could be enriched and elaborated. It was a discovery which worked a revolution in European literature, so it is not surprising that it was a gradual discovery.

The first of Scott's story-poems is *The Lay of the Last Minstrel,*[6] which is narratively the weakest. It has a frame structure, the main story being told by an Ossian-like minstrel to a lady and her maids. Each canto begins and concludes with a description of the hoary harper and the effect of his song upon his fair audience. Scott never completely dropped his use of formal introductions and conclusions, but he soon discarded the clumsiness of this rigid framework.

The plot of *The Lay of the Last Minstrel* is extremely simple, so simple that Scott can carry it through only five cantos and is forced to devote his final canto to a series of songs and ballads about the action already completed. He gives the action false complexity by introducing elements of "gramarye"—Lady Branksome's magic powers, Michael Scott's book, and the Goblin Page—which are, in fact, irrelevant to the development of the story but which do permit him to indulge in some Gothic wonder-mongering.

The poem is indebted to *Christabel,* part of which Scott had heard recited. One or two passages are outright plagiarism,[7] and the techniques of repetition and of rhetorical questions,[8] and the dialogue of the river and mountain spirits[9] all sound Coleridgean overtones. Scott's emphasis upon strange beliefs and superstitions as beliefs and superstitions and his extensive use of archaic words, much more marked here than in any of the later poems, probably reflect his own researches and the influence of other antiquarians rather than of Coleridge. All in all, *The Lay of the Last Minstrel* is apprentice work, crude and derivative and archaistic. But it bears the promise of Scott's peculiar development of the genre, particularly in its untiring raciness of execution, which makes one forgive him much that would be unpardonable in a more careful poet.

Marmion in part fulfills that promise. Here the minstrel framework is discarded, and in the long canto introductions addressed to several of his friends Scott assumes the role of minstrel himself. These introductions are concerned with the passage of time and with mutability, which are embodied in descriptions of Nature, the cycles of the seasons, and his personal memories of his younger days. We find an interest in how permanence encompasses change, and how the present relates to the past, the persistent concerns of all of Scott's best writing. These are introductions, then, less to the story of *Marmion* than to Scott's vision of life as historical process. We observe that his vision is hostile to the nostalgic melancholy (derived from *Ossian*) which had infected *The Lay of the Last Minstrel*. Scott's view seems to be that past history is interesting because it bears the same relation to modern civilization that an individual's previous experience bears to his present conduct. But our general knowledge of history is confused and fragmented. The artist's task when dealing with history (and what else does Scott deal with?) is to give form and meaning to the incoherence of our cultural memory, so to speak. That meaning does not consist of didactic moral lessons, but rather of the placing of our present problems and aspirations in a truer perspective and in a richer, more complicated context. One learns that human life is conditioned by its circumstances, but that these limitations are not oppressive to the thoughtful man, who finds in them the necessary cause for exercising his humane virtues—courage, honesty, good will. History as Scott writes it dramatizes the mature man's delight in the variety and vigor and nobility of human nature.

Most of this is implied rather than stated in the several introductory passages of *Marmion*.[10] But it is worthwhile to define Scott's view at this point where it first begins to take shape, for, fundamentally, his philosophic attitude, once established, never changes. What does develop is his ability to express his view of life.

The story of *Marmion,* while tinged with some of the apprentice manners of *The Lay of the Last Minstrel,* in most respects anticipates Scott's later methods. There is a complete and engaging story line in *Marmion* that appears fitful because clumsily welded to the actual history of Flodden Field. Scott was soon to become a master of mingling imaginative actions with historical events. Although he makes little effort at complex characterization in *Marmion,* his description of King James looks forward to the manner of his historical portraits in the later novels. He also treats details of manners, dress, and custom more straightforwardly in *Marmion* than in *The Lay,* where he had emphasized their quaintness and bizarreness, their exotic quality. In *Marmion* he is more assured; he presents historical details simply and naturally. He also plays down the supernatural features of his story. The trial in the monastery and the story of the ghostly knight are reminiscent of "Monk" Lewis, but Scott supplies the latter incident with a natural, but not overly rationalistic, explanation, and he treats the whole affair with restraint. He attempts, furthermore, to make the monastic trial illuminate the nature of the times for the modern reader as well as to thrill him with horror. All in all, *Marmion* marks Scott's first success (though only a partial one) at the kind of narrative which blends "real" history with imaginative romance.

In *The Lady of the Lake,* Scott's best narrative poem, the mingling of these elements is handled in masterly fashion. After a general invocation to The Harp of the North,[11] Scott reduces his canto introductions to one or two Spenserian stanzas. The narrative movement is fluent and coherent, though marked by several separate scenes of independent brilliance. The stag-chase opening, for example, is as skillful a beginning as one can find in narrative literature, and the fight between Roderick and James bears comparison with the concluding battle of the *Orlando Furioso,* of which it is reminiscent. Some of Scott's most attractive songs and the ballad *Alice Brand* are fitted easily into the course of the narrative to convey an idea of the practices and beliefs of the mountaineer clans. And, although some of the scenes are melodramatic and artificial, the carrying of the burning cross and Douglas's triumphs at the athletic contest,[12] for example, Scott has almost discarded the Gothic machinery that cluttered *The Lay* and, to a lesser degree, *Marmion.* More important, his descriptions of Nature are now less sensational, more realistic and richer in detail. Indeed, one of the most charming features of *The Lady of the Lake* is its evocation of the loch and bracken, crag and glen landscape of the Trossachs.

In this poem for the first time Scott creates believable characters. Though Douglas is a big stick and Graeme the shadow of a handsome shade, Roderick, James, and Ellen are living people. The principal weakness of these characterizations is that they are drawn only from the outside and at a distance. Scott never mastered the art, which the speed and compression of poetry demand, of swiftly dramatizing a character from the inside. It is a fair generalization that while few writers have ever observed human nature more shrewdly than Scott, many surpass him in the ability to enter into others' thoughts and feelings and then to make their readers share their experiences. Given the spaciousness of the novel and the relaxed rational structure of prose, Scott could build up the illusion of an interior vision, but in his narrative poems he depends on description and confines himself to simple and melodramatic personalities.

On the other hand, he is successful in *The Lady of the Lake* in conveying those aspects of character which are the result of physical environment and continued experience. For all his *joie de vivre,* James reveals the kind of small selfishness, capriciousness, and frivolity, combined with a love of the grand gesture, which one would expect of a pampered monarch. Ellen is likewise vivid, because Scott endows her with a mixture of the nobility requisite to a daughter of Douglas and the flirtatious gaiety of a girl who has spent much of her life in the rough and ready atmosphere of mountain camps. And with the simple but violent personality of Roderick he is at his best. Although more noble than Hagen, Roderick is a worthy compeer of that villain of the *Nibelungenlied,* for Scott evokes by suggestion the historical circumstances and experiences that create those primitively fanatical loyalties which are the essence of clan-leader Roderick-Dhu.

Scott is already moving toward a technique of characterization that depends upon the double perception of individual personality and social role, the same technique, in fact, which we observed in *Don Juan*. But whereas Byron is interested in the discrepancies between the two elements, Scott is more interested in the nature of their harmonious adjustment, in how the individual has adapted himself to the demands of his society. Scott's concern puts him at a disadvantage in the adventurous poetic tale, although in the novel form it opens the way to making his historical knowledge artistically functional.

It is noteworthy, however, that the characters of *The Lady of the Lake* never quite talk like real human beings, although for the first time many lines are devoted to dialogue. Most of this conversation is stilted and rhetorical, and that fault clings to the dialogue of most of Scott's upper-class characters even in his novels. Scott cannot achieve in poetry the kind of dramatically colloquial speech he later creates for humbler people like Jeanie Deans and Meg Merrilies. The best he attains in *The Lady of the Lake* is a formal gracefulness and reasoned balance, as in Ellen's denial of Roderick's passion to Allan-bane:

> To her brave chieftain son, from ire
> Of Scotland's king who shrouds my sire,
> A deeper, holier debt is owed;
> And, could I pay it with my blood,
> Allan! Sir Roderick should command
> My blood, my life—but not my hand.
> Rather will Ellen Douglas dwell
> A votaress in Maronnan's cell;
> Rather through realms beyond the sea,
> Seeking the world's cold charity,
> Where ne'er was spoke a Scottish word,
> And ne'er the name of Douglas heard,
> An outcast pilgrim will she rove,
> Than wed the man she cannot love.[13]

The trouble with *The Lady of the Lake,* of course, is that in it "ne'er was spoke a Scottish word." The dialect that looms so large in Scott's novels scarcely appears in his poetry. Upon the mastery of the colloquial mode, as we have seen, depends Byron's success as a novelistic narrative poet in the last cantos of *Don Juan*. Lacking Byron's purely poetic gifts, Scott could attain colloquial fluency only by turning to prose. But in prose he was able to develop the dramatic possibilities of ordinary, realistic speech much further than was Byron.

Most significant of all, in *The Lady of the Lake* Scott succeeds in making the process of history a functional part of his artistic design. The characters in the poem are more than individuals; they are embodiments of different kinds of civilization. *The Lady of the Lake* is not mere melodrama because the defeat of Roderick represents more than the death of a single chief. With him perishes the whole system of values which had animated the primitive civilization of Scotland. The circumstances of Roderick's death (he expires while listening to the minstrel's song of his clan's last, glorious, but hopeless fight) emphasize

Scott's meaning. At the same time the new civilization represented by James does not utterly destroy the values of the earlier culture. Through his romantic experiences in the Trossachs James learns the virtues of his country's older ways. He loves Ellen, admires Roderick's sense of honor, and admits that he had wronged Douglas. In triumph James learns humility, and with that lesson Scott expresses for the first time his concept of the proper relation of the individual to the forces of history.

History rolls relentlessly on, civilizations rise and fall. If we resist the new it will destroy us. But in moving on we must not completely abandon the values and virtues of older ways, for if we do, our new culture will be only different from the way of life it replaces, not better. That, in essence, is the conception upon which *The Lady of the Lake* is based. We may question whether it is well suited to expression in any narrative verse not manifestly epic in intention. To be presented convincingly it must include much factual detail and must concentrate upon social relations rather than upon individual heroism. In *The Lady of the Lake,* at any rate, Scott wavers between sacrificing the scope and significance of his theme to the demands of rapid continuity exerted by his story of adventurous romance and interrupting that continuity with dramatizations of the particularized historical forces that work upon the characters. On the balance, he favors his romantic story, which accounts for the unified coherence of the poem (as compared with *Marmion*) but its lack, also, of profundity.

He shifts the balance in *Rokeby,* and hence to the student of Scott's development *Rokeby* is his most significant poem. It fails at each point where Scott pushes beyond the limitations he had observed in *The Lady of the Lake.* The earlier poem begins with the simple but dramatic and exciting stag hunt which lands the incognito James lost and alone in the wilderness of the Trossachs. *Rokeby* opens with the timorous double-dealer Oswald waiting for Bertram's return from the battle of Marston Moor, where Bertram, at Oswald's instigation, has attempted treacherously to murder his commander. The increased complexity is obvious even in summary. The scene between the two equally black-hearted but temperamentally opposite villains, each suspicious of the other, is adequately handled, but one senses a contrivance and an artificiality not apparent in the stag hunt. The requirements of narrative poetry force Scott (because he is not a master of incisive and economical diction) to portray sketchily in the beginning of *Rokeby* a scene which cries out for the carefully detailed and cumulative treatment he employed later in his novels. In short, the opening of *Rokeby* focusses upon character, whereas that of *The Lady of the Lake* focusses upon an event.

The over-intricacy of the story of *Rokeby* as a whole springs from Scott's emphasis on character and his effort to pivot changes in the developing action upon characterization instead of situation. There are only two significant minor characters in *The Lady of the Lake:* Blanche, a crude forerunner of Scott's long procession of mad, outcast, but inspired women, and Allan-bane, a minstrel, a stylized figure. In *Rokeby* there are at least a half-dozen significant minor personages, and one of them, Edmund, is, like Allan-bane, a minstrel. But Edmund is skillfully individualized, and his adolescent and irresponsible yet sensitive nature is made to influence strongly the course of the story. All the characters in *Rokeby,* in fact, operate on mixed motives. If Matilda, for instance, is less vivid and attractive than Ellen, this is partly because Matilda is more complicated, more torn by doubts. She has a difficult choice to make between Redmond and Wilfrid, a choice not simply of emotional preference but affected by considerations of rank, loyalty, duty, and policy, which to her are real considerations that cannot be dismissed by melodramatic rhetoric. And Bertram, violent and unscrupulous as he is, lacks Roderick's monolithic unity and is tortured by conflicting loyalties.

Oddly, *Rokeby* is weakened by Scott's effort to bring history out of the background into the foreground of his presentation. In *Marmion* the story of the hero and the story of Flodden Field are, we might say, separate but equal. In *The Lady of the Lake* history and story are integrated but at the cost of some drastic simplification of the former. The story of *Rokeby* is determined by the battle of Marston Moor. In the first scene we are waiting for news from the battlefield, the nature of that news being the critical factor in the development of the private, romantic story line. In *Rokeby* the public event affects private experience, whereas in *The Lady of the Lake* the public event is affected by private experience. The importance of this reversal would be difficult to exaggerate. The earlier method encourages distortion of the historical forces involved in a particular story, the later does not. In fine, with *Rokeby* Scott makes his most decisive advance toward the form of the historical novel. We may observe that in *Rokeby* he goes beyond the military fact of the battle of Marston Moor and attempts to show how his characters and their actions are determined by the bitter chaos resulting from the religious and political implications of the military struggles between Roundheads and Cavaliers. But he is not yet in control of his new form. His invented story becomes confused by the sweep of history. Thus, although several of the exploits of the protagonists are as skillfully narrated as the adventures of Byron's early heroes, Scott's dramatic scenes strike the reader as separated interruptions of an historical continuity rather than (as is the case in Byron's Oriental tales) climactic personal experiences. Simply because Byron in his early tales is limited and concentrated we tend not to notice how blatantly melodramatic his situations are. The same tends to be true of *Marmion* and *The Lady of the Lake*. By giving us in *Rokeby* the sense of real historical forces at work, however, Scott makes us conscious of the artificiality, the sensationalism of the personal exploits he recounts.

It is well worth pointing out these sources of the defects of *Rokeby,* for the poem is in many ways Scott's most powerful one. Several of the characterizations are fascinating, the interpolated songs and ballads, notably *Brignal Banks* and *The Cypress Wreath,* are among Scott's best, and for the first time he enriches his nature descriptions with symbolic implications, the river Tees and its surrounding countryside, usually seen at night, representing evil, and the Greta, usually bright, rapid, and sunlit, representing virtue.[14] And in themselves some of the sensational incidents are masterfully handled. Bertram's flight up the cliff, the fight in the castle, and Oswald's death are swift, exciting, and pictorially brilliant.

Rokeby was a relative failure financially, partly because Byron's exotic Eastern tales were beginning to draw off Scott's audience. It was time, Scott insisted, for him to withdraw from narrative poetry and attempt a new genre. Hence *Waverley.*[15] There is probably much truth in this explanation of Scott's as to why he turned to the novel, but, as we have tried to suggest, *Rokeby* provides evidence that the natural development of his art was leading him away from narrative poetry toward the novel.

Nor did Scott surrender narrative poetry without a fight. *The Bridal of Triermain* shows him trying unsuccessfully to transform the mood and purpose of his verse stories. In this poem he aims for imaginatively sensuous effects and relies little upon naturalistic detail or direct narrative. *The Bridal* has a complex tripartite structure. The courtship of Arthur and Lucy takes place in the eighteenth century, and Arthur wins Lucy by telling her the story of a twelfth-century knight, Sir Roland de Vaux. Sir Roland finds and frees an enchanted princess, whose history (occupying a substantial portion of the whole poem) he learns from the sage Lyulph. As Lyulph's narration concerns King Arthur, the reader moves from the eighteenth century to the twelfth, to the seventh, back to the twelfth, and finally to the eighteenth century again.

Surprisingly, Scott manipulates this difficult structure with skill and tact. The Arthur-Lucy sections are light-hearted, realistic, and edged with satire. The story of Sir Roland is presented in the manner of a Spenserian allegory. Lyulph's story of King Arthur is Ariostan, impossible, immoral, charming. Throughout the poem Scott strives for opulent imaginative effects and a lush imagery different from that of his other narratives. Sir Roland's vision of the castle in the Vale of St. John is tinged by an evanescent, dream-like quality unique in Scott's poetry. The tournament at King Arthur's court, which Scott later resurrected in *Ivanhoe,*[16] evokes feelings of magical wildness and terror, visually dramatized by the blood splashing on the gown of the half-vengeful, half-frightened Gyneth, more characteristic of Coleridge than of Scott. And there is something suggestive of Leigh Hunt or the young Keats in the description of the maidens greeting King Arthur.

> Then o'er him mimic chains they fling,
> Framed of the fairest flowers of spring.
> While some their gentle force unite
> Onward to drag the wondering knight;
> Some, bolder, urge his pace with blows,
> Dealt with the lily or the rose.
> Behind him were in triumph borne
> The warlike arms he late had worn.
> Four of the train combined to rear
> The terrors of Tintadgel's spear;
> Two, laughing at their lack of strength,
> Dragg'd Caliburn in cumbrous length;
> One, while she aped the martial stride,
> Placed on her brows the helmet's pride;
> Then scream'd, twixt laughter and surprise,
> To feel its depth o'erwhelm her eyes. (I, xvii)

Such a passage illustrates, however, the weakness of Scott's sensuous imagination. He cannot submerge his jolting octosyllabic jogtrot in the lush details of Arthur's entrance into the "bower of bliss." Very likely a poem such as *The Bridal of Triermain* can be sustained only by the intricate dynamics of stanzaic verse. But stanzaic narrative was beyond Scott's capacity. To him the story, not the manner of its telling, was all-important.

It is this simplicity which places Scott at the center of the Romantic Movement while limiting the aesthetic value of his poetry. To the degree that the Romantic Movement is characterized by an interest in narrative forms Scott is the arch-Romantic, for he was of all his contemporaries the one most committed to the narrative mode. Indeed, so profound was his commitment that he was incapable of using effectively any technique which complicated the direct expression of his story. Coleridge, Byron, and Keats in their different ways worked to make the form of narrative verse an active element in the story being told. Such sophisticated complexity was beyond Scott. But the directness of his narrative impulse did enable him to make a transition from poetic to novelistic story, thereby extending the influence both of the narrative mode and of the Romantic style as none of his contemporaries could do.

The Bridal of Triermain is Scott's last fully serious effort at narrative poetry. Both *Harold the Dauntless* and *The Lord of the Isles,* written after his success with the novel, show signs of carelessness and half-heartedness. Scott apologized for having inadvertently used so Byronic a name for his hero in *Harold the Dauntless.*[17] It may have been a Freudian slip. In this poem Scott was making a good-humored attempt to adopt Byron's formula for success. Certainly the poem, set in the period of the Danish colonization, utilizes the kind of background of conflicting religions favored by Byron, and Harold himself, powerful, brooding, guilt-ridden, a man who fights gods as well as men, is Scott's one Byronic hero. But Scott is too down-to-earth to swallow Byronism solemnly, and not only does he treat Harold throughout the poem with lightness and irony, but he states flatly that Harold's final and most terrific adventure is purely imaginary.[18] Characteristically Scott supplies his Harold with plausible motives for his Cain-like existence—something Byron never provides his Harold with. Excepting some of the interpolated songs, which are vivacious and ringing, both the narrative movement and the versification of *Harold the Dauntless* suffer from Scott's ambivalence toward his subject and are perhaps more slack than in any of his other poems.

The Lord of the Isles is chiefly interesting for the light it throws upon Scott's novel *The Pirate*. Both poem and novel were inspired by a trip to the Western Islands,[19] and it is difficult to escape the conclusion that in *The Lord* Scott is simply finding an outlet for those visual sensations, emotions, and historical associations which would be inappropriate to the mood and plot of his novel. At any rate, he makes no effort to pull taut the story of his poem, and once having drawn a picture of Robert Bruce's romantic exile, he seems to lose all interest in his royal hero's career. And, although *The Pirate* is filled with lyrics, *The Lord* contains only one. While Scott conveys the misty desolateness of the Hebridian seascapes and draws a vivid portrait of the Coolins,[20] he seems to avoid the habitable landscapes he evokes in *The Pirate*. Poetry by this time in Scott's career has become the by-product or the servant of his novelistic art.

We have tried to suggest some of the ways in which Scott's long narrative poems point toward his novels, how, in particular, the deficiencies of these poems reveal an inherent novelistic bias in their author. We must now attempt to define the essential characteristics of the *Waverley* novels. Only by so doing can we hope to describe that narrative drive which, being central to Scott's art, most fully explains his role as the central figure of the Romantic Movement. In the *Waverley* series, moreover, that new style of novel which we have discussed in the two preceding chapters was realized in a specific and definite form. We have suggested that much narrative poetry of the late eighteenth and early nineteenth centuries is to be understood as a contribution to the enlarging and enriching of realistic fiction which reached so impressive a culmination in the Victorian novel. However much poets like Crabbe, Hunt, Hood, and Byron may have participated in that development, it was Scott who articulated the new novel, who gave novelistic shape to many of those forces which urged writers of his day toward narrative expression. To define the nature of the *Waverley* series is to isolate some causes of the impulse toward realistic narrative which found such diverse forms of expression during the early years of the nineteenth century.

Everyone knows that Scott "invented" the historical novel,[21] but the meaning of that invention is easily misunderstood. He did not merely make it possible to write novels about the Crusades; he made it possible to describe any society in its temporal dimensions. Before Scott the novel had been restricted to portraying social organization as static, as seen only in its contemporary aspect. Whether the novelist depicted the life of his own time or that of a different era, he represented one way of life without a significant past or future. Scott presents society as the product of past experiences and traditions which are in the process of becoming something different. Society to him is a moving current in the broad, continuous stream of history. The *Waverley* series did not teach later novelists how to resurrect the past. It taught them to see the present as it would appear to the future. For when Scott tells us a story of olden times, he treats those times not as statically quaint and remote but as the conclusion of still older ways and as the beginning of present ways.

In *Old Mortality,* for example, Scott does not paint an heroically antiquarian picture of life in the days of the Covenanters. Rather he shows the passions and principles which animated their way of life moderating into forms consistent with the changed conditions of a more modern British civilization. From a "reasonable" fanatic Burley is changed into an insane fanatic, because the tide of history flows ever more rapidly against the possibility of the success of his cause. Claverhouse, in his own way as fanatical as Burley, is forced to switch from the winning to the losing side by his refusal to accept the general movement toward moderation which characterizes this period of history. The characters who prosper are, like Morton and Cuddie, able to adapt in different ways to their changing society. Society in *Old Mortality* is conceived to be organically dynamic, some elements flowering, others decaying, and the stability of the whole dependent upon an ever-shifting balance of internal tensions.

This is why Scott's novels, as E. M. Forster has observed,[22] are organized about stories rather than plots. Scott's subject is the history of a society, not the dramatic interaction of particular individuals conceived without intensive reference to the historical conditions of their existence. The process of history works steadily in one direction only, and a more complex or dramatic representation of elements in the process than that provided by simple narrative would confuse or obscure the outline of the large development which it is Scott's purpose to portray. Scott's heroes tend to be nonentities, for their heroism, i.e., their success, derives from their moderateness. Morton in *Old Mortality* is typical. He is loyal to the ways of the past but he sees the necessities of the future. He suffers, not from a division in his soul, but from what one may call the political difficulties attendant on moderate behavior. His love of the past and his vision of the future are not warring contraries but two aspects of his unified view of the present state of changing society. His troubles arise from the actions of less clear-sighted men, who treat him as a fanatical reactionary or as a fanatical revolutionary. Morton is neither; he is a kind of seventeenth-century Kerensky.

Now Scott might have made heroes like Morton victims of the extremists, made his protagonists tragically unsuccessful. Had he done so twentieth-century critics would treat him with more respect. That he did not do so we may, of course, ascribe to his optimism, his conservatism, or his faith in rational progress. To us the fate of the moderate is the doom of Imre Nagy. But Scott is perhaps wiser, his view perhaps broader than we today can afford. To insist upon the inevitable destruction of the representatives of moderation would to him, we may deduce, have seemed a falsification of the very historical process which was his primary interest. In the long run of history moderation does triumph, the extremists do defeat themselves. Were this not the case history would not be—as it seemed to Scott to be—organic process. The cancerous growth or the monstrous aberration must be impermanent, unreproductive, at odds with the system of balances which is the structure of animate existence. Where we pity the individual, Scott celebrates the race.

We are not defending Scott's art except insofar as an explanation of its methods and purposes forces us to reject contemporary criticisms of the *Waverley* novels based on misreadings of the series. To condemn Scott for not providing his novels with dramatic organization and unified plot is as pointless as condemning Keats for not forming his lyrics about the kind of intellectually dramatic design favored by metaphysical poets. We are not arguing for any particular theory of what the novel or the lyric should be. Our position is that an art work succeeds or fails according to whether it realizes the purposes inherent in the form it assumes, and that our task is to elucidate the form and deduce its essential purposes. Scott's chosen form is the simple narrative, and his choice, like the similar choices of his contemporaries (in verse modes) seems predicated on a desire to represent life organically rather than formally, to embody its processes instead of asserting its patterns.

The Bride of Lammermoor illustrates this point, for the novel appears at first glance to be thoroughly dramatic, an appearance that is strengthened by its many Shakespearian borrowings. Closer inspection reveals that Scott is more concerned with the inner dynamics of cultural transformation than with a conflict of contrasting personalities. The Ravenswoods and Ashtons in *Lammermoor* bear a very different relation to one another from that of the feuding Montagues and Capulets in *Romeo and Juliet,* of whom they are reminiscent. The two families of Shakespeare's play are about equal in power and share the same moral code. The Ravenswood family belongs to an ancient order of civilization which is disintegrating. Its morality and code of conduct is being replaced by a new one represented by the Ashtons. Only by destroying the Ravenswood system of virtues, honor dependent on physical prowess, patriarchal loyalty dependent upon ignorance, can the Ashtons establish their own, which is based upon law and at least a degree of political emancipation. The love of Ravenswood and Lucy Ashton brings together two hostile ways of life, one of which must extirpate the other.

Bred to the sword and unbridled passions, Ravenswood cannot adopt the silky manners and legalistic thinking of the Ashtons. He cannot meet Mr. Ashton's schemes with counter-schemes nor his wife's manoeuvres with counter-manoeuvres. His instinctive response to the galling but legal usurpation of his hereditary estate is to attempt to murder the usurper, Mr. Ashton. When he gives over that plan out of love for Lucy, he is adrift. The promise of legal restitution held out by the Marquis is meaningless to him. It is not so much property as honor he has lost, and honor the law cannot restore.

Conversely, Lucy's love for Ravenswood is helpless against her mother's determination. Lucy lacks Ravenswood's independence, his value for personal initiative regardless of consequences. So she can resist only passively, in the end falling back on a kind of legalism: if Ravenswood does not return by a certain date their pledge will be null and void. Of course Ravenswood, to whom a promise is a spiritual rather than a legal commitment, returns too late to do more than drive her mad.

The key to *The Bride of Lammermoor* is Caleb Balderstone, the most thoroughly characterized representative of the old order and perhaps the one figure in the novel without a Shakespearian prototype. Caleb is superficially comic. His efforts to deceive Bucklaw, his raid on the cooper's kitchen, and his firing of the castle are funny. In retrospect, however, Caleb appears, if not tragic, at least pathetic. There is nothing funny about a man's being driven to hypocrisy, theft, and arson in order to preserve his principles. Caleb's ideals of hospitality may appear amusing in their antiquatedness and grotesque in their departure from the realities of Ravenswood castle, but they are ideals. The reader comes in the end, as is the case with Don Quixote, to admire Caleb rather than to laugh at him. His final device of setting fire to the castle in order to avoid having to exhibit its barrenness to the Marquis is at least magnificent in its absurdity.

The desperate actions of the comic-pathetic Caleb dramatize the disastrous nature of Ravenswood's passion for Lucy. Caleb's frantic efforts to supply even the basic necessities of life for his guests show, or should show, his master how little is left of the possessions upon which his code of conduct is founded. And the emptiness of the Ravenswood larder is symbolic of a more profound barrenness. So little is left of the Ravenswood way of life that that remnant can only be preserved, as Caleb repeatedly insists, by withdrawal, by refusing to let the new world of the Ashtons impinge upon it. Caleb's loss of his hereditary rights in town under the attack of a lawyer prefigures the disastrous consequences of his master's attempt to participate, through his love for Lucy, in the new order of civilization. The fatal attraction of new, powerful cultures to ancient and decaying ones could scarcely be better illustrated.

The Bride of Lammermoor, then, regarded as a dramatic opposition of individual personalities may seem mere melodrama, at its best only operatically sensational. Regarded as a story of changing styles of life in which the individuals are significant as representative of supra-personal forces, it appears both more interesting and more valuable. *Lammermoor* presents the case for understanding human behavior (and judging it morally) in terms of the cultural system under which it operates. To the eighteenth-century abstract constants of Reason and Passion it adds more specific variables, such as particular traditions in etiquette, special economic usages, and limited habits of thought and feeling. That is why *Lammermoor,* like so many other narratives of the early nineteenth century, is an exotic story of an unfamiliar way of life. It is a story of different cultural particularities. The difference between *Lammermoor* and Hunt's *Rimini,* however, is that in Scott's novel the exotic elements are functional, are, in fact, the essential forces in conflict. In Scott's hands the novel becomes the form best able to express the diversities and complexities of life which fascinated not only him but also all of his contemporaries. To literary men of the early nineteenth century life did not appear simple, orderly, and rational—as their Augustan predecessors had said that it should be—but wonderfully diverse and complex. One reason they turned to the relatively loose and simple form of narrative was to give unhampered expression to their pleasure in the richness and variety of human experience. Often they did no more than that and exposed themselves to not unjustified charges of moral anarchism. We have noted, for instance, the equivocations in *The Story of Rimini*. Narratives of the period are more typically flawed, however, by pointlessness, a tendency toward the unusual and the exotic for its own sake. That tendency, apparent in Scott's own poetry, sprang from the writers' desire to affirm the significance of the individual person and of his local experience. Even Crabbe's scientific realism, seemingly so un-Romantic, asserts through its detailed specificness the preciousness of particular, individual life. Scott, transforming the novel into a story of conflicting styles of life, by no means abandons that fundamental ideal of the early nineteenth century. He embodies the force of a particular cultural attitude in a specific individual—Cedric the Saxon in *Ivanhoe* provides a crude but clear example. These individuals who represent waning fashions, older ways, or localized concerns dramatize the right of the humble, the oppressed, and the singular to preserve their identity in some form against the pressure of conformity exerted by triumphant modern civilization. Chesterton is right in saying that all Scott's characters are kings in disguise, who at moments of crisis throw off their beggar's rags and stand forth in all the grandeur of their independent individuality.[23]

From his poetry one would never guess that Scott was trained as a lawyer, but law is the foundation of the *Waverley* series. The plots of almost all of the novels involve legal actions—the issuing of writs and warrants, the establishing of claims of possession, prerogative, or inheritance. The saturation with legalistic details is distinctive of the *Waverley* novels. Beyond that, there is in them an implicit questioning and testing of the whole concept of civilized law.

Scott was no anarchist. He was a Tory and a sheriff. He had respect for the intent of the law and for its forms. He was too intelligent and too experienced to doubt that law is the sturdiest pillar of civilized life. But as he matured he came to understand that those exotic traditions and historic events which had captured his fancy and had animated his early literary work raised some serious questions about the foundations of civilized life. He came to desire law based not on simple, abstract, and arbitrary principles but upon the complex realities of human life, realities discernible only to an historical vision. The same law for the lion and the ox is tyranny, was Blake's statement of this position. Scott argued less gnomically that the law which was not flexible enough to make allowance for tradition, for particular circumstances, for the inconsistency of private emotions was a kind of tyranny. The *Waverley* novels are an extended dramatization of the valuable diversities and complexities of mankind asserting themselves against laws too abstract, too rigid, too impersonal.

Scott was a Briton and proud of it, but he was also a Scotsman. He was, in other words, committed to the preservation of local traditions and values within the context of grander and more progressive British civilization. He pleaded for toleration, for a kind of cultural relativity, for moral judgments on the broadest and most humane level. Many of the finest moments in his novels are marked by the charity of victor to vanquished, as when Rob Roy protests against his clan's murder of the man who had betrayed him,[24] or when Campbell joins in the cheer for the Chevalier as he leaves England for the last time.[25] But the charity of the victors is only half of the total situation. There is, also, the assertion by the vanquished of the rights that remain to them as individual human beings.[26]

The peculiar heroism of Jeanie Deans's actions in *The Heart of Midlothian* springs from this kind of assertion. She succeeds in modifying the traditions of her people to accommodate them to the new conditions of present society without sacrificing any of their enduring virtues. She will, unlike her father, testify in a court of law, but she will not tell even a white lie to save her sister's life, and her truthfulness apparently dooms Effie. But Scottish society is progressing toward order and justice. The very existence of the court which condemns Effie, but which would not do so except on the basis of her sister's testimony, exemplifies that movement. The Porteus mob, too, has achieved its goal not by acting like a mob but by behaving with order and strict justice. Unlike her father (who represents a local tradition in its strict form) and her sister (who represents the surrender not only of the form of local tradition but also of its inspiriting principle), Jeanie understands that the need for the rigid structure of their code no longer exists.

"We are cruelly sted between God's laws and man's laws—what shall we do? What can we do?" cries Jeanie at first. Her decision is to prove that these laws are no longer incompatible. Truth can now be trusted to survive in the machinery of law and administration. Society is no longer controlled by arbitrary and capricious might but by a system of law founded upon truth. Scotland's legal institutions are adopting as their basis the principles of personal righteousness which had originally inspired the Cameronians to reject the authority of these non-ecclesiastical courts. And so, with as much determination and energy as the Porteus rioters, Jeanie sets out to save her sister by winning for her a legal pardon from the highest court of appeal—the Queen. Jeanie's success symbolizes the unification of individual righteousness and social lawfulness, which unification is the theme not only of *The Heart of Midlothian* but of all the *Waverley* novels. That theme, which first found expresson in Romantic verse narratives, was to become—largely through the influence of Scott—one of the central and characterizing preoccupations of Victorian prose fiction.

Chapter X

*

SUMMARY OF CONCLUSIONS

One principal assumption of this study has been that the critic does well to distinguish between the different kinds of narrative poetry which flourished during the early years of the nineteenth century. Insofar as we have established the validity of that assumption we are prevented from drawing general conclusions from our particularized analyses. But without denying that the different types of narrative verse must be criticized in and for themselves, and without falling back on a summary listing of our separate discoveries about ballads, poetic tales, adventurous narratives, and epics, we may suggest some causes for the recrudescence of the narrative mode during the early nineteenth century and some conclusions as to the significance of that mode within the Romantic style.

Probably the most enduring ot the early nineteenth-century experiments within the narrative mode was that which established the literary ballad as a respectable addition to the lyricist's repertoire. We have tried to show that Romantic treatment of the ballad is characterized by its anti-archaistic bias. To the Romantic poet imitation of a ballad is a means, not an end; what he strives for is a narrative lyricism. In Chapters Two and Three we observed several distinct causes for the emergence of this poetic ideal. We noted that the introduction of narrative elements into lyric verse permitted poets to be more personal and less formal, to stress actual, particularized experience as the originating matrix of their poetry, and, finally, to press toward a more intensely symbolic art. In short, Romantic poets used the ballad as a means of enriching all aspects of their lyricism. New subject-matter, new moral attitudes, and a new kind of singing voice were developed from a humble, primitive model. Whether it is possible to discover a single, all-encompassing, primary cause for this transformation—surely one of the most significant in English literature—we do not know; assuredly we have not found it. But one fact is plain: the causes (or *the* cause) are located within the dynamics of aesthetic change. When we study the rising fortunes of the literary ballad in the eighteenth and nineteenth centuries we need not seek for sociological, economic, or philosophical explanations. Art does not exist in a vacuum, and literary phenomena always affect and are affected by other cultural events. But the history of the literary ballad, like that of the sonnet, is above all a matter of aesthetic history. Its fascination and its difficulty arise from its intimate and almost exclusive association with the evolution of artistic sensibility.

This point deserves emphasis, because the other principal narrative development we have examined can be understood and evaluated only when related to non-aesthetic matters. Narrative, as we have insisted on several occasions, is a simple mode; it tends to respond swiftly to philosophic or social changes. More than that, it seems to be the mode toward which an experimenting, innovating poet, or a poet unsure of his traditions, perhaps even in rebellion against specialized literary conventions, will naturally turn—unless, of course, the heritage he is trying to escape is itself dominated by the story. Here, perhaps, lies the explanation for the cyclic recurrence of the narrative mode which we commented upon in Chapter One. In any event, the poetic story, in some respects the most characteristic Romantic genre, cannot be studied in isolation from the intellectual advances and the reformations of England's socio-economic life which took place during the latter half of the eighteenth century.

We have distinguished between two kinds of poetic story: the imaginative, moralistic narrative, and the adventurous, realistic narrative. The first kind appears to express a literary response to philosophic challenges raised by intellectual and scientific developments. The tendency of Blake, Coleridge, and Wordsworth to use brief poetic narrative as a means for combining objectivity with subjectivity as well as for expressing their conception of moral experience as dynamic process seems to arise from these poets' rejection of what they thought to be abstract and mechanistic cosmologies. In imaginative narrative they found a form well suited to their synthesizing aesthetic and to their preference for projective rather than responsive emotions. One strong impulse in the Romantic style was toward mythical art, a kind of art whose natural form is the simple story. The interdependence of this mythical tendency and the late eighteenth-century and early nineteenth-century fondness for verse narrative has, if anything, been slighted in our study. The Romantic poet rejects rationalistic and mechanistic explanations of the profoundest human problems but finds that his intellectual heritage has unfitted him for belief in older and more directly transcendental conceptions of human life and the cosmos—though he feels the attraction of these primitive states of mind. His creations tend to be mythically, not scientifically, ordered and directed, but his myths are original and private and take shape in the form of narrative that is deliberately simplified, a form that reacts against the immediately preceding formal tradition in literature and that allows freedom for his new vision to bring forth the full meaning of his particular experience of the natural world and of its transcendental significance. The evolution of this practice we traced through Wordsworth's art, noting how his transformation of conventional epic in *The Prelude* led, ultimately, into the more personal, more anti-prosaic, more visionary *Excursion*. We observed that his development illustrates a Romantic tendency to affirm the significance of poetry by making it express, not the traditions and aspirations of society, but the experience of an individual's journey through past errors and present confusions to a private intuition of universal harmony. It is a tendency that springs from—and at the same time is creative of—a conception of art as supra-rational discourse.

The Romantic interest in realistic or adventurous narrative, on the other hand, we think to be more closely connected with transformations within the economy and the social structure of Great Britain. We have drawn attention, for example, to the way in which realistic story poems of the early nineteenth century raise new moral questions instead of re-affirming traditional solutions to old problems, and to the accompanying tendency of these narratives to become extravagantly sentimental or grotesquely melodramatic. These characteristics we associate with the newly problematic relationship of the individual to his society. We have observed in Chapters Seven through Nine how Romantic narratives reveal an increasing consciousness of society as organic rather than mechanistic, and how that consciousness bears obvious affinities to Romantic aesthetics and Romantic philosophy. But it seems worthwhile here to stress that Romantic realistic narrative appears in conjunction with an assertion that the relationship of the individual to his social group is uncertain, unstable, fluid—is not absolutely fixed and defined by tradition.

Especially in the art of Byron and Scott, who were, we must remember, the two British writers who most significantly influenced the evolution of Romantic literature on the continent, this problematic relation is of the utmost importance. We have focussed attention upon the ways in which narrative for Byron became the means of combining lyricism with satire, naturalism with exoticism, objective description with subjective passion, real experience with idealized yearnings. In this Byron is typically Romantic. His search for a hero in *Don Juan,* a search based on his dissatisfaction with both the traditional hero and the traditional anti-hero, is his ironic, self-dramatizing method of exploring the same problem which lies at the heart of *The Prelude* and the *Waverley* novels. Similarly, Byron's flashy Oriental adventures, like Hood's tales of grotesque outsiders and Coleridge's stories of magical isolation, are based on a melodramatic, if not tragic, conception of the individual spirit in conflict with its society, a society which the individual may reject but cannot escape, for upon it depends his very existence as a human being.

Scott's contribution, which we believe to have been underestimated, consists in his transformation of the exotic into the culturally significant. To him not merely the individual but society itself becomes problematic. If his heroes are moderate, his societies are implacable, for what to Byron and, indeed, most of his contemporaries was the problem of individual survival and fulfillment was to Scott the problem of cultural survival and fulfillment. Yet this concern, which we have identified with the persistent theme of righteousness clashing with lawfulness in the *Waverley* novels, was founded upon and developed from Scott's Romantic preference for the personal, the particular, the local—his fascination with the thing-in-itself. Scott described the plume on Marmion's helmet, as G. K. Chesterton observed, not because the plume revealed anything about Marmion but simply because the plume was a plume. It has been insufficiently emphasized that this concentration upon the thing-in-itself is an adjunct to the organic view of life. The difference between an organism and a mechanism is that the unity of the former depends upon the functional co-ordination of parts possessing a high degree of individual, specialized integrity. Scott's advance from ballad to long narrative poem to novel, we propose, represents a characteristic development in the dynamics of the Romantic style: it is a progress toward larger and more encompassing organic unities, a progress founded upon an ever more intensified value for the specific, particularized details of the unified organism. Scott's particular genius led toward conceptions of cultural relativity and toward a vision of the historical unity of particular societies. He temporalized social history. This is why he needed, ultimately, the expansive scope of the novel. The *Waverley* series revolutionized novel writing, but the primary difference between the great eighteenth-century novels and Scott's is that the latter are simpler in structure, less formal in design, are based on the flexible, sequential order of story rather than on the dramatic, logical causalities of plot. In arriving at a fully temporal view of society Scott carried into his own province a tendency which, as Professor Lovejoy pointed out long ago, was central to all Romantic artists—the desire to temporalize that hierarchic cosmology (subsumed in the concept of the Great Chain of Being) which had dominated the thinking of preceding centuries. We need only add that such temporalizing is a necessary concomitant to the organic view, which implies growth, flowering, and decay as the primary order of existence—an order, we note, wherein simple sequence overshadows complex causality.

The value of distinguishing the various types of Romantic narrative verse is that such distinctions return us at last to an underlying paradox in all Romantic poetry: it is a poetry intensely original and individual, but both its originality and its individuality depend upon a sympathetic consciousness of earlier literary purposes, techniques, and traditions. Byron admired Pope, Keats admired Shakespeare, Shelley admired Homer, Scott and Wordsworth admired the folk ballad, and nothing literary was alien to Coleridge. It appears to us that the simplest, but in consequence most baffling, characteristic of the Romantic style, then, is the way in which it combines hospitality to a wide variety of literary traditions with insistence upon original, strongly individualized expression. It is perhaps true to say that the Romantics replaced the idea of art as imitation with the idea of art as creation, but it is also true that Romantic creativity cannot be separated from an unsystematized, non-doctrinaire admiration for past literatures and cannot be defined except in terms of its conscious exploitation of earlier poetic methods and ideals. In this regard, at least, Romantic literature foreshadows the dynamic eclecticism of the poetry of our own time.

Notes

****

Index

NOTES

Chapter One

1 Thomas Carlyle is perhaps the only major critic to dissent from this view. He argued in his review of "Lockhart's Life of Robert Burns," *Edinburgh Review,* December, 1829 (reprinted along with several other early critiques in *Early Critical Reviews on Robert Burns,* ed. John D. Ross [Edinburgh, 1900], pp. 256–313) that the poem reveals Burns's talent, not his genius (p. 279).

2 But the fact remains that in a letter to Mrs. Dunlop on April 11, 1791 (*The Letters of Robert Burns,* Vols. 7–10 of *The Complete Works of Robert Burns,* ed. Francis H. Allen [10 vols.; Boston and New York, 1927], IX, 29) Burns remarks: "Indeed, I look on your little namesake to be my *chef d'oeuvre* in that species of manufacture, as I look on "Tam o' Shanter" to be my standard performance in the poetical line." And in a letter to Alexander Tytler (*Letters,* III, 33) he says that "I am already revolving two or three stories in my fancy. . . ." Nor does there seem to be any reason to doubt, particularly in the light of Burns's desire to obtain a government position, that he was as conscious as Scott was later (*Early Critical Reviews,* p. 112) that his song-writing labors were a prostitution of his genius.

3 David Daiches, *Robert Burns* (New York, 1950), pp. 280–92, provides one of the most useful analyses of the poem. All quotations from *Tam o' Shanter* in this chapter are taken from the photo-chromolith reproduction of the original manuscript (London, 1870).

4 Ronald S. Crane, "The Plot of *Tom Jones,*" *Journal of General Education,* IV (January, 1950), 112–30, is the originator of this distinction and to his essay much of this first chapter is indebted.

5 Crane, p. 122.

6 Tam disregards his wife's advice, but Burns is careful to make us suspicious of both the motive for and the value of Kate's "sage advices." Burns credits Tam's decision to visit the kirk to the effect of whiskey. And Tam's shout, which brings out the witches, is the product of instinctive, irrational enthusiasm.

7 Despite Kate's prediction and the stormy night, Tam does not drown in the Doon; despite Tam's rashness (emphasized by Maggie's resistance) in approaching Kirk-Alloway, he enjoys what he sees through the window.

8 George Sherburn, "The Restoration and Eighteenth Century," *A Literary History of England,* ed. Albert C. Baugh (New York, 1948), p. 1107.

9 There may be, as Shakespeare proves, plenty of movement within a dramatic situation.

10 E. M. Forster, *Aspects of the Novel* (New York, 1927), pp. 44–51. Forster makes a distinction, to which we shall return later, between story and plot, the former stressing simple temporal succession of events and the latter stressing causal relationships between events. See Chapter Five below.

11 Louise Pound, *Poetic Origins and the Ballad* (New York, 1921), p. 111.

12 Nevertheless many dramatists from Aeschylus to Pirandello have worked such changes. One of Shakespeare's favorite devices is the play within the play.

13 Daiches, pp. 283–84.

14 The significance of Dr. Johnson's famous remark to the effect that a man who read *Clarissa* for the story would hang himself has never been appreciated sufficiently. Story *per se* was but little valued by Augustan critics.

15 On this point see Henri Peyre's fine study, *Le classicisme français* (New York, 1942).

16 Authentic belief in supernaturalism persisted longer in Scotland than it did in England. The Romantic poem closest to *Tam o' Shanter* is Wordsworth's *The Idiot Boy,* a narrative in which the protagonist's abnormal state of mind is used, as is Tam's drunkenness, to develop tension. Wordsworth, like Burns, employs humor to shift the reader's perspective at moments crucial to narrowing and sharpening expectations. (See John E. Jordan, "Wordsworth's Humor;" *Publications of the Modern Language Association,* LXXIII [1958], 81–93.) But Wordsworth's idiot lacks the authenticity of Burns's peasant; the implicit horror of the boy's condition is insufficiently developed to counterpoint the humor of the tale.

17 William Montgomerie, *"Tam o' Shanter," Robert Burns* (Glasgow, 1947), p. 70.

18 Art in *Tam o' Shanter,* in the form of singing, stories, and dancing, is either blasphemous or but a brief interlude which emphasizes the pervasive bitterness of life. Here, indeed, the "Muse her wing maun cour." See Montgomerie, pp. 79–80.

19 The narrator possesses only one pair of breeches, "that ance were plush"; the altar is desecrated with the relics of those crimes which are the products of degraded poverty; and there is point in Carlyle's complaint that the supernaturalism of the poem lacks traditional charm, "Shakespearian" quality (*Early Critical Essays,* pp. 278–79), and becomes "a mere drunken phantasmagoria." But what Carlyle objects to is the source of *Tam o' Shanter's* strength.

20 The remark was originally made by Edwin Muir in *Scott and Scotland* (Edinburgh, 1936). Maurice Lindsay, *Robert Burns* (London, 1954), p. 213, quotes the comment and discusses its applicability to the poem.

21 Burns differs from those precursors of Romanticism who are precursors because they praise the delights of Nature and of rural life. Burns is like Blake, almost his exact contemporary, who, though he damned London for each "chartered street" and attacked the "dark, Satanic mills" of the cities, did not

associate goodness and God with Nature and rejected the simplicity of the Cowperian formula: God-Nature is good, man-city is bad. Crabbe illustrated the horrors of rural existence and his verse also shows a mixture of Neo-classic and Romantic elements. But Crabbe lacked Burns's profound experience of peasant life, as well as his genius. See Chapter Seven below.

22 The chapter of this title in *Eras and Modes in English Poetry* (Berkeley and Los Angeles, 1957) makes an excellent case for the ballad as the primary stylistic model for Romantic poets.

Chapter Two

1 Henry A. Beers, *A History of English Romanticism in the Eighteenth Century* (New York, 1899), pp. 265–305; H. J. C. Grierson, *Lyrical Poetry of the Nineteenth Century* (New York, 1929), pp. 30–32; Josephine Miles, *Eras and Modes,* Chapter 7, "The Romantic Mode." Besides these representative general treatments of the subject, there are excellent discussions of the relation of the ballad to the polite literature of the eighteenth and nineteenth centuries in Sigurd Bernhard Hustvedt's *Ballad Criticism in Scandinavia and Great Britain during the Eighteenth Century,* Vol. II of *Scandinavian Monographs* (New York, 1916), and *Ballad Books and Ballad Men* (Cambridge, Mass., 1930). These are still the best books on the subject. All of Miss Miles's work is of course of the highest value to many aspects of the subject. Her adjective-noun-verb ratios for Wordsworth's contributions to the *Lyrical Ballads* as contrasted to her figures for the genuine ballads—10–16–10 and 5–12–10 respectively—illustrate concretely how different from "authentic" ballads the Romantic imitations were.

2 The technique used in this chapter and the next is to analyze carefully a few ballad-imitations selected as representative of the principal phases of ballad-imitating during the eighteenth and early nineteenth centuries. A less discriminating study of almost all ballad imitations of this period may be found in my unpublished doctoral dissertation at Columbia University.

3 Gordon Hall Gerould, *The Ballad of Tradition* (Oxford, 1932), p. 11.

4 The distinction is derived from William J. Entwistle, *European Balladry* (Oxford, 1939), pp. 56–60. Professor Entwistle also draws attention to three special categories: ballads dependent on previous literary traditions, ballads derived from classical antiquity, and religious ballads. These secondary classes have no relevance to the trends discussed here.

5 Entwistle, p. 60.

6 Francis James Child, *English and Scottish Ballads* (8 vols.; Boston, 1857–60), IV, 143–57. All quotations from *The Nutbrowne Maide* are from this edition.

7 Matthew Prior, *Poetical Works,* ed. John Mitford (2 vols.; Boston, 1875), I, 212–39. All subsequent references are to this edition.

8 Each speech ends with an Alexandrine.

9 Other versions of Emma's "refrain": "That I, of all mankind, will love but thee alone"; "That she, of all mankind, could love but him alone"; "To her, who of mankind could love but thee alone."

10 The ballad heroine, though admitting herself to be "ful febyl for to fyght,"

says she will "wythstonde" her lover's enemies "with bowe in hande,/ To greeve them as I myght." The best Emma can offer is:

> Though my inferior strength may not allow,
> That I should bear or draw the warrior bow;
> With ready hand, I will the shaft supply,
> And joy to see thy victor arrows fly.

11 Compare the ballad heroine's "devoyd of shame" lines quoted above with Emma's

> Let Emma's hapless case be falsely told
> By the rash young, or the ill-natur'd old:
> Let every tongue its various censures choose;
> Absolve with coldness, or with spite accuse:
> Fair truth at last her radiant beams will raise;
> And malice vanquish'd heightens virtue's praise.

12 Here the contrast is with stanza 26, ll. 289–300, of the ballad.

13
> Hear, solemn Jove; and conscious Venus, hear;
> And thou, bright maid, believe me whilst I swear;
> No time, no change, no future flame, shall move
> The well-plac'd basis of my lasting love.
> O powerful virtue! O victorious fair!
> At least excuse a trial too severe. (ll. 646–51).

14 One cannot but wonder if the ballad did not originate as a religious catechism, Christ's representative occupying the man's role, and the novice occupying the woman's. Such transformations of religious narrative into erotic are not uncommon. See Robert Graves's discussion of "iconotrophy" in his introduction to *The Greek Myths* (Penguin ed.; Baltimore, 1955), p. 21.

15 For the sake of clarity I have oversimplified. Pope undoubtedly regarded the fuss about Arabella Fermor's tress as ridiculous. But the final, unifying irony of *The Rape of the Lock* is that, while we read, the characters' absurdities and pettiness become exciting and important to us.

16 Hustvedt, *Ballad Criticism,* pp. 86–87, gives an amusing description of Prior's imitation and a good explanation for the poem's popularity during the eighteenth century.

17 Joseph Addison, *The Spectator,* ed. George A. Aitkin (London, 1898), I, No. 70, Monday, May 21, 1711, and No. 74, Friday, May 25, 1711.

18 No. 70.

19 No. 70.

20 E. K. Broadus, "Addison's Influence on the Development of Interest in Folk-Poetry in the Eighteenth Century," *Modern Philology,* VIII (1910), 123–34.

21 Hustvedt, *Ballad Criticism,* pp. 65–78.

22 No. 85, Thursday, June 7, 1711.

23 Thus establishing a *locus classicus* for ballad debate. See Chapter Three.

24 A thorough study of this unique literary phenomenon is provided by O. F. Emerson's *The Earliest English Translations of Bürger's "Lenore"* (Cleveland, 1915).

25 For one important aspect of Gay's influence see Edmond McAdoo Gagey, *Ballad Opera* (New York, 1937).
26 *The Poetical Works of John Gay,* ed. G. C. Faber (London, 1926), pp. 357–58. Spelling modernized.
27 The significance of this incongruity between matter and manner can best be appreciated, perhaps, if one contrasts *The Beggar's Opera* with Burns's uproarious "Cantata," *The Jolly Beggars.*
28 *The Poetical Works of William Wordsworth,* ed. de Selincourt and Darbishire (5 vols., 2nd ed.; Oxford, 1952), I, 233. Hereafter cited as *Poetical Works,* ed. de Selincourt.
29 Ian A. Gordon, *Shenstone's Miscellany, 1759–1763* (Oxford, 1952), pp. xvi–xviii.
30 Quoted by Hustvedt, *Ballad Criticism,* p. 161.
31 *The Letters of William Shenstone,* ed. Marjorie Williams (Oxford, 1939), p. 596.
32 *The Poetical Works of William Shenstone,* ed. Rev. Gilfillan (New York, 1854), pp. 164–66.
33 Stages in the process by which Neo-classic standards yielded to the pressure of changing economic and social conditions are illustrated by three popular plays, each of which is based on a ballad story. Rowe's *Jane Shore* (1714) manages to be both classical and Shakespearean; Rowe treats his ballad story in the same way that Prior treats his. Lillo's *George Barnwell* (1733) is moralistic and aimed not at sophisticated literary men but at bourgeois businessmen. John Home's *Douglas* (1757) is a piece of extravagant, sensational archaizing.

Chapter Three

1 William Powell Jones, *Thomas Gray, Scholar* (Cambridge, Mass., 1937), p. 22.
2 Leah Dennis, "Thomas Percy: Antiquarian *vs.* Man of Taste," *Publications of the Modern Language Association,* LVII (1942), 142.
3 Jones, pp. 15–16. See also Donald M. Foerster, "Thomas Gray," *The Age of Johnson* (New Haven, 1949), pp. 217–26.
4 Edward D. Snyder, *The Celtic Revival in English Literature* (Cambridge, Mass., 1923), Chapter 3, esp. p. 68.
5 See Foerster, p. 224.
6 His Norse "translations" provide particularly interesting examples of this technique.
7 *The Works of Thomas Gray,* ed. Edmund Gosse (4 vols.; London, 1884), II, 316.
8 Hustvedt, *Ballad Criticism,* p. 148.
9 Herder's great collection draws heavily on Percy's work.
10 A horrifying picture of Percy's treatment of his sources is drawn by Walter Jackson Bate, "Percy's Use of His Folio-Manuscript," *Journal of English and Germanic Philology,* XLIII (1944), 337–48.
11 *Reliques,* Series I, Book III, Introduction. In the easily available Everyman

edition (2 vols.; London, 1906) this passage is found on p. 227 of Vol. I and the subsequent quotation on p. 238.

12 That this arrangement was deliberate and planned to suit the convenience of the general reader Percy makes clear in his general preface to the first edition of the *Reliques.*

13 Dennis, p. 142.

14 Hustvedt, *Ballad Criticism,* p. 302.

15 *The Complete Poetical Works of William Wordsworth,* Cambridge Edition (Boston, 1904), p. 814.

16 Even Burns participated in this purifying process, e.g., *Green Grow the Rashes, O.*

17 *The Rowley Poems,* ed. Maurice E. Hare (Oxford, 1911), a reprint of Tyrwhitt's Third Edition, pp. 58–59.

18 Characterization scarcely exists in the ballad, for the delineation of individual personality is possible only in a reasonably stable and ordered environment. While cause and effect operate (often ferociously) in the ballad, there is no system of cause and effect. To call the ballads tragic, therefore, is misleading; ballad disasters are presented as if they were unfortunate accidents—even when they are not.

19 "Rhetoric" with its adjective "rhetorical" has been so bandied about recently that it is perhaps necessary to state definitely the rather old-fashioned meaning I apply to the term. When I refer to a poem with rhetorical organization I mean one composed so that the reader's or listener's perception of its meaning depends upon his understanding of the interrelation of its parts. In rhetorical organization structure is not merely apparent but crucial. Only through a perception of what the structure is can one apprehend the poem satisfactorily. Structural organization occurs wherever meaning and structure are not immediately distinguishable. With a symbolic narrative, which requires structural organization, the audience is aware that there is coherence but cannot say what that coherence is until they have grasped the meaning of the total narrative, for the meaning is the coherence. Obviously, all poetry of any worth possesses both kinds of organization, and there does not seem to me any difference in value between poetry which stresses one kind of organization over the other. The distinction is useful to the critic, however. A poet, for instance, who has given his work a predominantly rhetorical organization is probably conscious of a specific audience in a way that a man writing a structurally organized poem probably is not.

20 Gerould, *The Ballad of Tradition,* p. 109.

21 Gerould, p. 110.

22 Earl Wasserman, *The Finer Tone* (Baltimore, 1953), pp. 67–68. The subsequent analysis of the structure of *La Belle Dame* is derived from Dr. Wasserman's persuasive study, which indicates how much Keats enriched and refined the stylized rhetorical form of the popular ballad.

23 Wasserman, p. 82.

24 Wasserman, p. 66.

25 Wasserman, p. 67.

26 Wasserman, p. 67.

27 Wasserman, p. 79.

28 Wasserman, p. 79. The analysis of the structure of this movement, granted Professor Wasserman's version of the poem, is excellent. "In stanza four it is noticeable that the only actor is the knight. In the next stanza the knight controls the action of the first two lines, and the lady that of the second two. In stanza six he truly governs only the first line. . . ."

29 It is the direct imitation of this literalism by poets who do not hold such beliefs which spoils most eighteenth-century ballads (such as *Hengist and Mey*) which attempt to deal with supernatural subjects.

30 In keeping with the practice established in the second chapter I am limiting myself to the most important poets. For Scott see Chapter Nine.

31 *Complete Poetical Works,* p. 798. The following quotation is from the same paragraph.

32 *Complete Poetical Works,* p. 791.

33 *Complete Poetical Works,* p. 791.

34 See Chapter Six below.

35 Stanzas seven and eight of *Lucy Gray* illustrate the way in which Wordsworth combines in the same poem a learned and studied choice and arrangement of words (note "wanton stroke" and "disperse" as well as the sudden intrusion of the present tense in seven) with simple language and syntax (stanza eight is almost identical with the first stanza of *The Babes in the Wood*).

> Not blither is the mountain roe:
> With many a wanton stroke
> Her feet disperse the powdery snow,
> That rises up like smoke.
>
> The storm came on before its time:
> She wandered up and down;
> And many a hill did Lucy climb:
> But never reached the town.

36 Wordsworth's theory of diction is, of course, based on a more significant premise, which all the Romantics accepted, namely, that rustics, sailors, and members of the lower classes of society in general were worthy of serious treatment in sophisticated literature. In Augustan art the rustic, or the beggar, is usually treated as comic or is idyllically stylized; in the ballads such characters are often treated seriously and realistically and that kind of treatment provided another reason for the Romantics' sympathy for the simple, narrative form.

37 See my article " 'The Rime of the Ancient Mariner' as Stylized Epic," *Transactions,* Wisconsin Academy of Sciences, Arts, and Letters, XLVI (1957), 179–87. The form of Coleridge's story is itself a large, encompassing symbol. This, more than anything else, distinguishes his poem from the eighteenth-century tradition of "strange" and primitive poetry from which *The Ancient Mariner* derives. Macpherson's *Ossian* is an important part of that tradition. But, ex-

actly contrary to *Ossian, The Ancient Mariner* does not celebrate the primitiveness it describes. The poem does not invite us to marvel at the wonders of ancient and relatively uncivilized life; it engages us in its magical events. Macpherson tries to make us conscious of the strangeness of the strange, whereas Coleridge familiarizes it (this was, we remember, his task in the *Lyrical Ballads,* to which *The Ancient Mariner* was his most substantial contribution) by making us participate in the mariner's adventure. Coleridge transforms the exotic into the symbolic, the marvellous into the mythical.

38 Coleridge's own critical statements have tended to obscure this point.

39 No genuine ballad has the variety of stanzaic and metrical forms exhibited by *The Ancient Mariner,* but Coleridge's ear seems to have caught one element in genuine ballad rhythm that had escaped his predecessors, namely, the technique of emphasizing alternate stresses. See Gerould, p. 129.

40 Quotations from *The Ancient Mariner* are from the text of I. A. Richards' *The Portable Coleridge* (New York, 1950).

41 Probably because the Romantics were not specially interested in the ballad *per se,* they preferred the adventurous ballad to the historical. Even such an extended and epical poem as *The Ancient Mariner* develops symbolically what would have been an adventurous folk ballad. A few comments on the methods and purposes of that development may be helpful. (The fullest discussion of Coleridge's emendations is to be found in the article of B. R. McElderry, Jr., "Coleridge's Revision of 'The Ancient Mariner,'" *Studies in Philology,* XXIX [1932], 68–94).

As has been observed, Coleridge consistently modified or deleted the sensational features of the poem, e.g., the arms of the seraphs burning like torches, toning down those elements most immediately reminiscent of the supernaturalism of the "horror" ballads (McElderry, p. 89). The character of the mariner Coleridge stylized, discarding his more quaint and ludicrous aspects, e.g., the opening scene with the Wedding-Guest. He reduced to a minimum the balladic formulae which had predominated in the original poem. He retained those formulae—phrases like "To Mary Queen the praise be given," repetitions like "Water, water, every where," and internal rhyme—which are not so specifically balladic as suggestive of the generic qualities of popular literature. All of Coleridge's revisions can be understood as efforts to emphasize the symbolic and universal aspect of his poem and to de-emphasize the peculiarities and idiosyncrasies of his ballad model.

His one major addition, the prose gloss, not only provides an extra temporal dimension, but also supplies a perspective of sophistication (see Huntington Brown, "The Gloss to *The Rime of the Ancient Mariner," Modern Language Quarterly,* VI [1945], 319–24). It is an artistic device which serves to make the primitiveness of the verse immediately available to the civilized reader. The naïveté, linguistic and intellectual, of the learned prose commentator is about midway between the barbaric naïveté of the poem and the sophistication of the modern reader. The gloss functions as a medium of transmission. But the gloss bears a more dynamic relation to the versification. It enriches the simplicity of the brief verse narrative by making the totality of the poem a complex interplaying of prose and verse forces. The prose gloss asserts rhythms—musical, emotional, dramatic—different from those of the verse. The prose sometimes retards the movement of the poetry (e.g., ll. 103–6), sometimes accelerates it (e.g., ll. 119–23, 164–70). Usually the gloss is more literal than the verse (ll. 224–27), but occasionally the prose evokes a richer imaginative context than the poetry, as in lines 199–200.

As to Coleridge's purpose, R. C. Bald's long and richly annotated monograph, "Coleridge and *The Ancient Mariner:* Addenda to *The Road to Xanadu*" in *Nineteenth-Century Studies,* ed. by Herbert Davis, William DeVane, and R. C. Bald (Ithaca, 1940), pp. 1–45, leaves little room for doubt that at the time Coleridge began to compose *The Ancient Mariner* he was not only thinking about epics and the requirements of heroic poetry but was also seriously considering undertaking an epic himself, as Charles Lamb urged him to do in his letter of January 10, 1797. It appears to me that Bald's evidence supports the validity of his addenda to Lowes, the basic argument of which is that "Lowes has shown how Coleridge's proposal for a series of Hymns to the Sun, Moon, and the Elements sharpened his eyes to certain details in his reading, but these details were incidental discoveries rather than the objects of his search. A more grandiose plan, which determined the direction of his reading, lay at the back of Coleridge's mind: he hoped to write an epic" (p. 16). If, as I have suggested elsewhere, Coleridge did write a kind of epic, he accidentally fulfilled his own requirement for the length of time demanded for composition of an heroic poem. "I should not think of devoting less than 20 years to an Epic Poem" (quoted by Bald, p. 18). The final version of *The Ancient Mariner* did not appear until 1817, almost exactly twenty years after the poem was begun.

Chapter Four

1 See Chapter Six, especially the commentary on the difference between *The Prelude* and *The Excursion,* where the significance of Romantic faith in private, visionary experience is discussed in relation to longer, "more-than-lyric" poems.
2 *Poetical Works,* ed. de Selincourt, II, 208–9.
3 "The Statesman's Manual," *Biographia Literaria and Two Lay Sermons* (reprinted from the original editions [London, 1891], p. 332); *Coleridge's Miscellaneous Criticism,* ed. Thomas Middleton Raysor (Cambridge, Mass., 1936), Lecture VIII, p. 99.
4 See especially Elisabeth Schneider, *Coleridge, Opium, and Kubla Khan* (Chicago, 1953), particularly p. vii and pp. 241–43.
5 In strong contrast, for example, to Pope's famous conclusion to *The Dunciad.*
6 The distinction between spontaneous and responsive emotions is not, of course, absolute. I mean by spontaneous emotions those that a poet brings to a situation and projects into it, thus coloring and shaping his immediate environment. By responsive emotions I mean those aroused in him by the stimulation of surrounding circumstances. Obviously the two kinds always overlap, but one can distinguish a bias in one direction or the other.

7 The two conceptions are not mutually exclusive; indeed, all fine poetry both conveys an immediate impact and provokes further contemplation. But changes in emphasis do occur. Though *The Rape of the Lock* is enjoyable on its fiftieth reading, its power of almost perpetual delight springs not so much from the new meanings re-reading reveals as from the fascination provided by perfect accomplishment of intricate design and graceful form. Read often enough, Mr. Eliot's *The Waste Land* reveals considerable strength and intricacy of form, although no one would persist long enough to discover this had the poet not from the first intrigued him by the mystery of the poem's meanings. That is why Mr. Eliot's notes (like E. K.'s to *The Shepherd's Calendar*), although a sign of artistic immaturity, are by no means wholly inappropriate: they urge the value of persistent study. A thorough discussion of this matter from a different point of view is to be found in Sir Herbert Read's Chapter "Obscurity in Poetry" in *The Nature of Literature* (New York, Evergreen Books, 1959). Sir Herbert is probably correct in attributing to Vico the origination of the modern critical theory of poetry as a method of discourse necessarily different from that of rational communication.

8 Warton's *The Pleasures of Melancholy* and Keats's ode on the same subject provide an equally illuminating parallel.

9 *The Poetical Works of Mark Akenside,* ed. Alexander Dyce (Boston, 1864), pp. 323–24.

10 All quotations from Keats's poem are from *The Poetical Works of John Keats,* ed. H. Buxton Forman (London, 1908), pp. 230–32.

11 Here, and elsewhere in this chapter, my references to evolution, development, and the like are not meant to imply any simple chronological sequence, either in the work of individual poets or in the poetry of the era as a whole. While it is true and important that Wordsworth's contributions to the *Lyrical Ballads* preceded his *Intimations* ode, and that Keats wrote *La Belle Dame* before he wrote his great odes, and that Coleridge, Wordsworth, and Scott experimented more frequently with balladic forms than did the second generation of Romantics, the process I am concerned with is too large and too fundamental to be reduced to an easy, schematic system.

12 Yet a memory or echo of narrative can be found in most of the best Romantic odes, which, contrasted to Neo-classic or early seventeenth-century odes, are story-like in total structure and often contain straight narrative passages.

13 The comparison of *Kubla Khan* to *Sailing to Byzantium* suggests that I have as low an opinion of Coleridge's poem as Dr. I. A. Richards (see his introduction to *The Portable Coleridge* [New York, 1950], p. 34). On the contrary, I think any student of literature ought to be fascinated by Coleridge's unparalleled success at interweaving the romantic suggestiveness of proper names and traditional motifs (a device most commonly associated with Milton and Virgil) with the elusive music of highly original sound and rhythm patterns, the effortless complexity of which makes the experiments of a militant innovator such as Hopkins look like fumbling amateurishness.

Chapter Five

1 I. A. Richards, *The Portable Coleridge* (New York, 1950), pp. 33–34. All quotations from *Christabel* are from this volume.
2 *Aspects of the Novel* (New York, 1927), p. 130.
3 J. Bronowski, *William Blake, 1757–1827: A Man Without a Mask* (London, 1944), p. 97.
4 Bronowski, p. 97.
5 This is not, of course, to deny unity to such forms as the drama. But the unity of a dramatic action is more indirect and less immediately apparent than that of narrative. In a play, for example, a character's statement of his motives for behaving in a particular way contributes to the unity of the action only through our judgment of the truth or falsity of his statement on the basis of his personality as it appears to us through his previous and succeeding acts. On the contrary, when the narrative poet ascribes a motive to a particular character, we have no choice but to accept that judgment as true to the narrator's vision.
6 Particularly recommended as a study of Blake's early poetry is M. R. Lowery's *Windows of the Morning* (New Haven, 1940).
7 Robert F. Gleckner, "Blake's *Tiriel* and the State of Experience," *Philological Quarterly,* XXXVI (April, 1957), 195–210. My reading of *Tiriel* is deeply indebted to Professor Gleckner's careful and lucid interpretation.
8 See Gleckner, pp. 199–201. Quotations from *Tiriel* are from The Modern Library *Poems of William Blake,* ed. W. B. Yeats.
9 Ijim I take to be physical strength unenlightened by intellectual capacity and Zazel to be intellect without strength. In any case, both are products of Tiriel's previous tyranny.
10 As this is not a book about Blake, I cannot take time to examine any of his longer narratives. What is said of *The Mental Traveller,* however, I believe to be applicable to his longer, later, and more mysterious narrative poems.
11 "Without contraries is no progression," wrote Blake.
12 Hence directly contrary to Chaucer's progress, for example. Chaucer, beginning with imaginative and symbolic stories, arrived at realistic narrative. The Romantic narrative development we are tracing is not identical with that of other eras. But see Chapters Seven through Nine for a contrasting development.

Chapter Six

1 See Charles E. Mounts, "The Place of Chaucer and Spenser in the Genesis of *Peter Bell,*" *Philological Quarterly,* XXIII (1944), 108–15, for Wordsworth's rejection of Renaissance "marvellousness."
2 *Poetical Works,* ed. de Selincourt, I, 119.
3 D. G. James in "Wordsworth and Tennyson," *Proceedings of the British Academy,* 1950, pp. 113–29, urges us to recognize in Wordsworth a developing tendency to find "in *dereliction,* in extreme dreariness . . . a visionary

quality." In respect to this tendency *Guilt and Sorrow* is an important forerunner of *The Prelude.* In note 53 there are references to some other works treating this point, but no one, so far as I know, has considered the progress of Wordsworth's art as part of a general Romantic development.

4 Not published complete until 1842. In the intervening years Wordsworth worked a number of changes, which, though to the advantage of the versification and diction, weakened the passion of his social criticism. For a description of the four versions see the *Poetical Works,* pp. 333 ff.

5 In lines 971–80 the ass is explicitly associated with Christ. The unusualness of this reference deserves comment in the light of what is said below about the "un-Christian" quality of *The Prelude.* "Christ" or "Jesus" is mentioned in all of Wordsworth's poetry just twenty times, according to the Lane Cooper Concordance, and most of these mentions occur in the translation of Chaucer's *Prioress's Tale* and the *Ecclesiastical Sonnets.* There is one passing reference in *The Prelude* (VI, 484) and two in *The Excursion.*

6 Poems like *The Idiot Boy* made Wordsworth an easy target for this charge.

7 Though why events occur *in the order* that they do is here, as in *Tiriel,* made manifest. Wordsworth's development in narrative parallels Blake's.

8 Chapter Two.

9 Compare Chapter Three above.

10 All quotations from *Michael* are from *Poetical Works,* ed. de Selincourt, II, 80–94.

11 A comparison Wordsworth deplored in the preface. The significance of his deliberate effort to transform the Scottian romance can scarcely be overestimated.

12 For more sympathetic views see O. J. Campbell, "Wordsworth's Conception of the Esthetic Experience," *Wordsworth and Coleridge,* ed. E. L. Griggs (Princeton, 1939), pp. 26–46, and Ellen D. Leyburn, "Radiance in *The White Doe of Rylstone,*" *Studies in Philology,* XLVII (1950), 629–33.

13 Florence Marsh, *Wordsworth's Imagery: A Study in Poetic Vision, Yale Studies in English,* Vol. 121 (New Haven, 1952), approaching the poem in terms of figurative patterns, reaches a similar conclusion. "The weeds and spear grass of *The Ruined Cottage* may fail to persuade one of the unreality of Margaret's suffering but they are convincing as weeds and spear grass. The white doe is less convincing as doe . . . . Like the landscape in *Tintern Abbey* the white doe is idealized so that the natural rises into the spiritual, so that the natural *is* spiritual. Unlike the landscape, however, the doe is never really natural" (pp. 62–63).

14 Not literally true, of course. Keats's *Isabella,* for example, is a simple poetic tale. But both Keats and Shelley attempted visionary personal epics much earlier in their careers than had the first generation of Romantics. *Endymion* and *Alastor,* moreover, originate in a confidence in the validity of personal vision as truth and of private myth as an appropriate form for that truth, a confidence which Wordsworth attained only in *The Excursion.*

15 I am thinking specifically of Wordsworth's two longest poems, Shelley's *The Revolt of Islam,* and Keats's *Hyperion,* though several other Romantic nar-

ratives might be considered in this connection. Let me repeat, however, that to analyze adequately the verse narratives of Shelley and Keats alone would require another book. However like their immediate predecessors they may be, they worked changes in narrative practice that are important to the history of the Romantic style and perhaps even more important to the history of the influence of that style upon later nineteenth-century poets. To mention but one minor instance: Shelley and Keats were by no means averse, as the earlier Romantics had been, to using old stories and old mythologies as the basis of their "original" visions. (Wordsworth's *Laodamia,* written after *The Excursion,* provides an important exception which seems almost literally to prove this rule.) It is apparent that Tennyson, Browning, and Morris developed and enriched Shelley's and Keats's method rather than returning to the inventiveness of the earlier Romantics.

16 But see Donald M. Foerster, "The Critical Attack upon the Epic in the English Romantic Movement," *Publications of the Modern Language Association,* LXIX (1954), 432–47.

17 There are now many fine studies of the nature of epic, most notable perhaps among works in English those of Bowra, Chadwick, Lewis, Routh, and Tillyard. But in some ways even more valuable is Lascelles Abercrombie's brief essay *Epic* in *The Art and Craft of Letters* Series. To this essay my discussion of epic problems is indebted. Professor Abercrombie, for example, renders suspect the hoary distinction between primary and secondary epic, upon which rests the major argument of even so recent a book as Professor C. S. Lewis' brilliant *Preface to Paradise Lost.*

18 An exhaustive study of Augustan epic criticism is Hugh Thomas Swedenberg's *The Theory of Epic in England, 1650–1800* (Berkeley, 1944).

19 This is, possibly, why Addison's *Spectator* papers on *Paradise Lost* are still interesting. Addison seems to have been deeply impressed by Milton's poem and his enthusiasm infects the rather mechanical form of his critique.

20 W. Macneile Dixon, *English Epic and Heroic Poetry* (London, 1912), pp. 242–43.

21 Douglas Knight, *Pope and the Heroic Tradition, Yale Studies in English,* Vol. 117 (New Haven, 1951), pp. 82–110.

22 Knight, p. 107.

23 And later, since all of Southey's epics, for example, belong to the eighteenth-century tradition of historical narrative.

24 The remarks in Chapter Three on Coleridge's anti-historical procedures are relevant to this discussion. In note 37 to that chapter I have tried to suggest one of the ways in which *Ossian* is important for an understanding of Romantic handling of ancient subjects, but limitations of space forbid the kind of thorough analysis which this matter deserves. Part of its complexity has been hinted at in note 41 to Chapter Three, and its significance is clearly brought forth by Keith Stewart in his article "Ancient Poetry as History in the 18th Century," *Journal of the History of Ideas,* XIX (1958), 335–47, which discusses that "kind of poetry whose truth (in the sense of historical fact) was on numerous occasions taken to be of a significance at least equal

to that attached to it conventionally as art" (p. 347). See also Lois Whitney, "English Primitivistic Theories of Epic Origins," *Modern Philology,* XXI (1924), 337–78. To my mind, however, all studies in this area must consider A. C. Bradley's "The Long Poem in the Age of Wordsworth," *Oxford Lectures on Poetry* (2nd ed.; London, 1923), which sensitively and perceptively investigates Matthew Arnold's assertion that the peculiar characteristics of early nineteenth-century long narratives are the result of their authors' lack of knowledge.

25 Some of Milton's greatest difficulties arise in *Paradise Lost* at those places where his commitment to the biblical story as historically true cramps the imaginative freedom of his conception. Virgil's advantage in this respect lies precisely in the amorphousness of his legendary material.

26 I oversimplify. History is an art, too.

27 Among others see Ernest de Selincourt's introduction to *The Prelude or Growth of a Poet's Mind by William Wordsworth, Edited from the Manuscripts* (Oxford, 1926), esp. p. xxvii (from this edition are taken all subsequent quotations from the 1850 version of *The Prelude*), Sir Herbert Read, *Phases of English Poetry* (New York, 1929), and Abbie Findley Potts, *Wordsworth's Prelude* (Ithaca, 1953). Of special interest is R. A. Foakes's chapter "The Unfinished Journey" in *The Romantic Assertion* (New Haven, 1958). Mr. Foakes's treatment of *The Prelude* as an epic journey, his comparison of it to *The Ancient Mariner,* and his explication of several imagaic patterns, notably those of the journey, the sea, and the mountain, are substantially identical with my observations and conclusions in the original version of this chapter, which was written before Mr. Foakes's book appeared. Consequently I have eliminated, insofar as was possible, anything in my discussion that duplicates his lucid and reasonable exegesis, and I urge interested readers to consult his excellent chapter. My interpretation of Wordsworth's poem, however, is very different from Mr. Foakes's, though complementary, I hope, rather than antagonistic.

28 Following Havens and Foakes; see in the latter's book note 1 on page 67, an excellent summary of the evidence. But compare also de Selincourt, *Poetical Works,* I, 328, for a discussion of the relation of this image to its model in the 1793 version of *Descriptive Sketches,* ll. 492–511.

29 "Preface," Cambridge Edition, p. 794.

30 This is probably why we all secretly sympathize with Milton's Satan, although we all know better, and why we have difficulty in estimating the heroism of Aeneas at its proper worth. It is to me significant that it was not until the beginning of the nineteenth century that literary men began genuinely to prefer *The Iliad* to *The Aeneid,* though of course since the time of Petrarch Homer had been paid lip service.

31 The time of the first book, like that of the last books, is the mature present. *The Prelude* forms a complete circle.

32 Foakes, p. 63.

33 Arthur Koestler, *Darkness at Noon* (New York, 1941), Chapter Four.

34 Fiction aside, it is the crisis of Milovan Djilas.

35 Ignazio Silone, *Bread and Wine,* trans. Gwenda David and Eric Mosbacher (New York, 1937), Chapter Four.

36 It is suggestive that Nejdanov, Hyacinth Robinson, and Rubashov do *not* recover and that they are *not,* like Spina and Wordsworth, from the country.

37 Ignazio Silone, *The Seed Beneath the Snow,* trans. Frenaye (3rd ed.; New York, 1942), Chapter Two.

38 One may wonder why there is so much speculation about causes for the deterioration of Wordsworth's later poetry, when simple physiological changes, such as hardening of the arteries in the brain, would be sufficient to explain such a decline. Probably literary critics do underestimate physiological factors. Yet the artist is almost by definition the man who overcomes the physical debilities of increasing age. Sophocles and Titian may be extreme cases, but their ability to keep on producing in their old age art qualitatively equal to that they created in their earlier years is typical of most artists. One would expect sculptors, for instance, to lose the sheer physical strength necessary for their work, but in general this does not happen. One suspects, consequently, that Wordsworth's case is like that of Tolstoy, who in later life lost none of his skill but who pursued purposes and techniques which we do not understand or approve of in art, partly because they differ from the purposes and techniques to which his early work has made us accustomed.

39 Sir Herbert Read, *Wordsworth* (London, 1930), p. 247.

40 Judson S. Lyon, *The Excursion, A Study, Yale Studies in English,* Vol. 114 (New Haven, 1950), p. 30.

41 Lyon, p. 31.

42 Lyon, p. 138.

43 Lyon, p. 139.

44 *The Complete Poetical Works of James Thomson,* ed. J. Logie Robertson, Oxford Standard Authors, "Winter," ll. 704–13. The argument to "Spring" quoted above is from this edition.

45 An illuminating discussion of Thomson's use of science and the literary traditions within which he utilized it is provided by Alan Dugald McKillop, *The Background of Thomson's Seasons* (Minneapolis, 1942).

46 Maurice Quinlan in his article "Cowper's Imagery," *Journal of English and Germanic Philology,* XLVII (1948), 276–85, in support of his contention that Cowper "disliked conscious imitation, and . . . read very little poetry" quotes this passage from one of Cowper's letters to Newton in 1782: "I reckon it among my principal advantages, as a composer of verses, that I have not read an English poet these thirteen years. . . . Imitation, even of the best models, is my aversion; it is servile and mechanical."

47 *The Complete Poetical Works of William Cowper,* ed. H. S. Milford (London, 1907), *The Task,* ll. 8–21, p. 129.

48 Hence there are, relatively, few Miltonisms in the poem.

49 Lyon, pp. 46–52, lists and describes these.

50 *"The Ruined Cottage* and *The Excursion," Essays Mainly on the Nineteenth Century, Presented to Sir Humphrey Milford* (London, 1948), p. 1.

51 Lyon, pp. 130, 132 ff.

52 See Lyon, p. 130. The entire chapter on style, pp. 122–38, particularly the discussion of Wordsworth's use of inversions and extended similes, is valuable.

53 This dividedness is commented upon in detail by Marsh, *Wordsworth's Imagery,* pp. 48–51, 60–61, 82–83, 94, 109–10, and is in fact the principal ground for her disapprobation of Wordsworth's later poetry. Her chapter, "Landscape—Light and Dark," illustrates in detail the more philosophical judgments of A. C. Bradley in *Oxford Lectures on Poetry* and D. G. James in *Scepticism and Poetry* (London, 1937).

54 Jeffrey asked: "Why should Mr. Wordsworth have made his hero a superannuated Pedlar? . . . Did Mr. Wordsworth really imagine, that his favourite doctrines were likely to gain any thing in point of effect or authority by being put into the mouth of a person accustomed to higgle about tape, or brass sleeve-buttons?"—Francis Jeffrey, *Contributions to the Edinburgh Review* (4 vols. in 1; Philadelphia, 1852), p. 457.

55 One may go further. In the *Duddon* series there is an actual river; in the *Ecclesiastical Sonnets* there is no actual river, but the fundamental and unifying symbol of the later series is that of a stream. The literal is transformed into the envisioned. Marsh, *Wordsworth's Imagery,* pp. 93–94, has pointed out, in fact, that *The River Duddon* can be read as "almost *The Prelude* in reverse." But unless one is ready, as I am not, to adopt Professor Marsh's assumption that all Wordsworth's poetry after 1807 is inferior, it is impossible to deal briefly with the complexities of his later long poems. Both their intrinsic value and the significance of their influence can be assessed fairly, it seems to me, only in the light of a study of their relationship to Shelley's and Keats's more ambitious poems, with which they are contemporaneous. For that reason I have made no effort in this chapter to do more than suggest the general outline of Wordsworth's development revealed by the differences between *The Prelude* and *The Excursion* as formal entities, defining those differences in terms of the poems' transformations of an earlier tradition.

56 This is one of the matters I hope to study in detail in a later work, for the problems it raises are complicated. For instance, one difference between Shelley's and Keats's use of mythical narrative and Tennyson's is that the earlier poets have confidence in their private visions, whereas Tennyson is anxious to affirm the objective validity of imaginative intuition.

57 See Charles Williams, "Wordsworth," *The English Poetic Mind* (Oxford, 1932), and G. Wilson Knight, "The Wordsworthian Profundity," *The Starlit Dome* (New York, 1941)—the discussion of Wordsworth's tendency to replace concrete imagery with "eternity structures."

Chapter Seven

1 Crabbe was born in 1754; Hunt died in 1859.

2 Apprenticed by his father to a surgeon in Suffolk, Crabbe threw up his position and travelled to London to try his fortune in literature. At first he was completely unsuccessful. Starving and destitute, he wrote a despairing but manly letter to Burke enclosing a sample of his writing. Burke befriended

him at once, took him into his house, gave him money, arranged for the publication of *The Library,* pulled strings to have him ordained, and used his influence to find other patrons for him, notably the Duke of Rutland and Lord Thurlow. Throughout his life Crabbe was dependent on moral, financial, and critical patronage, Francis Jeffrey supplying much of the last.

3 Both the vigorous descriptive force of Crabbe's verse and its abstract, rationalistic quality are well illustrated by the following lines from *The Village:*

> Such is that room which one rude beam divides,
> And naked rafters form the sloping sides;
> Where the vile bands that bind the thatch are seen,
> And lath and mud are all that lie between,
> Save one dull pane, that, coarsely patch'd, gives way
> To the rude tempest, yet excludes the day.
> Here, on a matted flock, with dust o'erspread,
> The drooping wretch reclines his languid head;
> For him no hand the cordial cup applies,
> Or wipes the tear that stagnates in his eyes. (I, 262–71)

All references are to A. W. Ward's edition, *Poems,* Cambridge English Classics (3 vols.; Cambridge, 1905–7). Undoubtedly the most carefully considered critical analysis of Crabbe's artistic strengths and weaknesses is Lilian Haddakin's *The Poetry of Crabbe* (London, 1955), though she underestimates changes in Crabbe's practice.

4 I, ll. 226–346.

5 This hiatus would be unusual in any artist's career, and it is particularly puzzling in Crabbe's, for he worked in an artisan-like manner, assigning himself a certain number of lines per day. René Huchon, *George Crabbe and His Times,* trans. Frederick Clark (New York, 1907)—probably the most thorough and impartial study of Crabbe's life and work—Part III, Chapter I, describes Crabbe's life during this period and stresses his interest in science as a distracting influence. Huchon also calls attention to the three lengthy verse tales on non-Augustan topics (a story of the prophet Elisha, of a gipsy band, and of the legend of a supernatural treasure hunt) which Crabbe offered for publication but which were rejected. During the same period Crabbe wrote, and destroyed, three novels. These abortive efforts suggest experimentation with a new form of artistic unity, narrative, and perhaps a new conception of realistic art.

6 *Form and Feeling* (New York, 1953), pp. 264 ff.

7 *The Borough* was the first of Crabbe's poems after *The Village* to be more condemned than praised (see Huchon, pp. 304–6). This is interesting, because *The Borough* provides some of Crabbe's most famous passages and his one story that is generally known today, "Peter Grimes." The reviewers accepted at face value Crabbe's announced purpose, which was to present a larger and more comprehensive version of *The Village.* So judged, *The Borough* fails. An excellent discussion of the relation between *The Parish*

Register and *The Borough* is to be found in Arthur Sale's "The Development of Crabbe's Narrative Art," *Cambridge Journal,* V (1952), 480–98. See also Haddakin, pp. 81–90.

8 Sometimes Crabbe gives us stories within stories within stories in a way that looks forward to Emily Brontë's technique in *Wuthering Heights,* particularly as Crabbe, like Brontë, likes to use narrators of different social classes.

9 Huchon, p. 422.

10 P. 427.

11 Almost all of Byron's narratives, for example, concern a moral impasse which is not resolved even though the story embodying that impasse is complete. See G. Wilson Knight's chapter on Byron, "The Two Eternities," in his *The Burning Oracle* (London, 1939).

12 P. 301.

13 "Ruth," for example, because told by the heroine's mother is invested with grief-stricken nostalgia. Sometimes in the later stories the protagonist is not fixed in the traditional social hierarchy but operates within an area of social mobility. "The Brothers" concerns a tradesman who has become a gentleman and is subjected to embarrassment by a brother who has not advanced socially. In the posthumous "Danvers and Rayner" we find love not only perplexed by shifts in the social status of both hero and heroine but complicated in an almost Austenian fashion by the characters' unsureness as to the meaning and value of social position. And as Crabbe grew older his interest in the irrational aspects of normal personalities increased. "Villars" suggests, if only sketchily, the transformation of hate into love and the illogical recrudescence of suppressed passion.

14 A splendid analysis of Crabbe's verse techniques is to be found on pages 481–88.

15 See the following chapters for development of this point.

16 Hunt, like Hood afterwards, was a journalistic writer, all his life dependent not upon the direct patronage which Crabbe enjoyed but on the assistance of friends influential in the literary world and upon his ability to cater to popular taste. Hence it is impossible to make the kind of correlation between his life and his work that one can establish for a writer like Crabbe. In large measure the story of Hunt's life is the social history of his time.

17 Necessarily my discussion of Hunt's career must be cursory and one-sided. I am conscious of slighting both his personal charm and the courage of his early journalistic career as well as the selflessness with which he championed Shelley and Keats, who, we must remember, would in all probability not have been so violently attacked by conservative critics had they not been regarded as his protégés. For a brief and lively survey of Hunt's early journalistic career Edmund Blunden's *Leigh Hunt's "Examiner" Examined* (London, 1928) is recommended. Blunden makes it plain that the government was almost forced into bringing charges of libel against Hunt, but he also quotes Brougham's defense, which includes the following summary of Hunt's political interests, a summary that represents fairly the essential temperateness of his reforming spirit. "Among the political topics which

occupy his attention ... the system of Military Punishments in this country; the Criminal Justice of it ... the Liberty of the Press, and fair Discussion; the purity of the Principles of our free Constitution; the Abolition of the Slave Trade; the Amelioration of the present Condition of the Poor. ..."

Carl R. Woodring, "The Hunt Trials: Informations and Manoeuvres," *Keats-Shelley Memorial Bulletin,* X (1959), 10–13, not only makes clear the procedures of libel trials in the first years of the nineteenth century but throws light upon the legal and political skirmishing between the Hunts and the government that produced the bitterness of the "great trial" in 1812.

18 Though Hunt's reputation as a poet has declined precipitously since his death, his stature as a man of letters has risen considerably in recent years, thanks largely to Edmund Blunden's *Leigh Hunt and His Circle* (New York, 1930), Louis Landré's exhaustive *Leigh Hunt* (2 vols.; Paris, 1935–36), and Clarence D. Thorpe's introduction to *Leigh Hunt's Literary Criticism,* ed. by L. H. and C. W. Houtchens (New York, 1956). All three critics stress Hunt's skill as a translator, and it is relevant to our purposes to note that many of his translations are of narrative poems. Worthy of special attention are his passages from *The Iliad,* the Homeric Hymn to Bacchus, and the Medoro and Cloridano episode from the *Orlando Furioso.* If one compares parallel passages from Pope's *Iliad* with Hunt's translation one observes at once that the later poet, although much less sure in his diction, is far better at catching the rush and movement of action of the original. A fascinating contrast about this point is made by Landré, II, 237–38.

19 Landré, II, 267.

20 In general Boccaccio softens and sentimentalizes Dante's austere moral passion.

21 All quotations from Hunt's poetry are taken from *The Poetical Works of Leigh Hunt,* ed. Milford (London, 1923).

22 *Rimini,* I, 243–47, II, 28, III, 86–87; "aught," "glade," "lightsome": I, 215–16, 129, III, 143. Landré, II, 275 ff., provides a thorough analysis of Hunt's diction and metrics.

23 As revealed by *The Story of Rimini.* What is said in this paragraph, I realize, cannot be equated exactly with all of Hunt's critical statements about the nature of poetry and its appropriate techniques (for which see *Hunt's Literary Criticism,* ed. Houtchens and Houtchens, cited above). But the importance of the conflict between Hunt's criticism and his practice (more apparent than real, I believe) should not be exaggerated. It is partly the result of his anomalous position as "gentle reformer" and partly the result of his contradictory character, which combined a neither powerful nor incisive critical mind with subtle taste and sensibility. As a critic Hunt suggests what Coleridge might have been without metaphysical capacities. It seems to me fairest to Hunt to judge his conception of poetry not merely on the basis of his critical statements but also in the light of his practice. Nevertheless, in essays such as *What Is Poetry?* we find him defining poetry in terms close to those I have used. For example: "Poetry begins where matter of fact or of science ceases to be merely such, and to exhibit a further truth; that is to say,

the connexion it has with the world of emotion, and its power to produce imaginative pleasure . . . in poetry feeling and imagination are necessary to the perception and presentation even of matters of fact. They, and they only, see what is proper to be told, and what to be kept back; what is pertinent, affecting, and essential. Without feeling, there is a want of delicacy and distinction; without imagination, there is no true embodiment."

24 Quotations from Hood's poetry are from *The Complete Poetical Works of Thomas Hood,* ed. Walter Jerrold (London, 1906). By far the most complete and perceptive study of the relation of Hood's art to Keats's is Alvin Whitley's "Keats and Hood," *Keats-Shelley Journal,* V (Winter, 1956), 33–48. Professor Whitley provides an excellent listing of studies of this relationship (p. 39, note 53) and is particularly interesting in his comments on Hood's version of *Lamia* and *La Belle Dame* (*The Water Lady* in Hood).

25 Even the most superficial comparison between Hood's version of the Hero-Leander story and Hunt's will make this point clear. See also Douglas Bush, *Mythology and the Romantic Tradition in English Poetry* (Cambridge, Mass., 1937), pp. 189–92. Professor Bush quite rightly stresses parallelisms between Hood's poem and the works of Shakespeare, Marlowe, and Spenser, though his insistence upon Hood's poem as an "almost complete reproduction of the narrative manner of the Elizabethan Ovidians" (p. 192) seems to me misleading.

26 The relevance of these literary antecedents will become clear to anyone who consults the illustrated edition of *The Dream of Eugene Aram, the Murderer,* published by Charles Tilt in London in 1831. The woodcuts emphasize Aram's psychological distress (of which there is little sign in the actual murderer's own defense, which is included in the volume), and Hood's preface credits his success in the poem to the "uninvoked inspiration" of a "terrible dream" that carried "an overwhelming sense of obligation . . . some awful responsibility, equally vague and intense, and involving, as it seemed, inexpiable sin, horrors unutterable, torments intolerable,—to bury my dead. . . ."

27 In Crabbe's later tales the satiric impulse weakens noticeably as something like the tolerant spirit of comedy usurps its place.

28 G. K. Chesterton, *Charles Dickens, The Last of the Great Men* (New York, 1942—a reprint of the 1906 *Charles Dickens*), p. 184. For an exceedingly interesting and stimulating discussion of the non-poetic quality of eighteenth-century novels, see Graham Greene's "Fielding and Sterne" in *From Anne to Victoria,* ed. Bonamy Dobrée (New York, 1937), pp. 279–89.

29 The effect is, perhaps, most clearly visible in the language of novelists like Dickens, which, though now recognized as providing the foundation for many of the most extreme modern experiments, to many Victorians seemed shocking, vulgar, and inartistic. See George H. Ford, *Dickens and His Readers* (Princeton, 1955), especially pp. 110–18. Ford is, so far as I know, the first scholar to call attention to the significance of David Masson's remarkable study of the style of Dickens and Thackeray. For the importance of Byron's "colloquial mode" in *Don Juan* see the following chapter.

30 Though Crabbe tried his hand at the novel and failed, both Hunt and Hood tried and succeeded. Significantly, Hood's *Tilney Hall* (which foreshadows Dickens) is much more readable than Hunt's *Sir Ralph Esher,* which looks back, through Scott, to the eighteenth century.

31 Byron's narrative art is treated in the next chapter and Scott's in the one following.

Chapter Eight

1 *The Works of Lord Byron, Poetical Works,* ed. E. H. Coleridge (7 vols.; London and New York, 1898–1904), I, 313–14. All references to Byron's poetry, except *Don Juan,* are to this edition.

2 Certain epic characteristics of *Childe Harold* are discussed below.

3 Canto I, stanzas xv–xix.

4 I, lxxii–lxxix.

5 I, lxxxvi–lxxxix.

6 I, lxxx.

7 III, xxxvi–xl.

8 II, lxv–lxix.

9 I, lxxxiii.

10 T. S. Eliot, "Byron," *From Anne to Victoria,* ed. Dobrée (New York, 1937), pp. 601–20; Robert Escarpit, *Lord Byron, un tempérament littéraire* (2 vols.; Paris, 1955–57), esp. II, 197 ff.

11 II, xxiv.

12 Byron's technique in *The Giaour* owes something to Rogers' method in *Columbus.* Cf. Coleridge's note, *Poetical Works,* III, 76.

13 Escarpit, II, 197, 207.

14 Excellently analyzed by Escarpit, II, 202.

15 Quoted by E. H. Coleridge, III, 323–24, n. 2.

16 Hunt's poem was conceived before Byron's tales were written but was not published until after Byron's success.

17 See esp. ll. 846–53. A decade later Hugo treated the same subject symbolically.

18 Quoted by E. H. Coleridge, IV, 157.

19 As many commentators have observed. See, for example, C. M. Bowra, *Heroic Poetry* (London, 1952), Chapters Five through Seven.

20 Three very different modern critics who have in one way or another stressed this point are Van Meter Ames, *Aesthetics of the Novel* (Chicago, 1928), Lionel Trilling, "Manners, Morals, and the Novel" in *The Liberal Imagination* (New York, 1950), and Erich Auerbach, *Mimesis,* esp. Chapters II, XIV, and XIX in the Anchor Edition, trans. Willard Trask (New York, 1957).

21 Truman Guy Steffan and Willis W. Pratt, *Byron's Don Juan* (4 vols.; Austin, Texas, 1957). Quotations from *Don Juan* are from this edition, referred to as "Variorum." Present reference is to Steffan's commentary, I, 185 ff.

22 For a discussion of this point, see H. J. Hunt, *The Epic in Nineteenth-Century France* (Oxford, 1941), Appendix I, p. 407.

23 See, for example, his letter to John Murray of April 6, 1819.

24 *Byron's Don Juan* (New Brunswick, 1945), p. 59.

25 Boyd, p. 35.
26 For example, Boyd, p. 34.
27 Lermontov's *A Hero of Our Own Times,* the first of the great Russian prose novels, draws not only on Pushkin's poem but directly on *Don Juan.* See W. J. Entwistle, "The Byronism of Lermontov's *A Hero of Our Time,*" *Comparative Literature,* I (1949), 140–46.
28 Variorum, I, 193.
29 The episode begins with Juan's "baptism" in the sea, and continues with his death-like trance from which he awakes to find his "Eve." Particular echoes of the paradise story are to be found, for example, in the following stanzas: II, 117, 172, 179, 188, 189, 192, 193, 204, 213; III, 2, 10; IV, 8, 10. Throughout these cantos reminiscences of *Paradise Lost* are frequent.
30 That context, of course, being created principally by sardonic authorial comments.
31 Miss Boyd was, so far as I know, the first to examine this point at length. See pp. 36 ff.
32 S. T. Coleridge, *Biographia Literaria,* ed. J. Shawcross (2 vols.; Oxford, 1907), II, 186–87.
33 Notably Helene Richter, *Lord Byron: Persönlichkeit und Werk* (Halle, 1929).
34 A distinction must be drawn between Cantos V and VI, for the latter is more flippant and digressive than the former. Also a year and a half intervened between the composition of the two cantos. Despite the more lighthearted tone of VI, I think Professor Steffan goes too far in treating the canto as an almost worthless joke (*Variorum,* I, 215–21). Partly the frivolousness and triviality of the sixth canto is introduced as a change of pace, a relaxation from the efficient comic rapidity of Canto V and a gentle prelude to the severe satire of Canto VII. I would contend that Byron had studied Italian Renaissance epic sufficiently to have understood the necessity for modulations in tone and tempo in a poem such as *Don Juan.* Furthermore, Byron can afford to linger and digress in VI. Juan, disguised as a girl, is going to spend the night in a harem. Until the reader finds out what happens, he will not let a few hundred lines of digressive commentary stop his reading. And Byron's presentation of what does happen, it seems to me though not to Professor Steffan, is arranged with far more comic tact than the Juan-Julia episode of Canto I. Finally, it should be observed that the "joke" of Canto VI, like Juan's and Haidée's love affair in Cantos III and IV, is surrounded and conditioned by the threat of danger and disaster. The last stanzas of Canto VI are not harsh, compact, and rapid-moving only because, as Professor Steffan feels, Byron is preparing to write about the siege of Ismail. Those last stanzas return to the mood and manner of Canto V, quite appropriately, for the joke of Juan in the harem is also a difficult and dangerous game played for the stakes of life and death. The Sultan is a pompous fool, but he is perfectly capable of having Juan killed. Gulbeyaz, too, has the power, and perhaps the inclination, to end Juan's career. It is this tension—increased by the fact that the situation has gotten beyond the control of

either Baba or Juan—that makes Byron's fooling in Canto VI more genuinely comic perhaps than his burlesque in Canto I.

Despite the foregoing, I should like to express here my gratitude to Professor Steffan, who is the first critic of Byron's poetry to present us with a complete and painstaking study of *Don Juan* as a whole.

35 The anti-epic quality of Cantos VII and VIII is emphasized by the apostrophe to Homer, VII, 78–80.

36 VIII, 13, 15, 88.

37 VIII, 92.

38 VIII, 121.

39 VIII, 83–85.

40 VIII, 33–41.

41 XV, 44–47.

42 Miss Boyd has contrasted in a somewhat analogous manner the supernaturalism of *Lara* to that in the final cantos of *Don Juan* (pp. 154–55).

43 See Marius Bewley, "The Colloquial Mode of Byron," *Scrutiny,* XVI (March, 1949), 8–23, which corrects Ronald Bottrall's "Byron and the Colloquial Tradition in English Poetry," *Criterion,* XVIII (1938), 204–24. Mr. Bewley's article, to which the present discussion is indebted, is the first modern study, so far as I know, to draw attention to the excellence of Francis Jeffrey's criticism of Byron's style and to the significance of Jeffrey's distinction of that style from both the "satirical vein" of Pope and the "burlesque" manner of Samuel Butler.

44 Alexander Pope, "Epistle III," Twickenham Edition, III, ii, ll. 342–98.

45 Probably worthy of a detailed study in its own right is Byron's last shorter narrative poem, *The Island*. Though written very late (1823), it seems to superficial inspection a throwback to Byron's earliest narrative manner. That it is not, in fact, M. Escarpit has shown in his interesting discussion of the poem (II, 230 ff.). M. Escarpit may somewhat overrate the artistic value of *The Island,* but he is certainly right to insist upon it as a forerunner of the popular and highly romantic fiction of the nineteenth century with which the name of Jules Verne is inextricably associated. The one observation I have to add to M. Escarpit's analysis and commentary is that the double plot, the odd mixture of realism and lurid romance, and the new treatment (for Byron) of the Nature-civilization opposition may owe something to the fact that this is the first of Byron's poems seriously to exploit the clash between different civilizations, and consequently that it may be understood best in its relation to Scott's novels, for which see the succeeding chapter.

Chapter Nine

1 Hesketh Pearson, *Walter Scott* (London, 1954), p. 88.

2 Walter Allen, *Six Great Novelists* (London, 1955), p. 78.

3 *Sir Walter Scott Lectures, 1940–1948,* intr. by W. L. Renwick (Edinburgh, 1950), p. 86.

4 The anti-epical tendency of a genuine historical sense is discussed at the beginning of Chapter Six.

5 The introduction to "The Lay of the Last Minstrel," in *The Poetical Works of Sir Walter Scott,* ed. J. Logie Robertson (London, 1913), pp. 50–51. This is the introduction of 1830. See also the preface to the first edition (nearly twenty years earlier) of *The Bridal of Triermain,* pp. 285–86. My references to Scott's poetry and prefaces throughout this chapter are to this Oxford Edition.

6 The order of Scott's narrative poems: *The Lay of the Last Minstrel,* 1805; *Marmion,* 1808; *The Lady of the Lake,* 1810; *Rokeby,* 1812; *The Bridal of Triermain,* 1813; *The Lord of the Isles,* 1815; *Harold the Dauntless,* 1817, although in part written before *The Lord of the Isles.*

7 Canto II, xxvi and xxvii.

8 III, i.

9 I, xv–xvii.

10 See particularly the introductions to Cantos II, III, and V.

11 In this story the minstrel figure becomes a character within the action.

12 III, i–xxiv; V, xxii–xxvi.

13 II, xiii.

14 Compare I, i–iii, with III, viii, for example.

15 Introduction to *Rokeby,* pp. 380–81.

16 Compare II, xxiii–xxv, with the description of the tournament in Chapter 12 of *Ivanhoe.*

17 Introductory Note to the Edition of 1833, Oxford Edition, p. 475.

18 VI, i.

19 Introduction to the Edition of 1830, *The Lord of the Isles,* p. 474. Scott himself draws the parallel to *The Pirate.*

20 IV, i–x.

21 George Saintsbury, "The Historical Novel," *The Collected Essays and Papers of George Saintsbury, 1875–1920* (London, 1923–24), II, 1–20, reduces the fanaticism of origin-seeking to absurdity by arguing plausibly that the first historical novel is the *Cyropaedia.* His point is that the evolution of art is qualitative. What matters is not whether there were forerunners to Scott's historical novels or whether Richardson had models for his epistolary novel. Richardson and Scott possessed the genius to establish particular literary forms as means of successfully expressing significant aesthetic values. To that degree they remain inventors, regardless of how many predecessors scholarship unearths.

22 E. M. Forster, *Aspects of the Novel* (New York, 1927), pp. 51–61.

23 Chesterton, *Charles Dickens,* p. 177.

24 *Rob Roy,* Chapter 34.

25 *Redgauntlet,* Book II, Chapter 17.

26 Nicol Jarvie's refusal to be browbeaten out of his common decency by Helen MacGregor (*Rob Roy,* Chapter 32) provides a striking instance of such assertion.

INDEX

*